MW01618611

Drawing Music II

The La Musica

International Chamber Music Festival

Sketchbook

For Ellen with my best wishes

1987 – 2013

Sol Schwartz

The Art of
Sol Schwartz

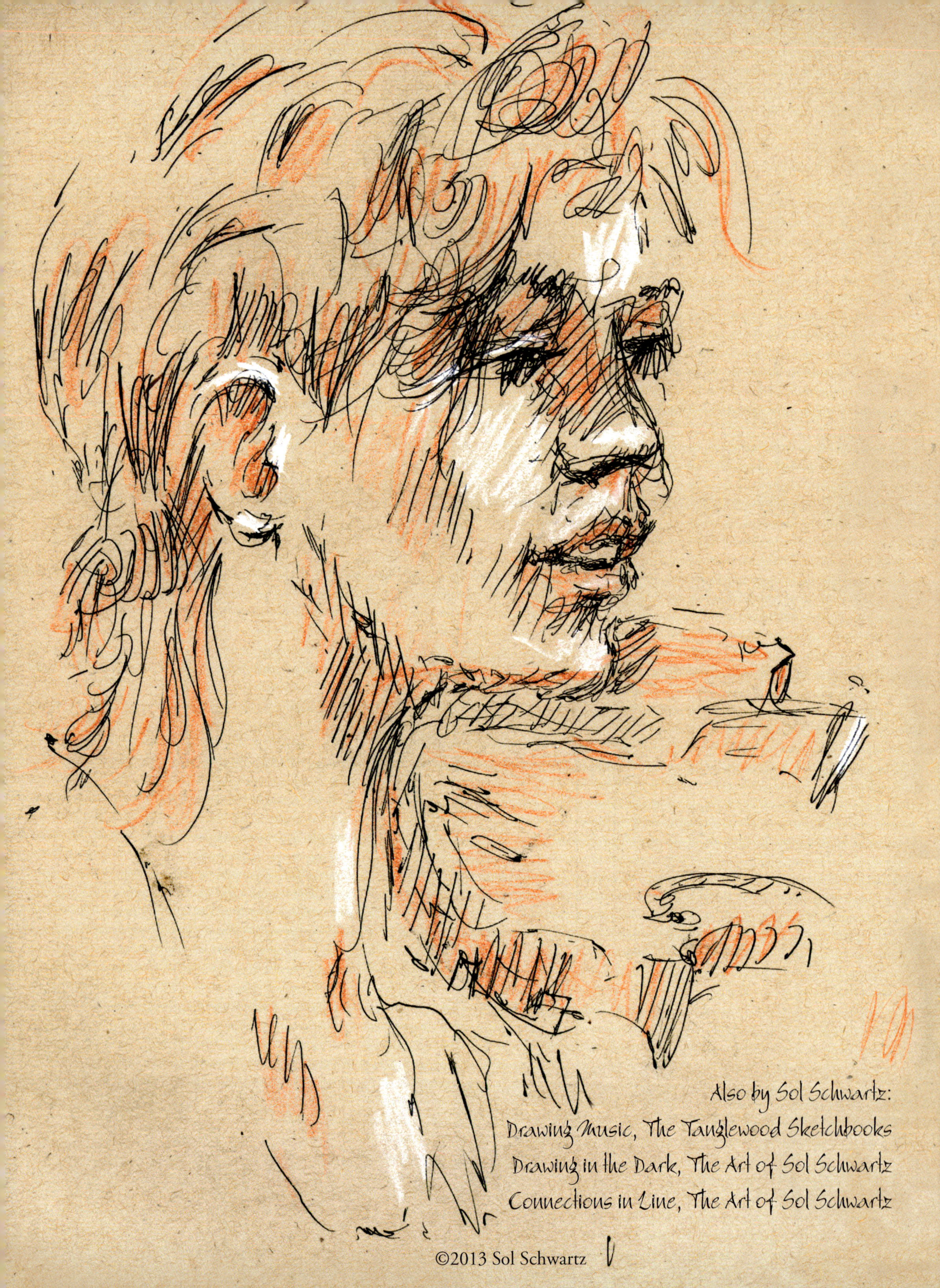

Also by Sol Schwartz:

Drawing Music, The Tanglewood Sketchbooks

Drawing in the Dark, The Art of Sol Schwartz

Connections in Line, The Art of Sol Schwartz

This book is dedicated to
All lovers of Music and Art.

– Sol Schwartz

Acknowledgements

I wish to acknowledge Studio Two and it's founder, Kevin Sprague, who has worked with me on all four of my books. I wish to also thank Heather Rose, Design Director at Studio Two. Her skill, expertise and infinite patience with me has made this book possible.

In addition, Michelle Bruback, Tom Sokolis, Marek Pietrucha, Katie McTeigue, Kate Brown, Risa Schwartz, David Schwartz and Nan Thompson, have all been of great assistance and support.

– Sol Schwartz

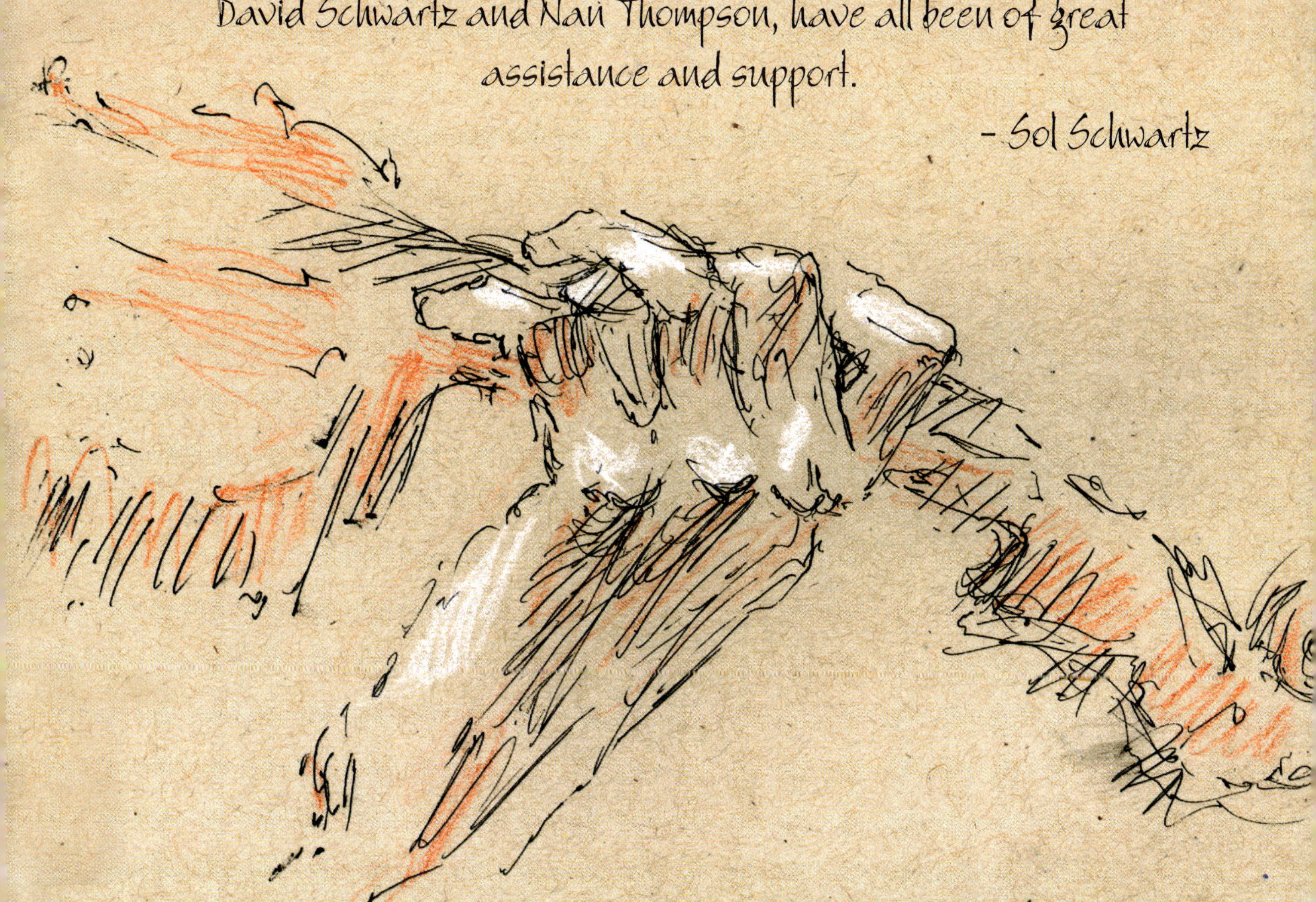

Drawing La Musica Introduction
Sally Faron

"For 26 years, La Musica has been bringing together outstanding European and American musicians for two and one-half weeks of intense music making, in which differing traditions and ideas are discussed, clarified, and presented in five concerts of superior quality.

Among the annual events are pre-concert lectures, open rehearsals, special community events and appearances as well as the five concerts. La Musica has established itself as an artistic and critical success and become an outstanding American cultural institution. Guided by Artistic Director Bruno Giuranna and Associate Artistic Director Derek Han, the Festival presents exciting programs of familiar and unusual chamber music, communicating a joy in performance to enthusiastic audiences.

Drawing Music is not only a reminder of La Musica's history but also a visual celebration of this joy, for throughout those 26 years, the artist was there. And now, in its 27th year, this book is presented in honor of the 80th birthday of its Artistic Director, Bruno Giuranna.

During its years, La Musica has had another purpose: to draw people together into the creative process. Through its open rehearsals, its collaboration with other cultural organizations, both national and local, its presentation of premiered and commissioned works, La Musica has explored ways in which music relates to other art forms and cultural movements. Drawing Music so aptly fulfills this purpose.

To those of us who for many years have watched Sol Drawing La Musica, what a flood of memories return! The vibrancy and joyfulness of his portraits speak to us once again of the same qualities in those musical performances. And we happily look forward to more!"

– Sally Faron,
Executive Director

"Sol's sketches provide an extraordinary tribute to chamber music, and become more special now that our La Musica musicians are captured in performance. What a wonderful collaboration of art and music. Thank you, Sol, for your creative genius!"

– Frederick M. Derr,
Board President

Artist's Prelude

I have been drawing the artists at the La Musica Festival for the past 25 years. I did this sketch in front of the Opera House while waiting in line for tickets.

Prior to relocating to the Opera House, the Festival was held at the Historic Asolo Theatre in the Ringling Museum.

The drawings commemorated in this book were done at the Asolo, the Opera House, and at the Sainer Pavillion during rehearsal.

It has been my great pleasure to capture both the preparatory rehearsal time and the actual performances and to see the difference between artists dressed in shorts and sandals discussing how the work will be performed and then to see them in full dress at the actual performance.

Maestro Giuranna has gathered the finest chamber music players from Europe and The Americas and this international combination of artists has made this Festival unique.

I have been fortunate to have been able to record many of these rehearsals and performances and to be able to present them here for your pleasure.

– Sol Schwartz

Schwartz

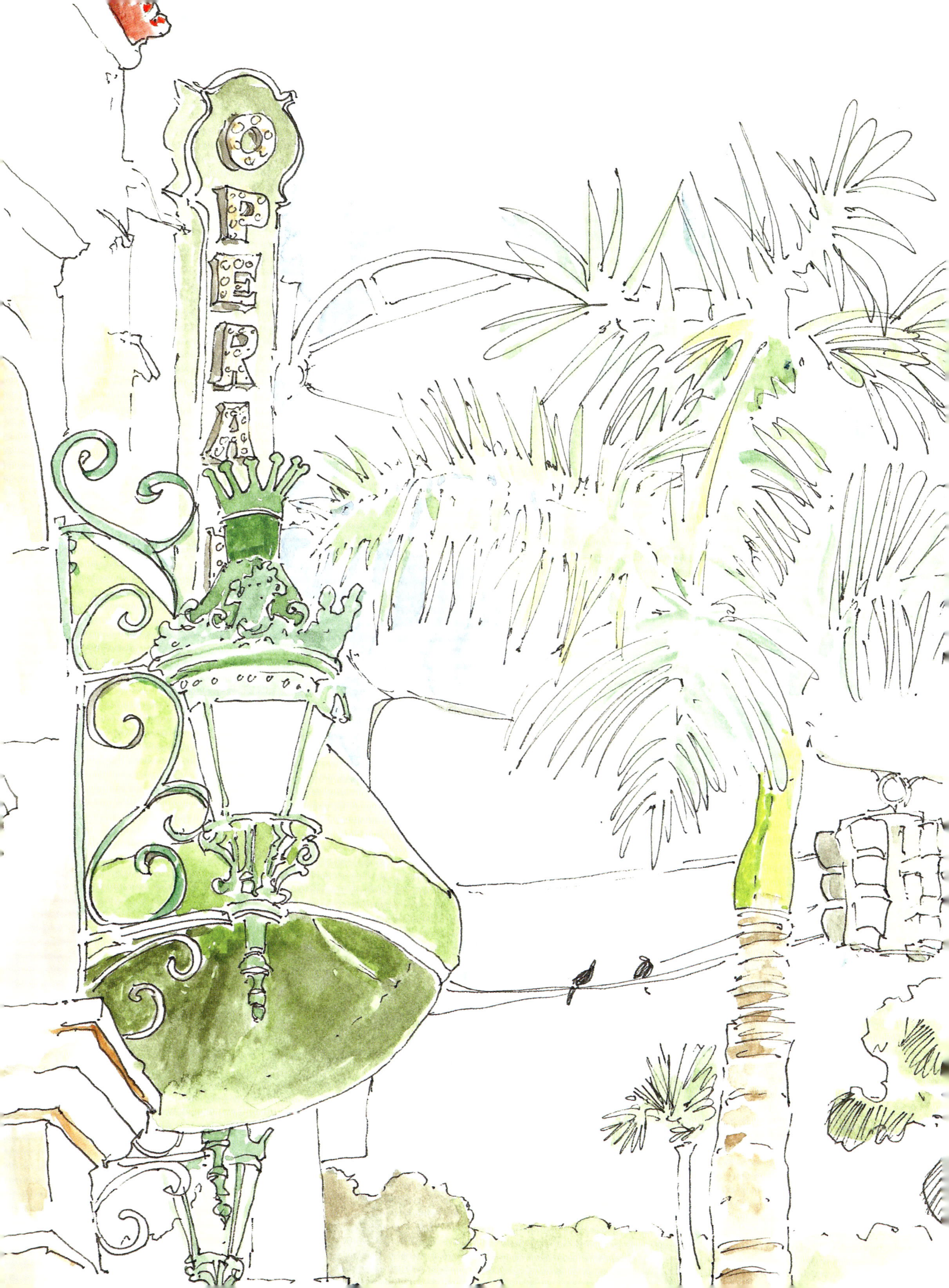
OPERA

This book is presented to Bruno Giuranna
on his 80th birthday.

Maestro Giuranna has devoted the last
27 years to the founding and flourishing of the
La Musica di Asolo Festival in Sarasota, Florida.

His direction, guidance and artistic sensibility have made
this festival an international attraction.

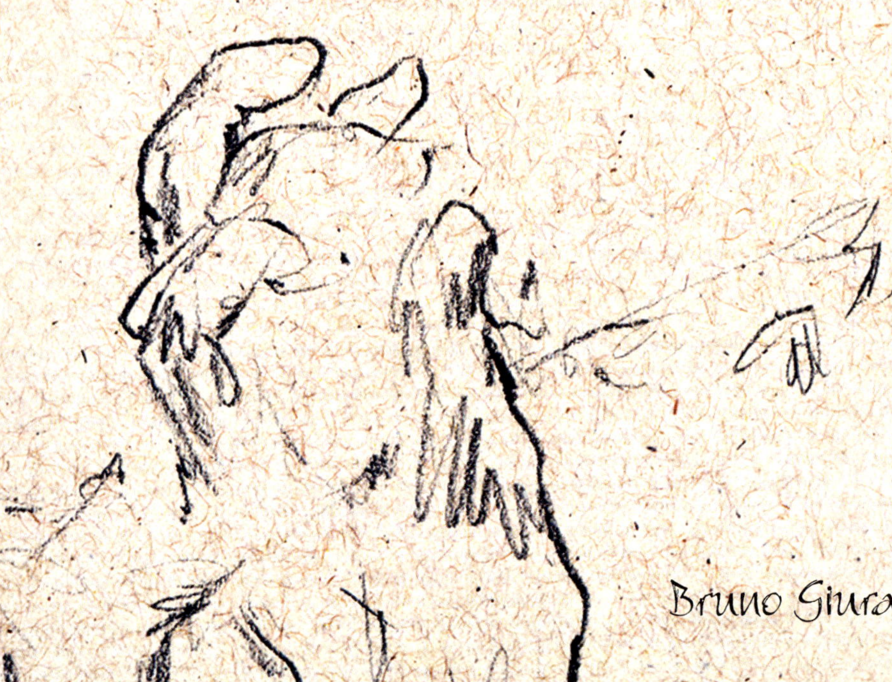

Bruno Giuranna, 1996

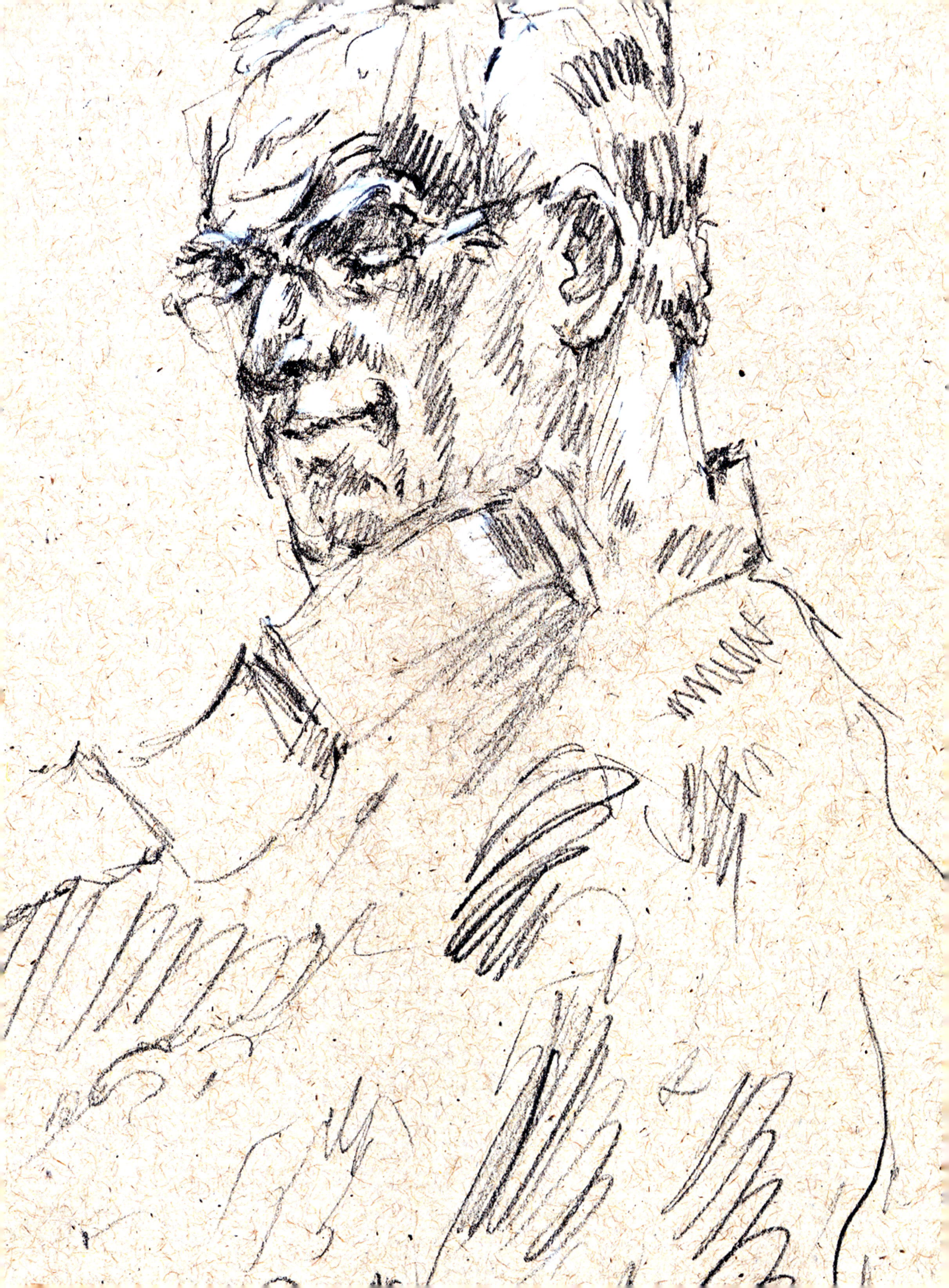

The following set of drawings all include Maestro Giuranna with a variety of artists done during rehearsal and the actual performance on stage.

You might have fun trying to identify some of the players yourself.

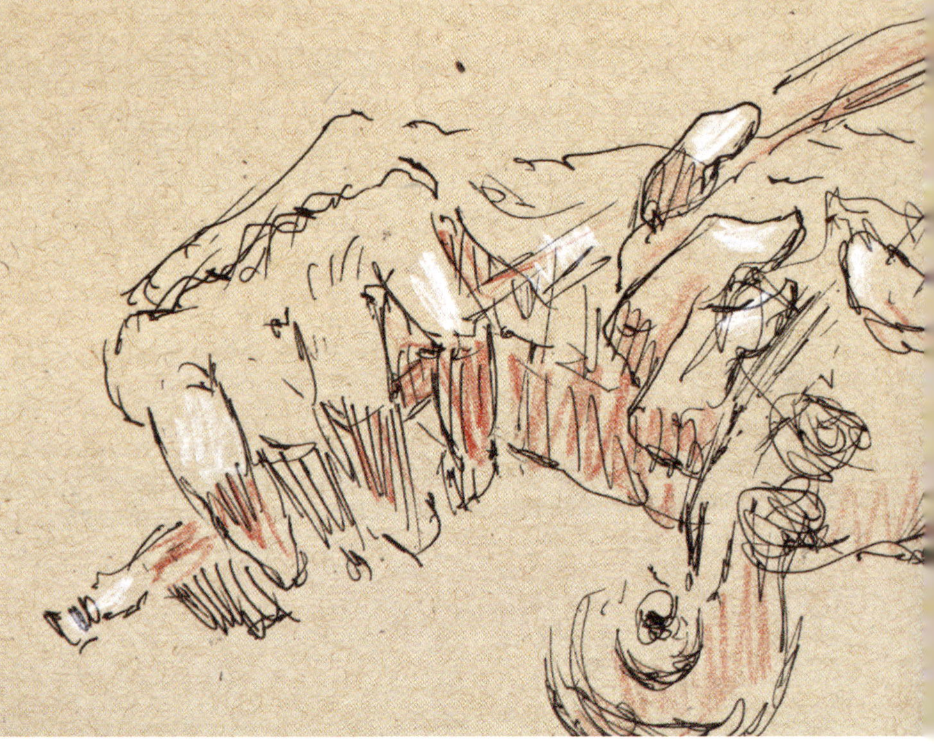

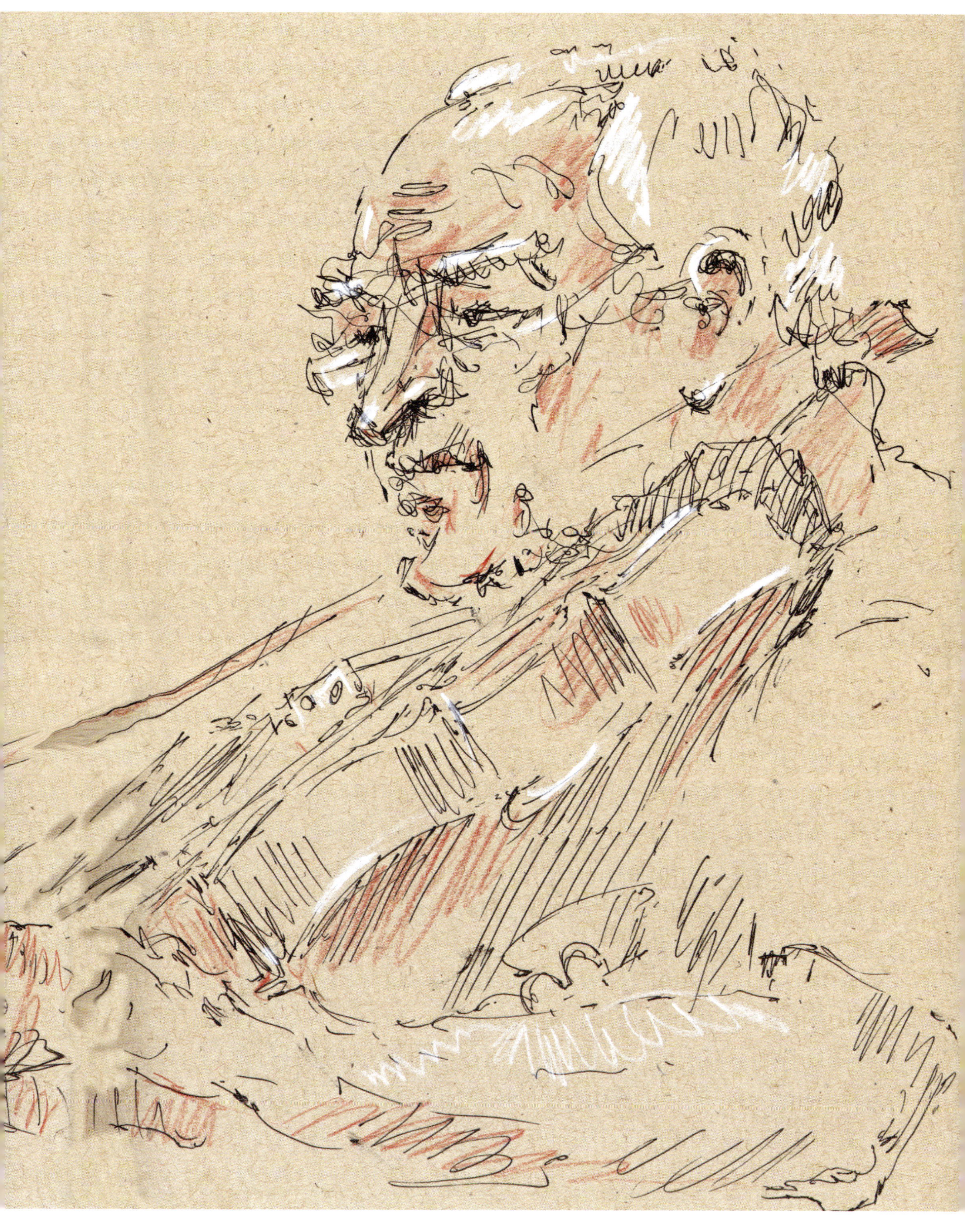

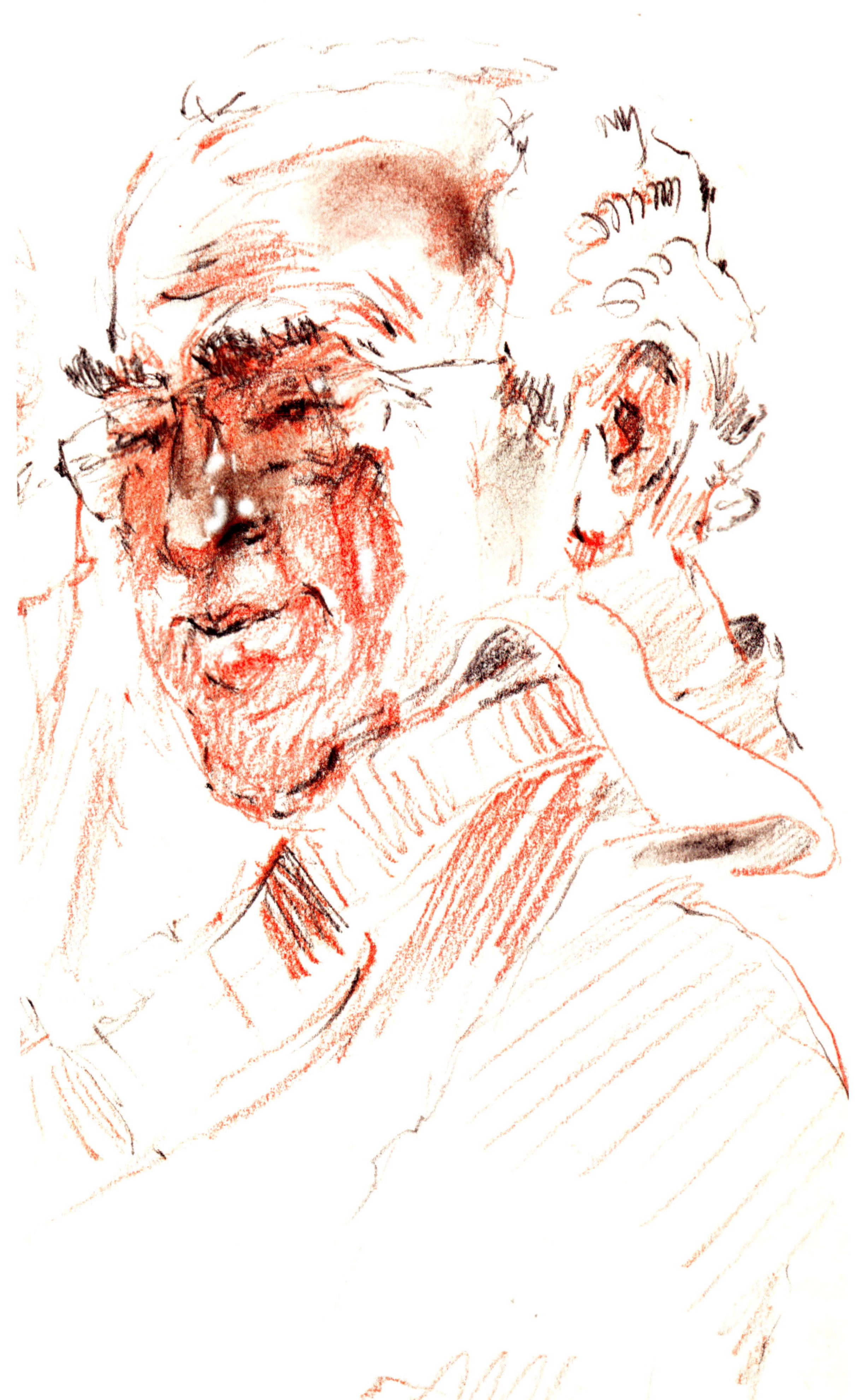

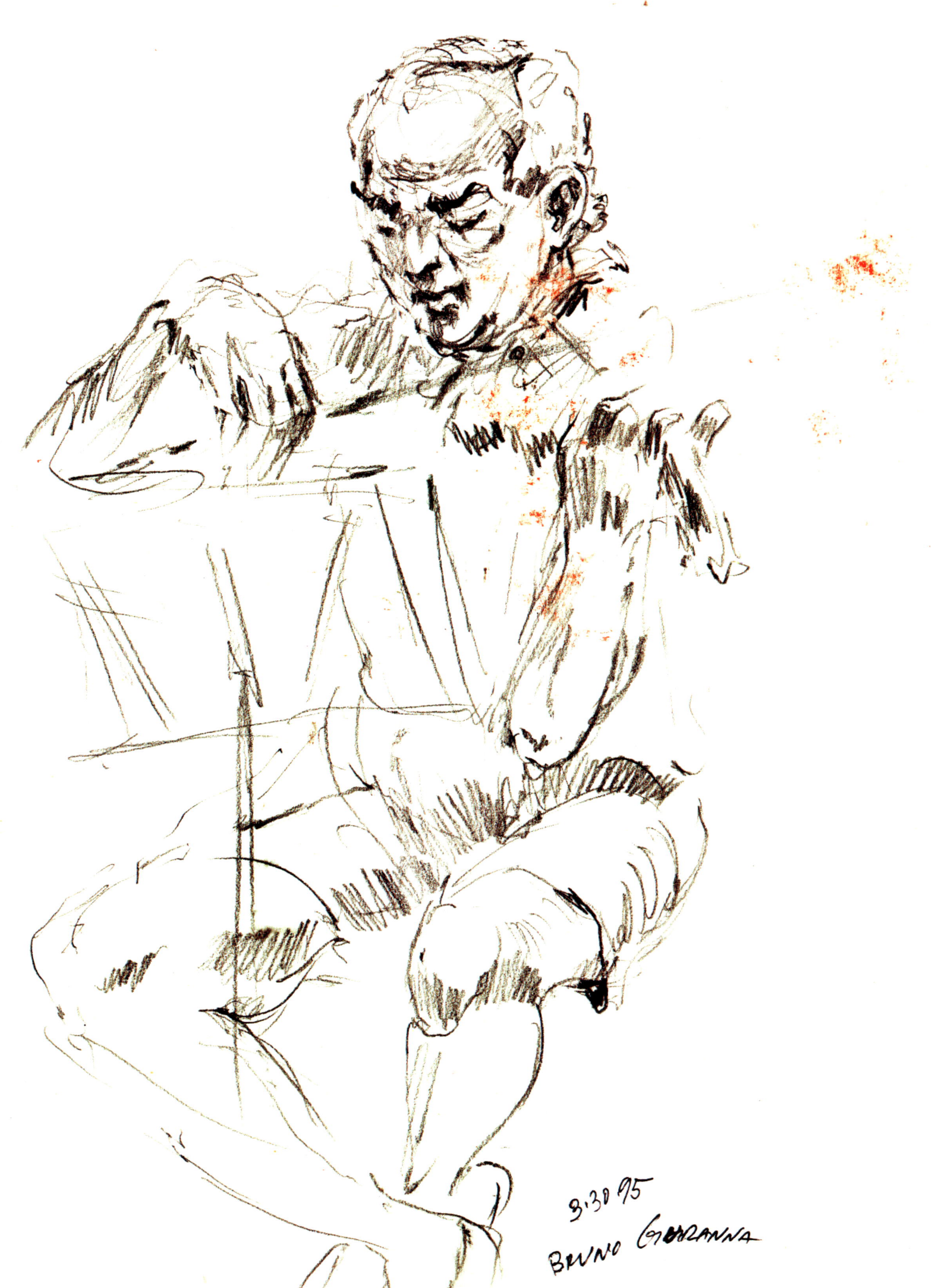
8.30 95
BRUNO

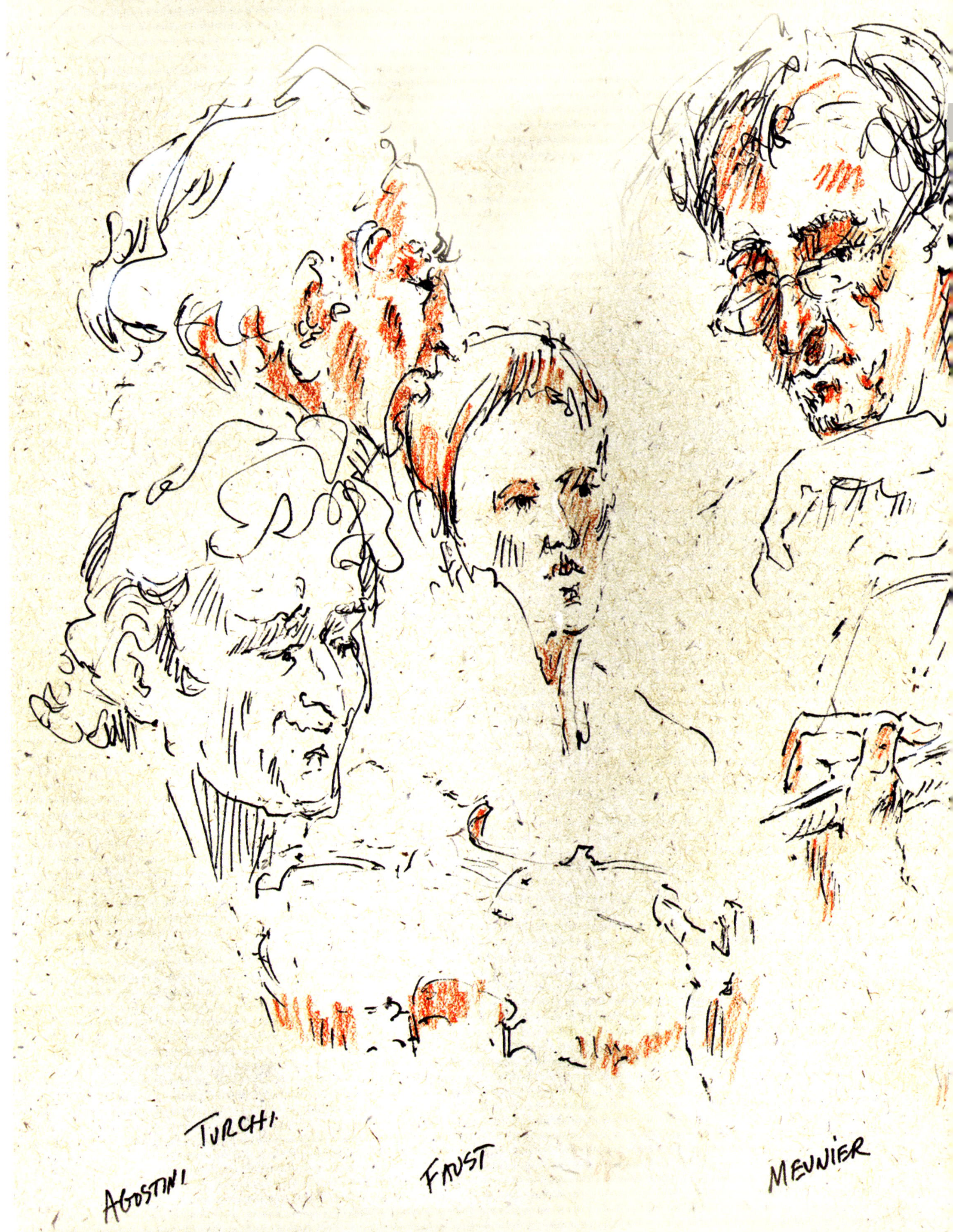
TURCHI
AGOSTINI
FAUST
MEUNIER

Schwartz 4.16.00

GIURANNA

TELLMANN

REHEARSAL

GUIDO TURCHI – STRING QUINTET
WORLD PREMIERE

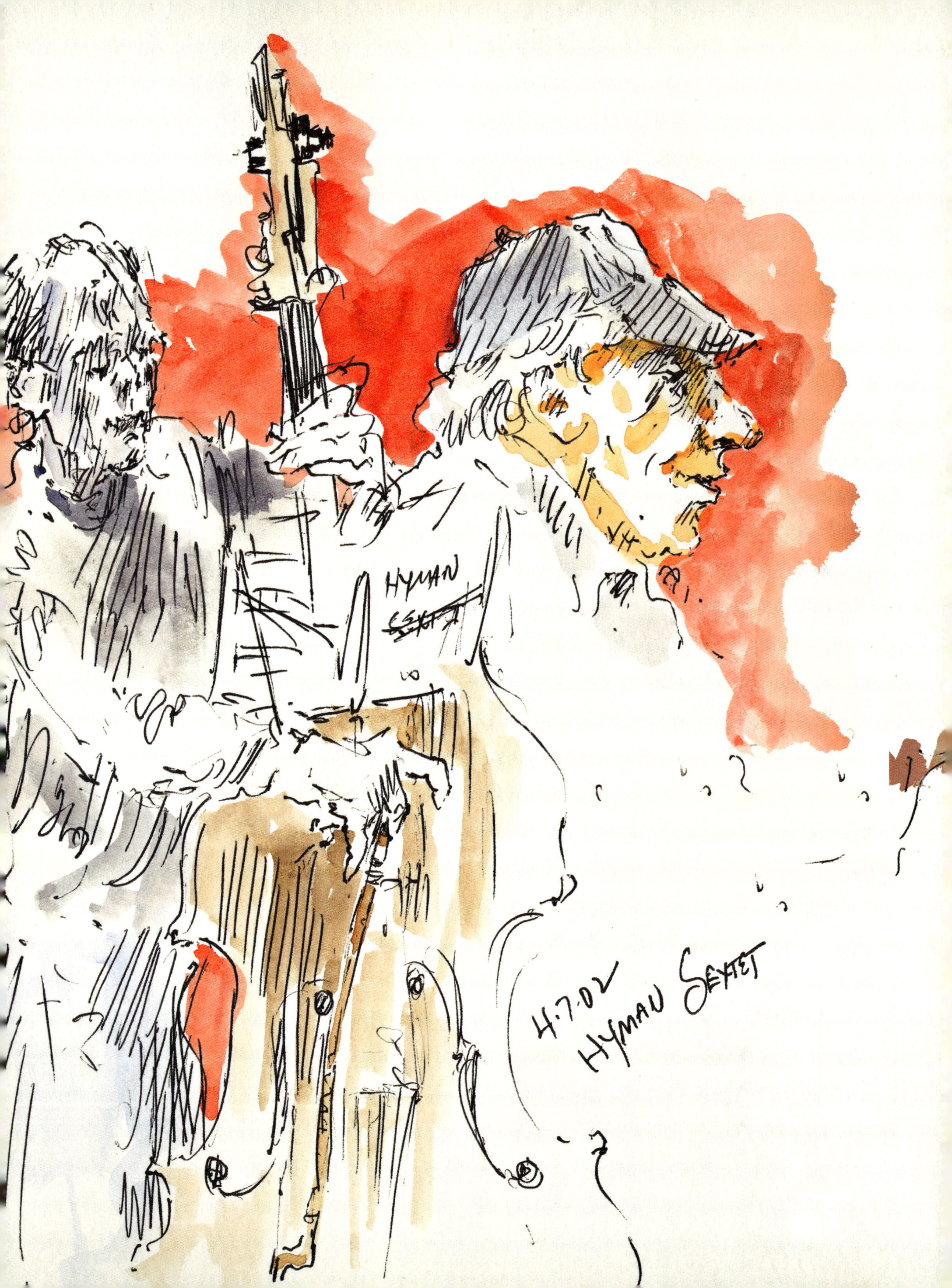
HYMAN SEXTET
4.7.02
HYMAN SEXTET

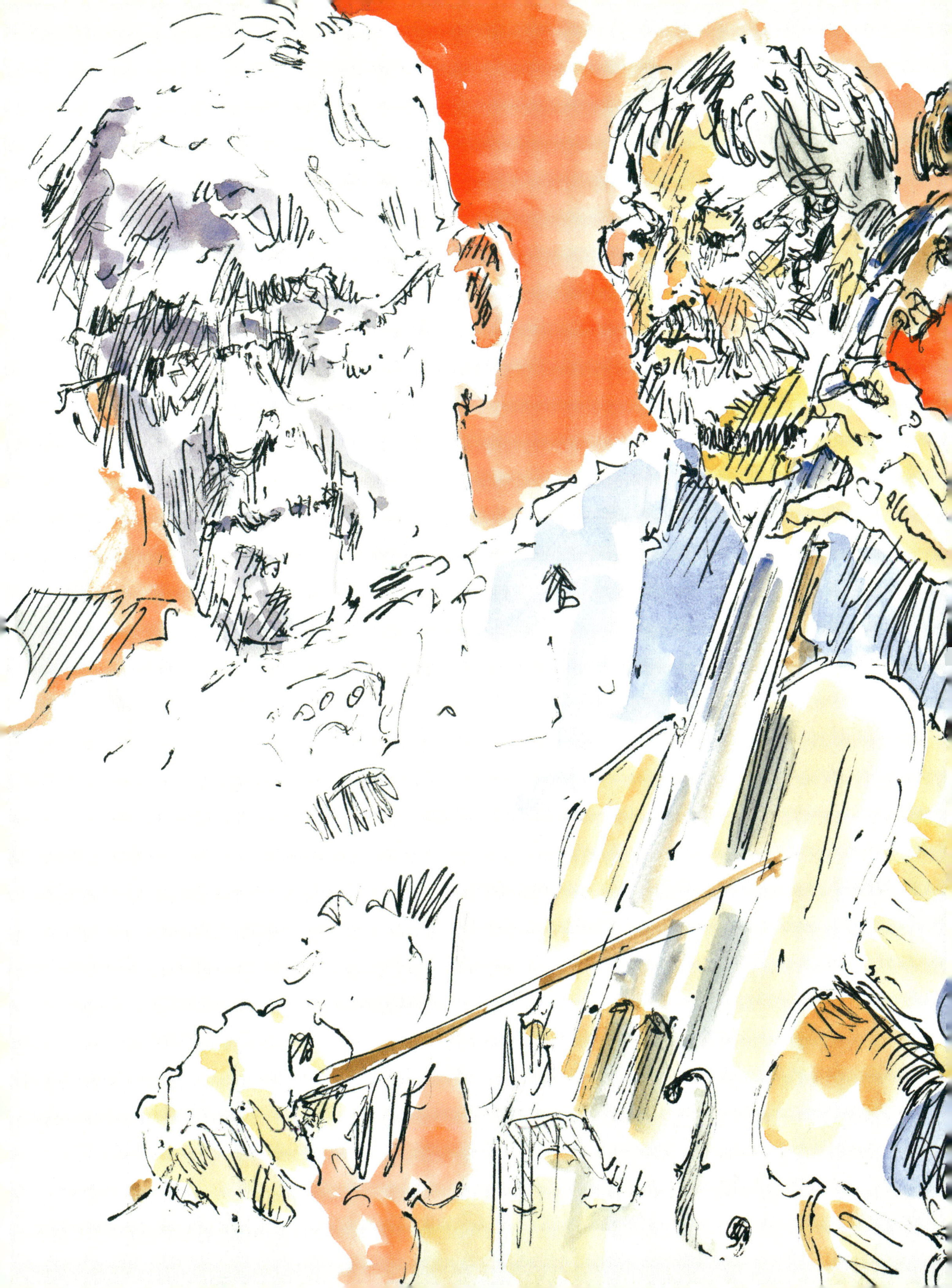

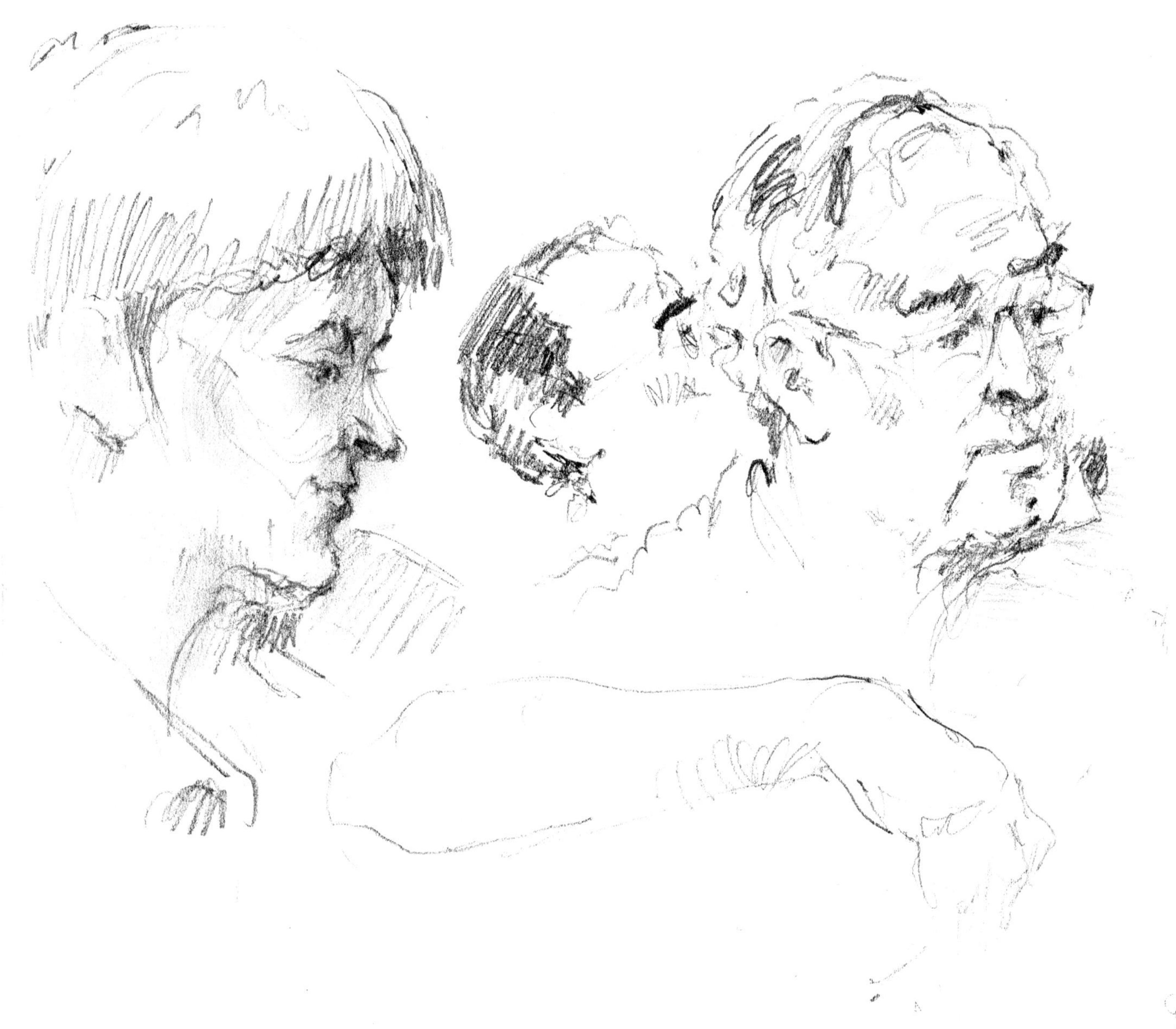

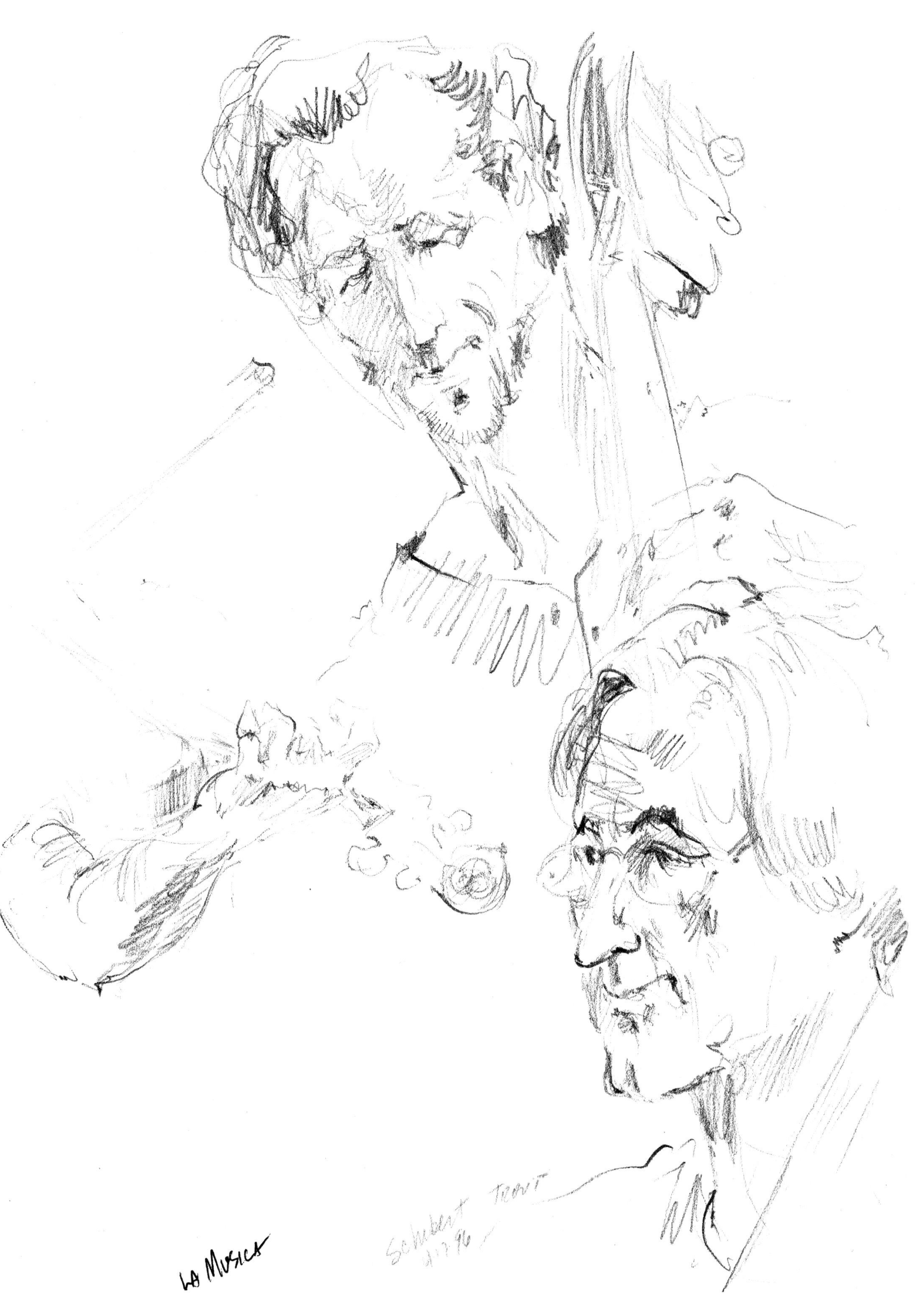
Schubert Trout
La Musica

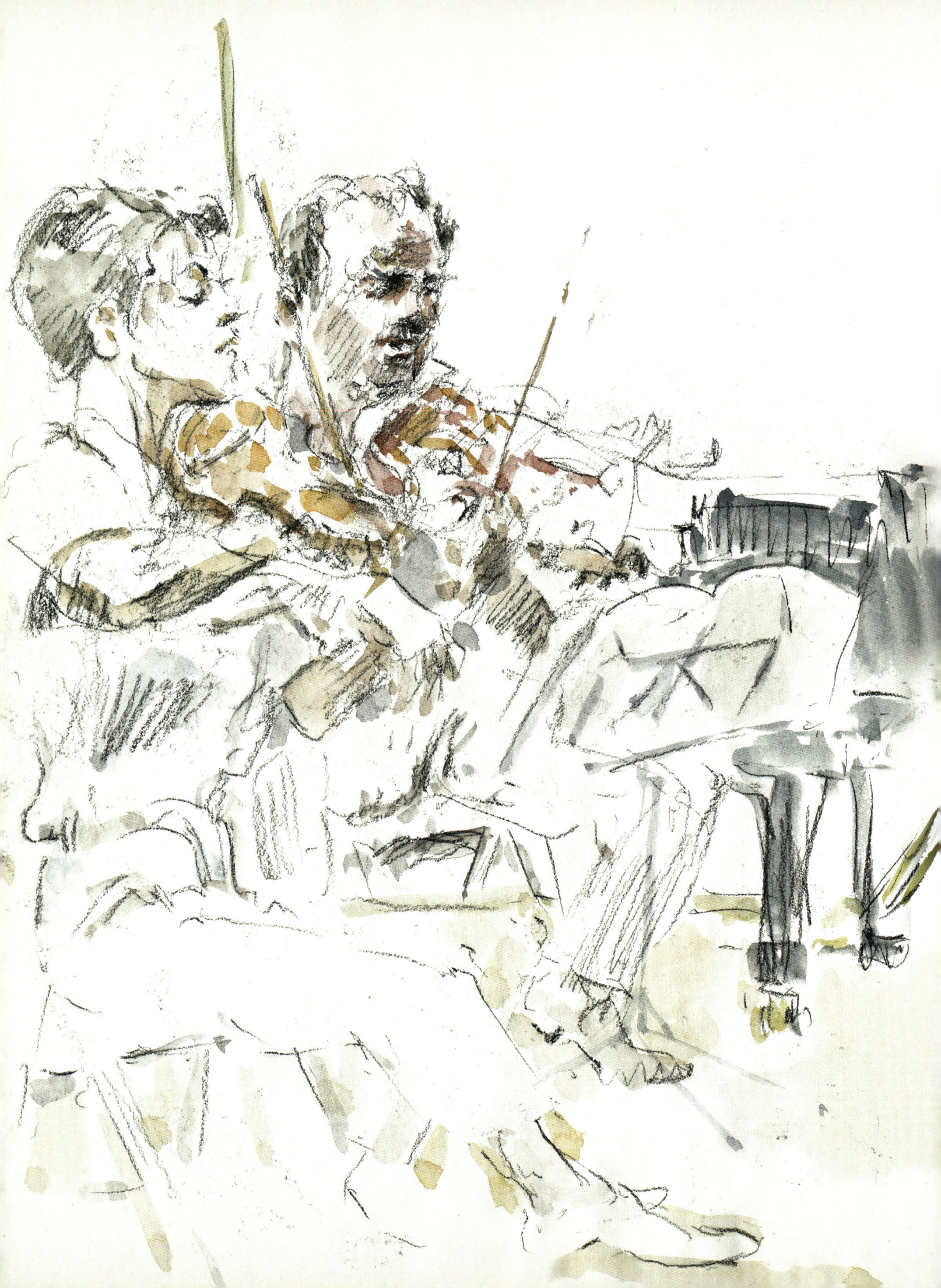

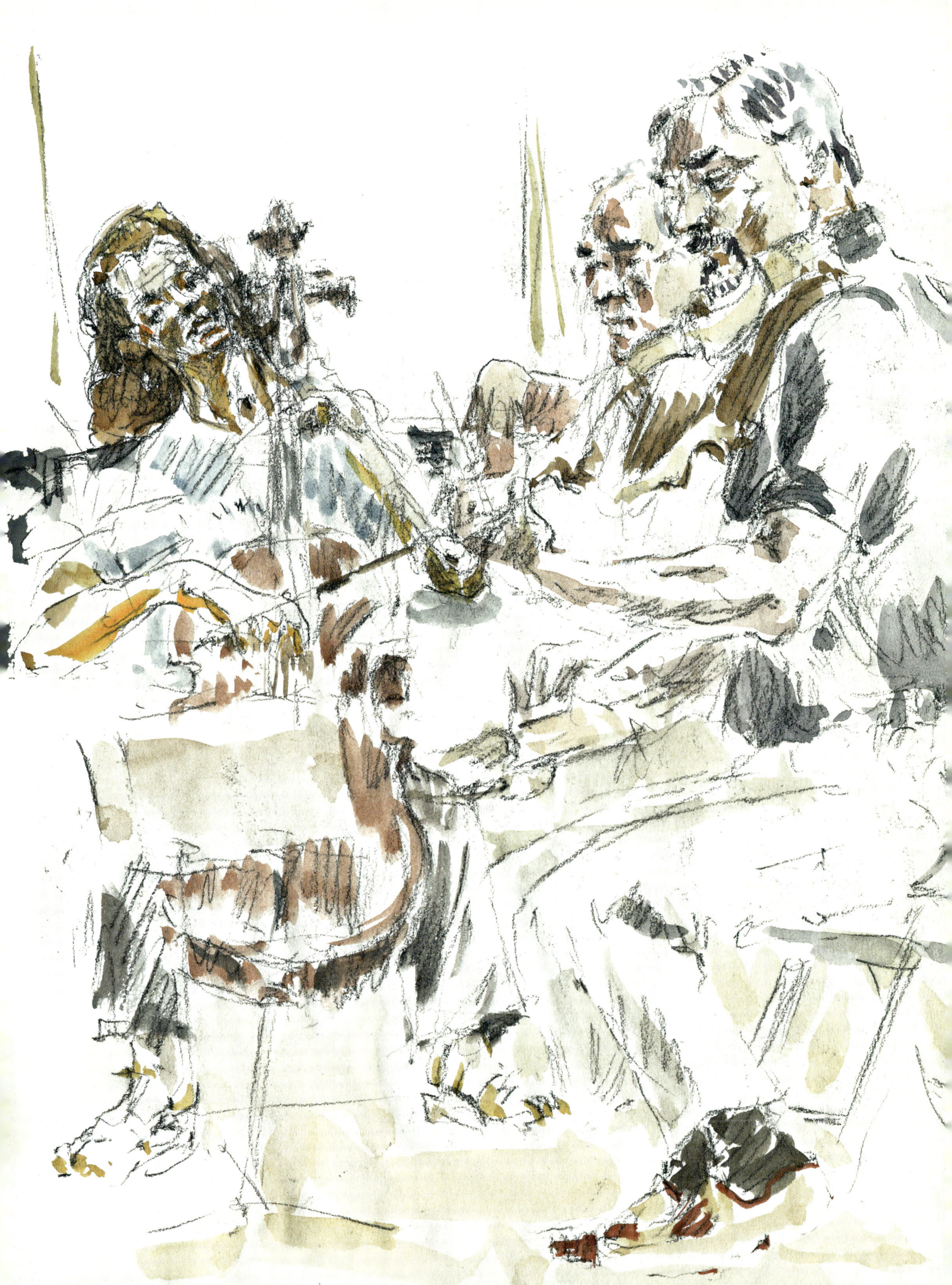

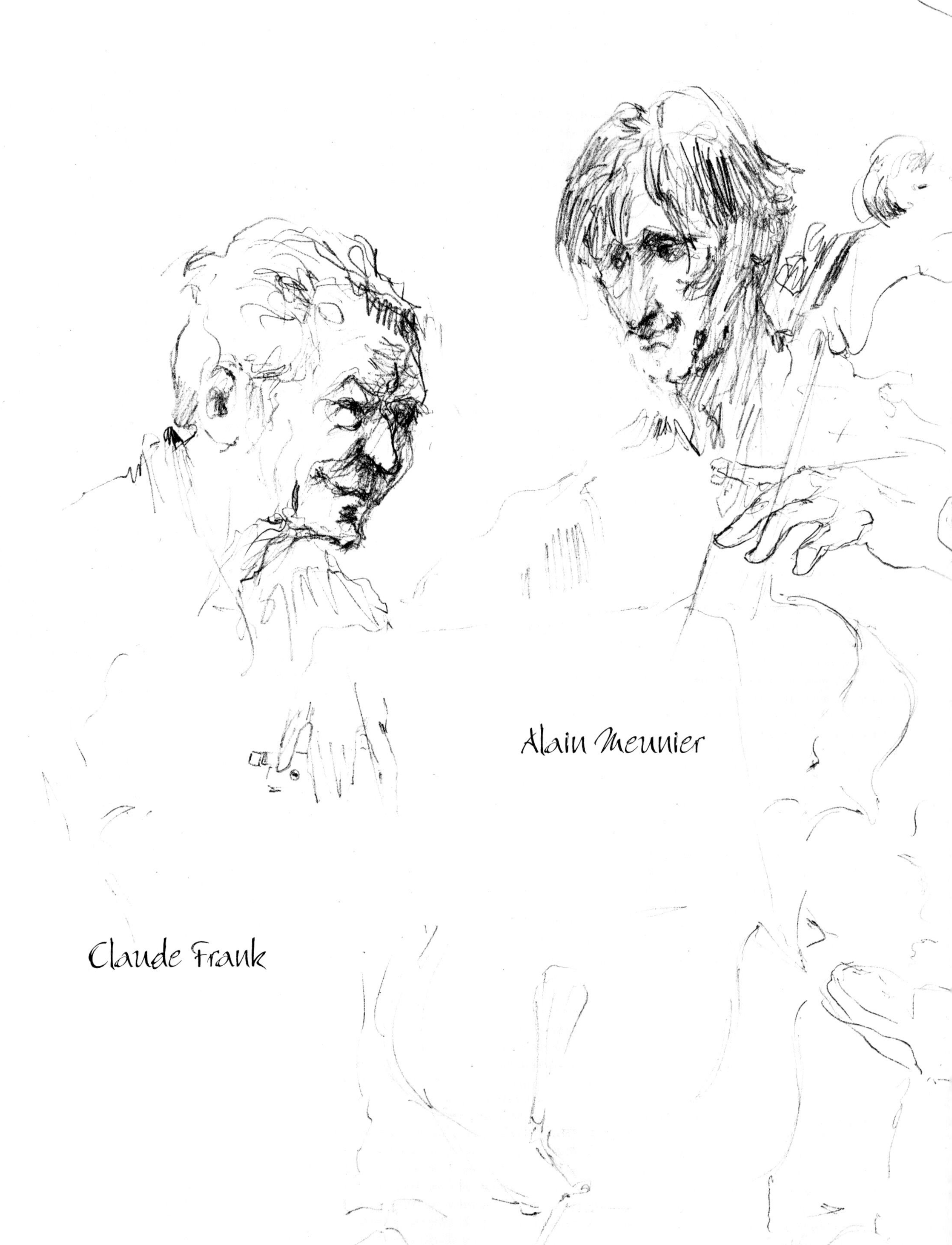
Alain Meunier
Claude Frank

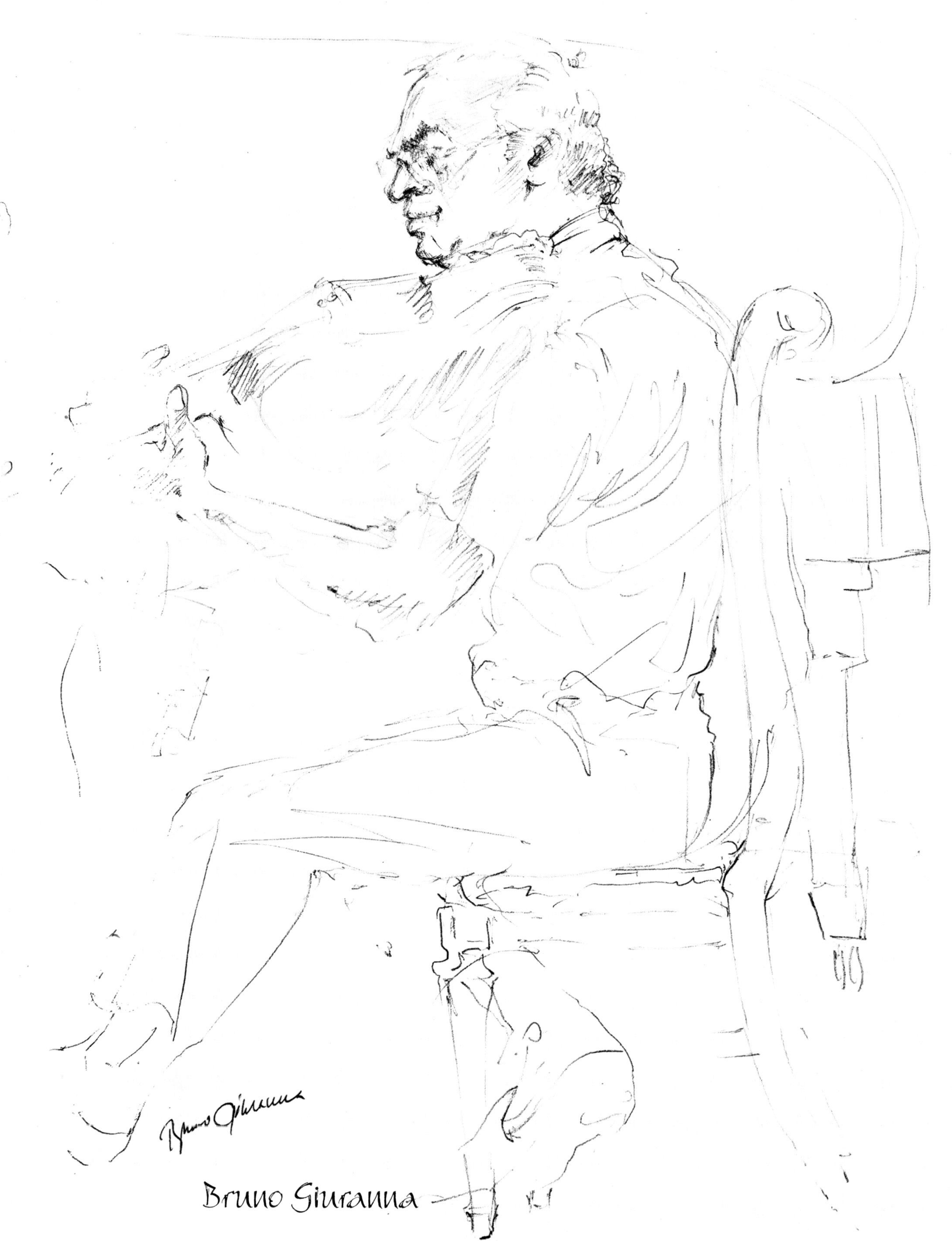

Bruno Giuranna

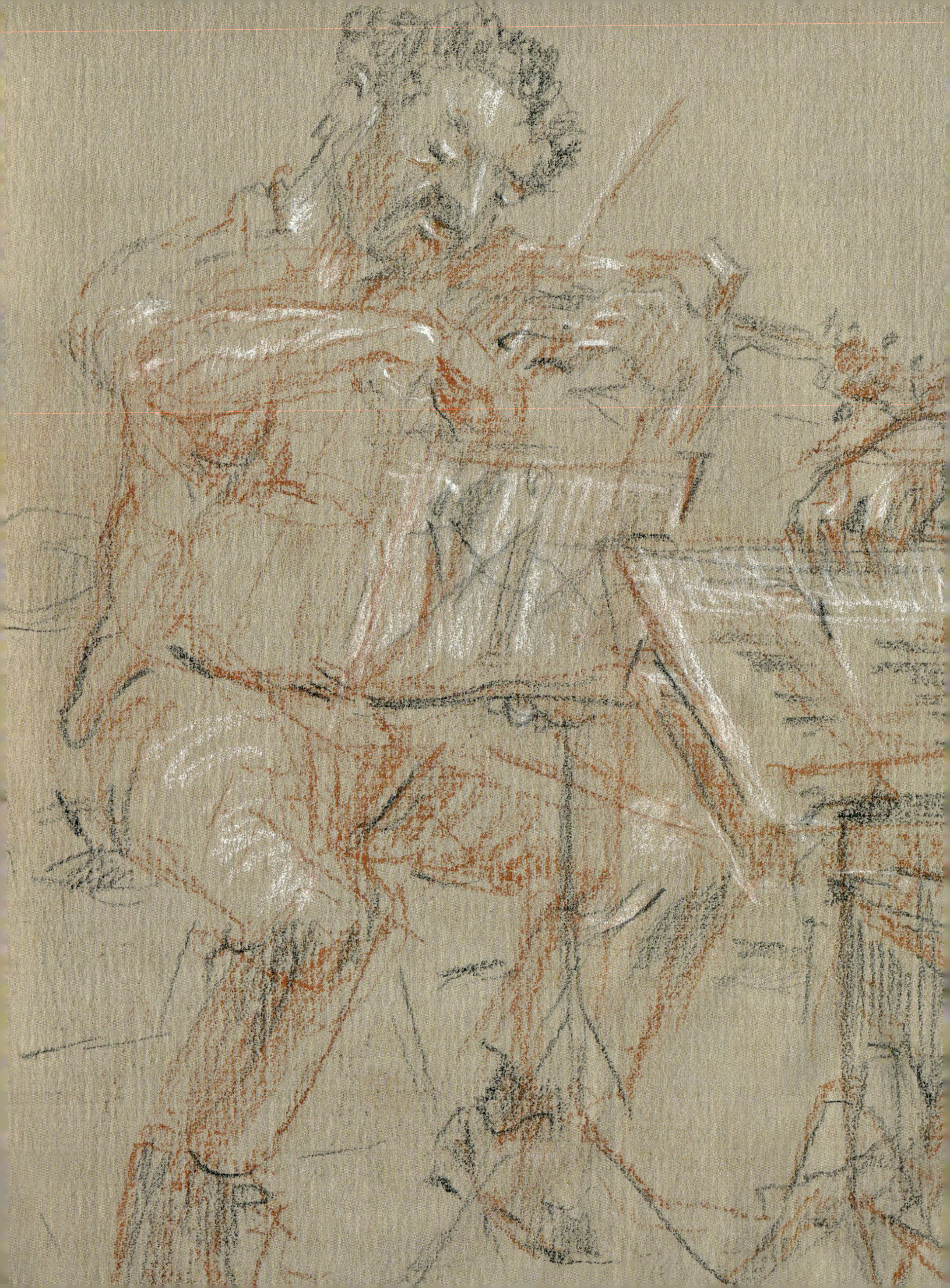

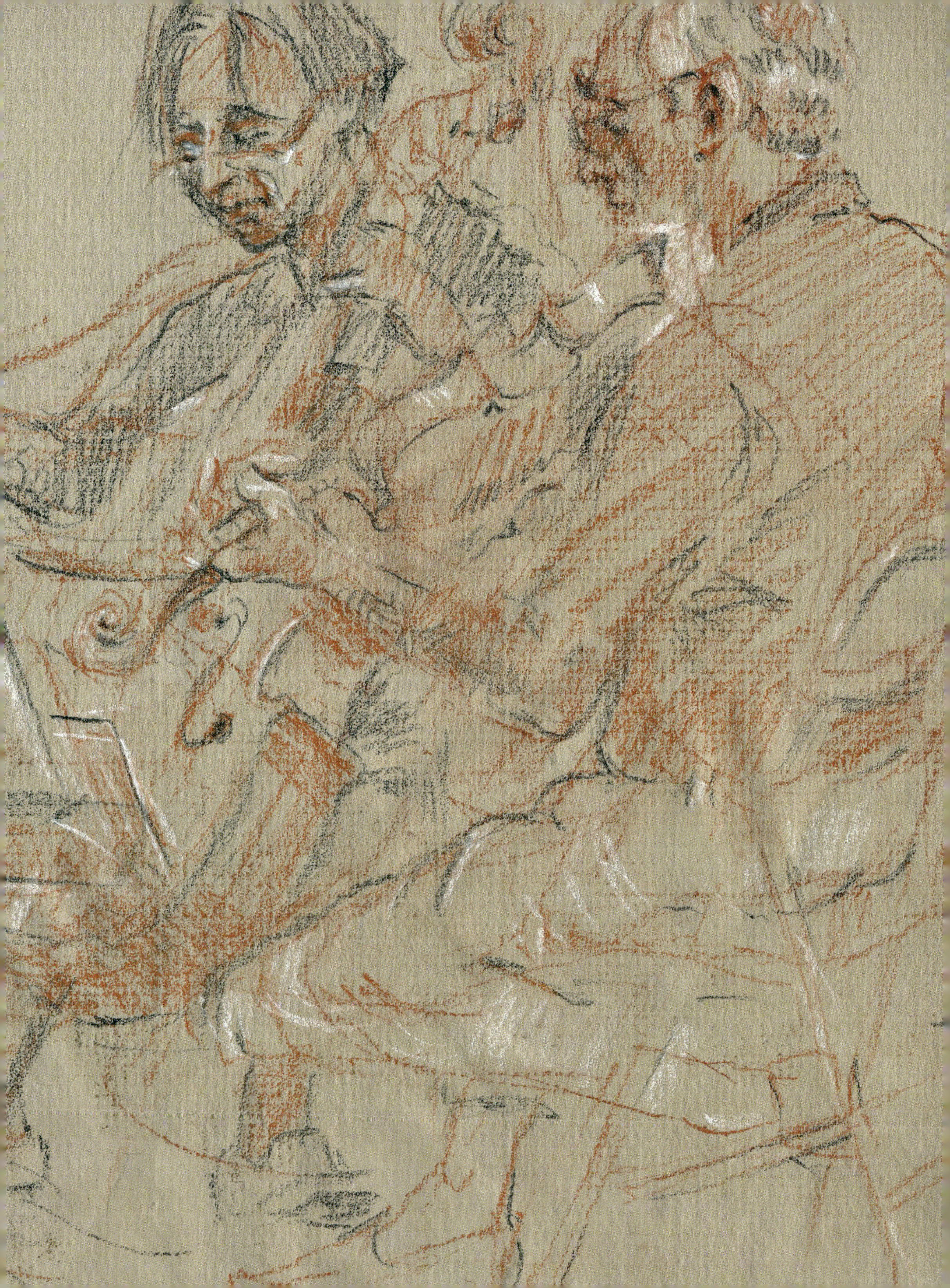

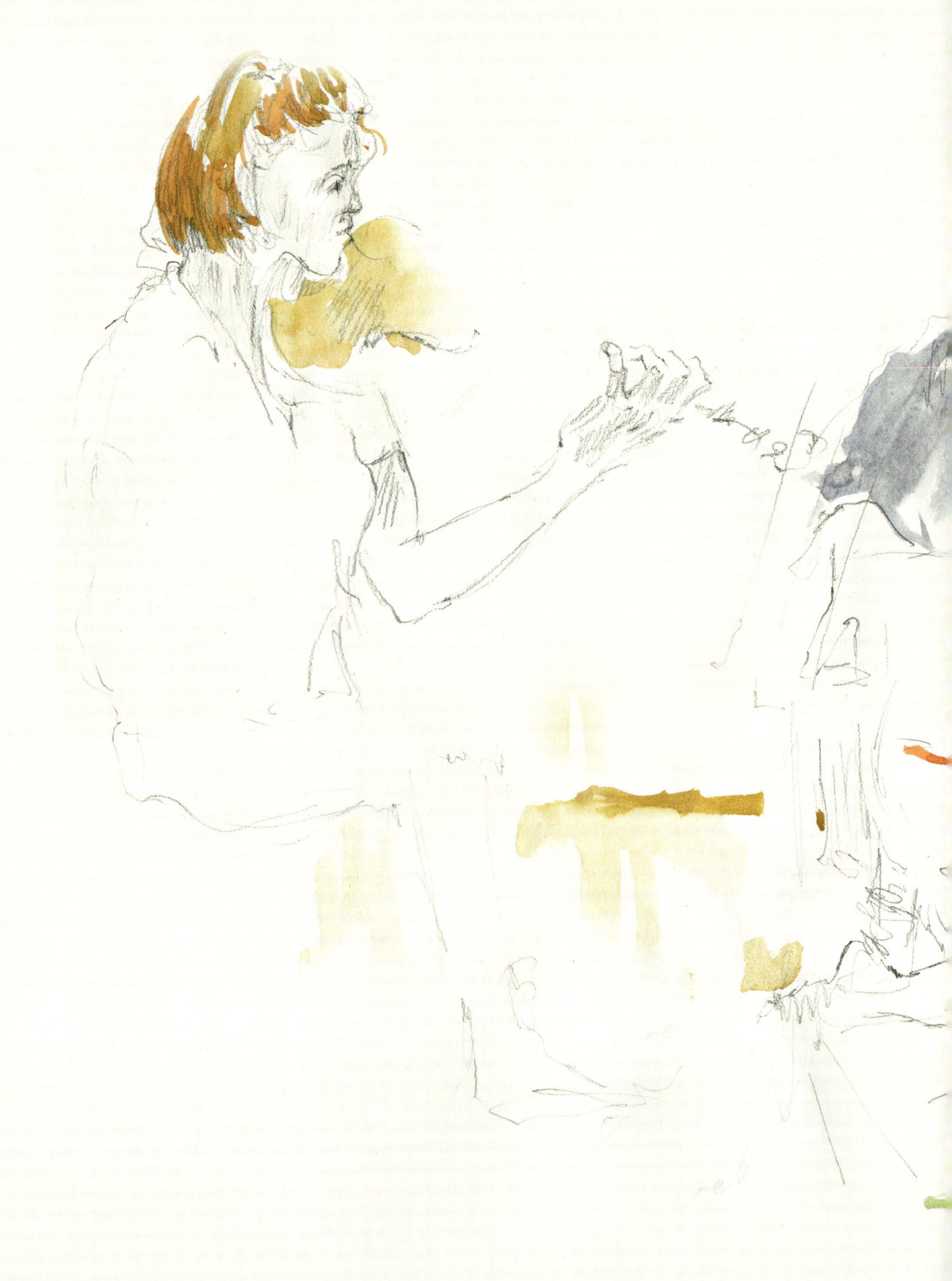

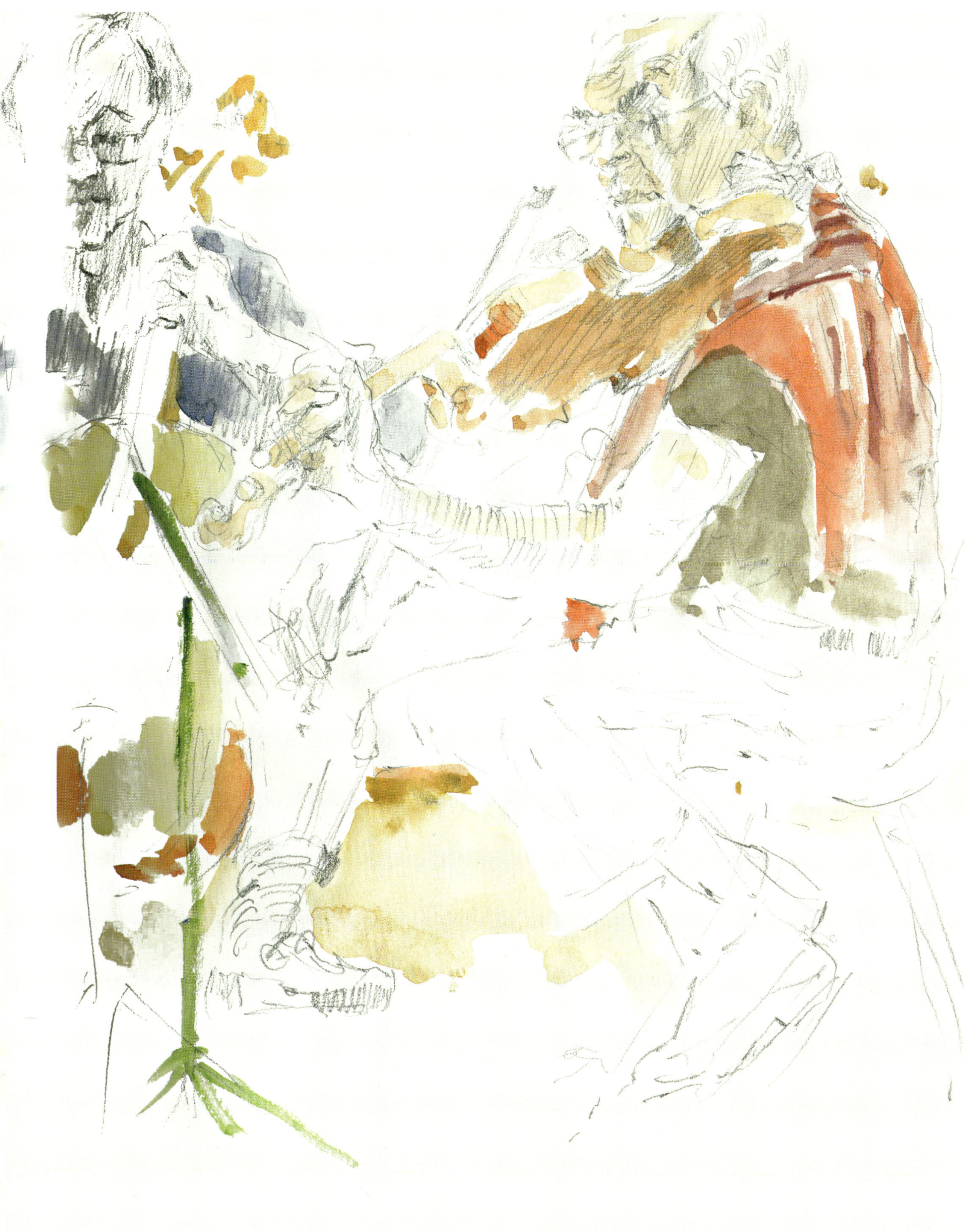

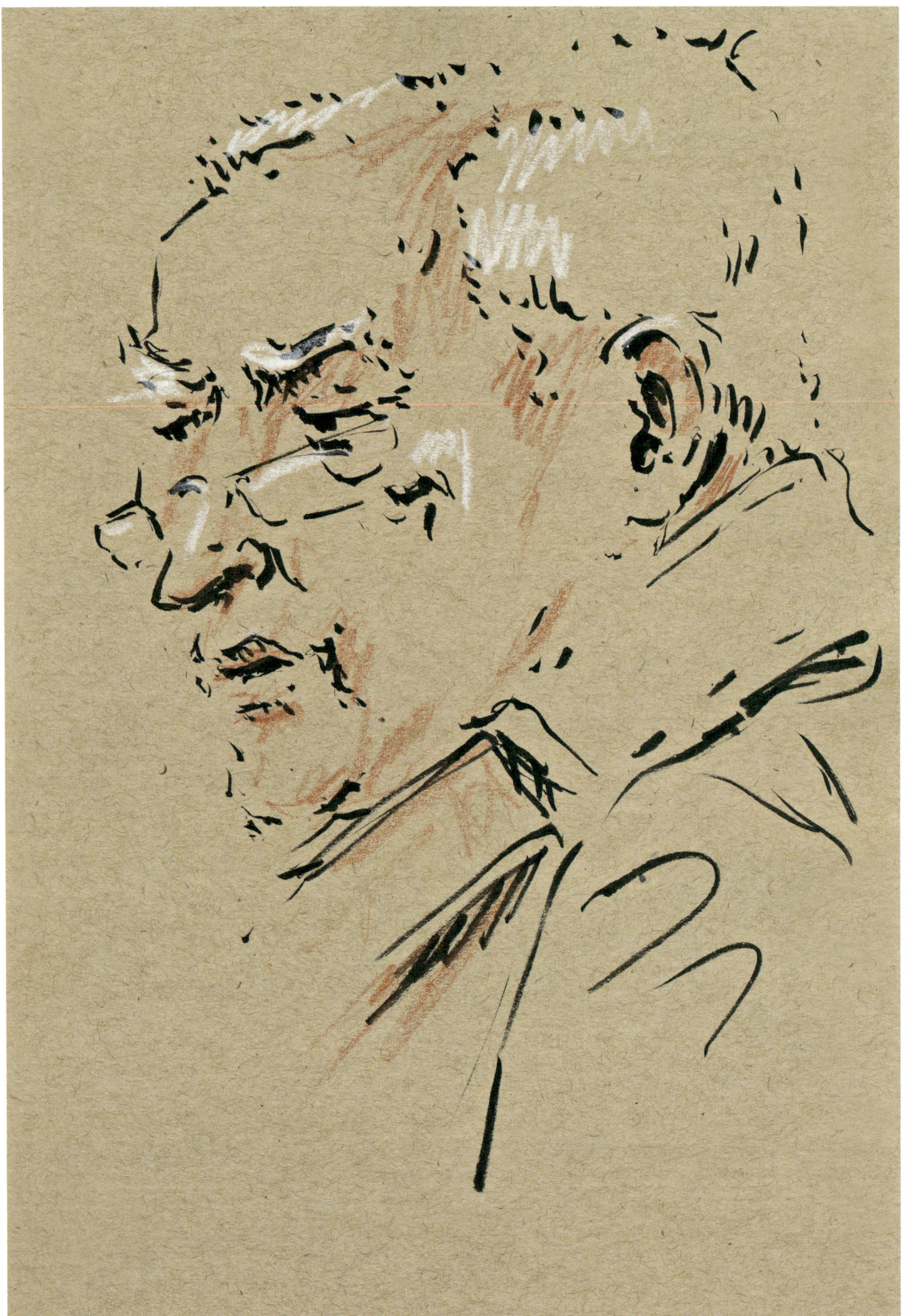

The next group of drawings are arranged in chronological order starting at the Historic Asolo Theatre in 1989.

Within the chronological order the drawings are grouped to feature a particular artist like Pia Gerlach, a beautiful young cellist who participated in the earliest concerts. You'll see her turning pages for Derek Han at the old Asolo and rehearsing with Francesco Petracchi the renowned bass player.

Pia Gerlach was a student at Juilliard of Nancy Streetman who now lives in Sarasota and was also my cello teacher. I had the pleasure of meeting Pia when she was performing here.

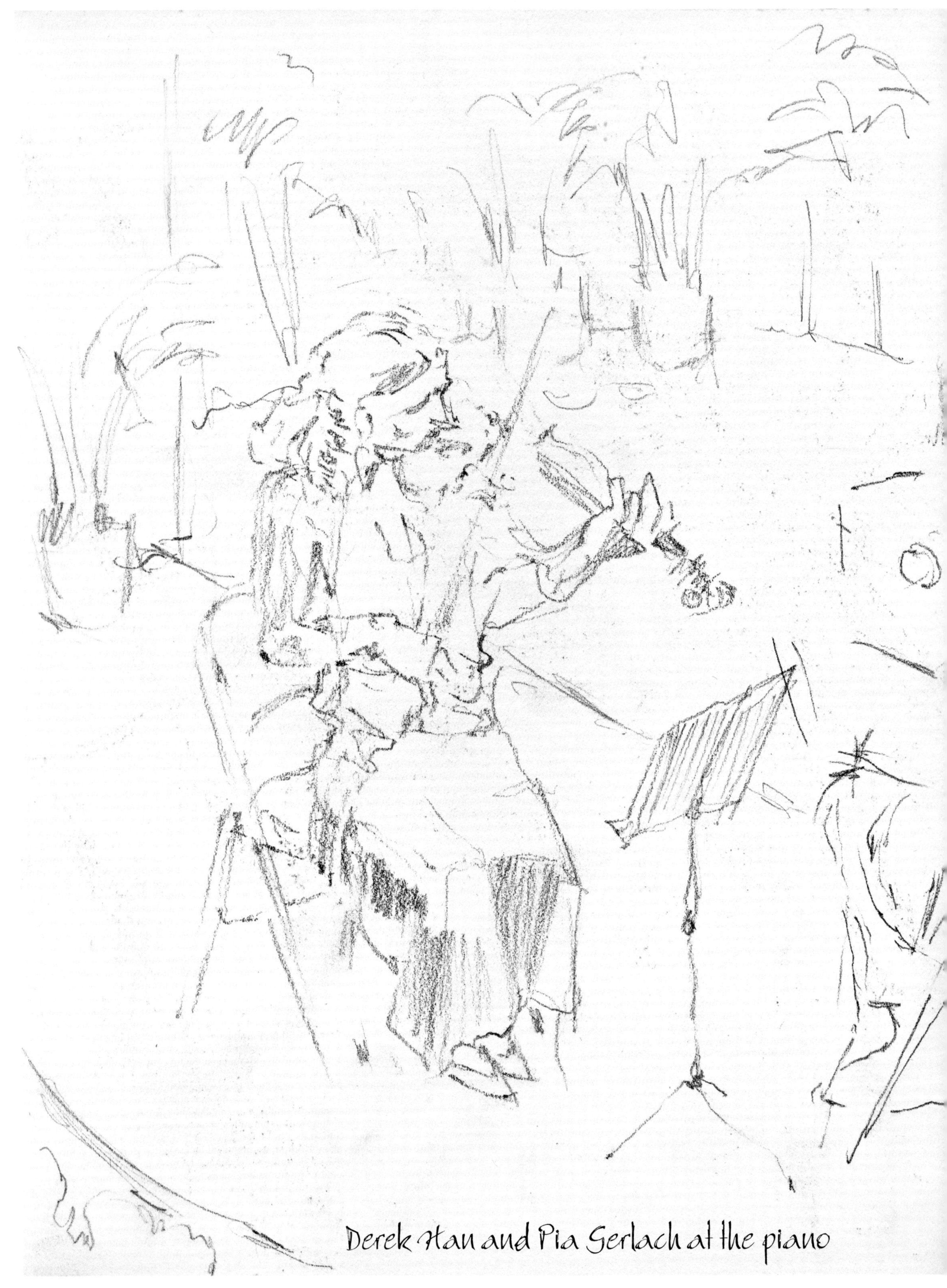

Derek Han and Pia Gerlach at the piano

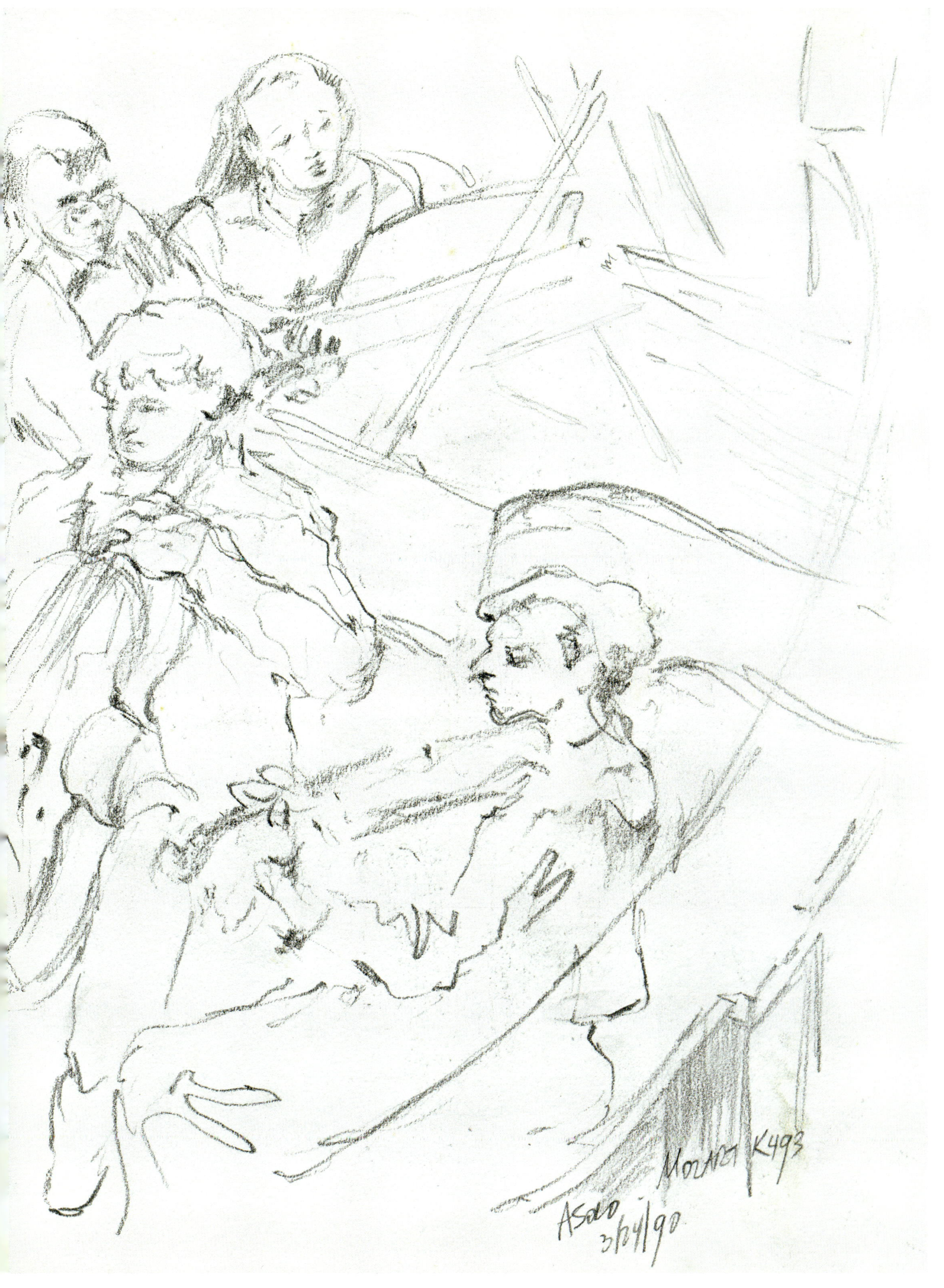
Mozart K493
Asolo
3/24/90

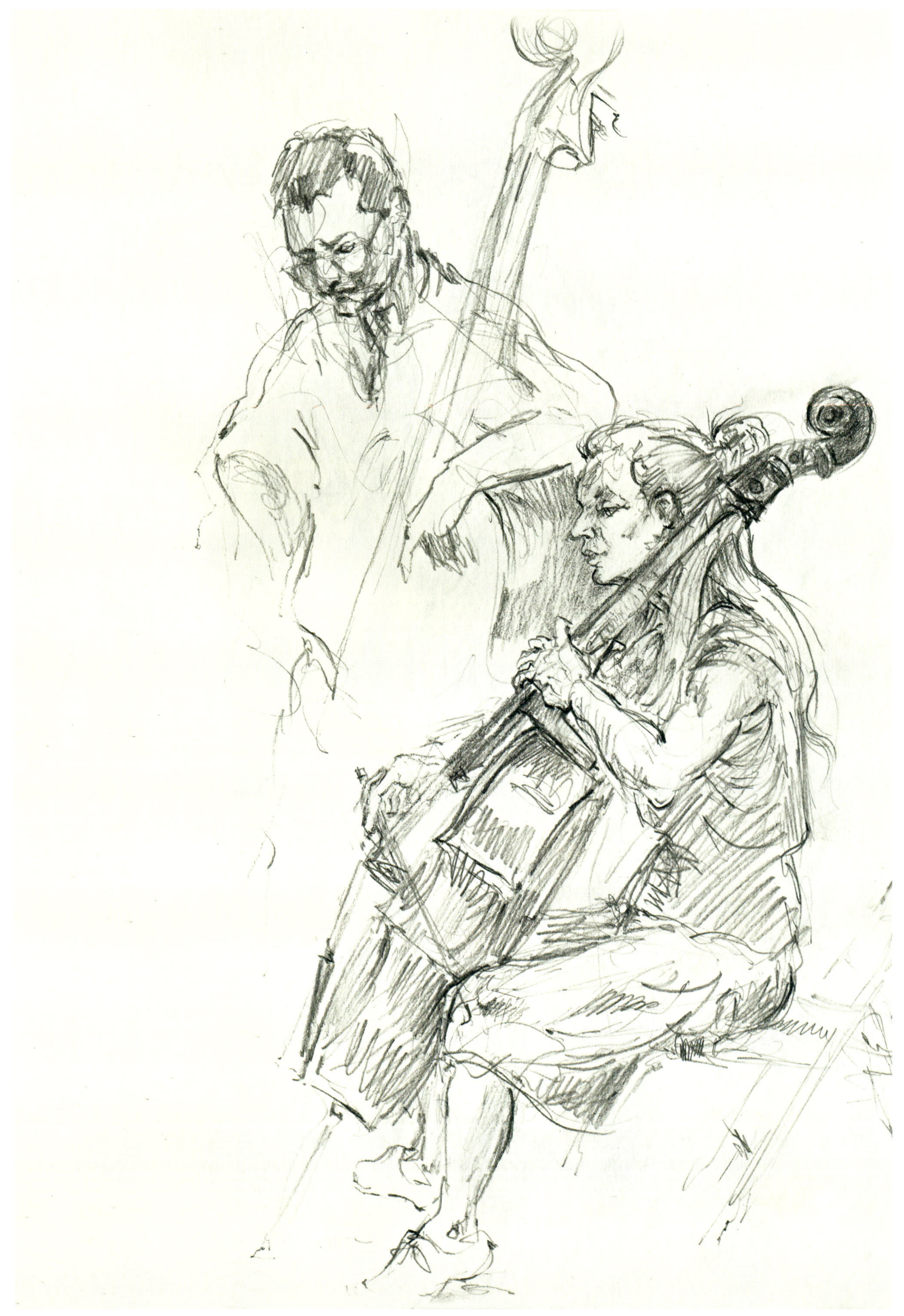

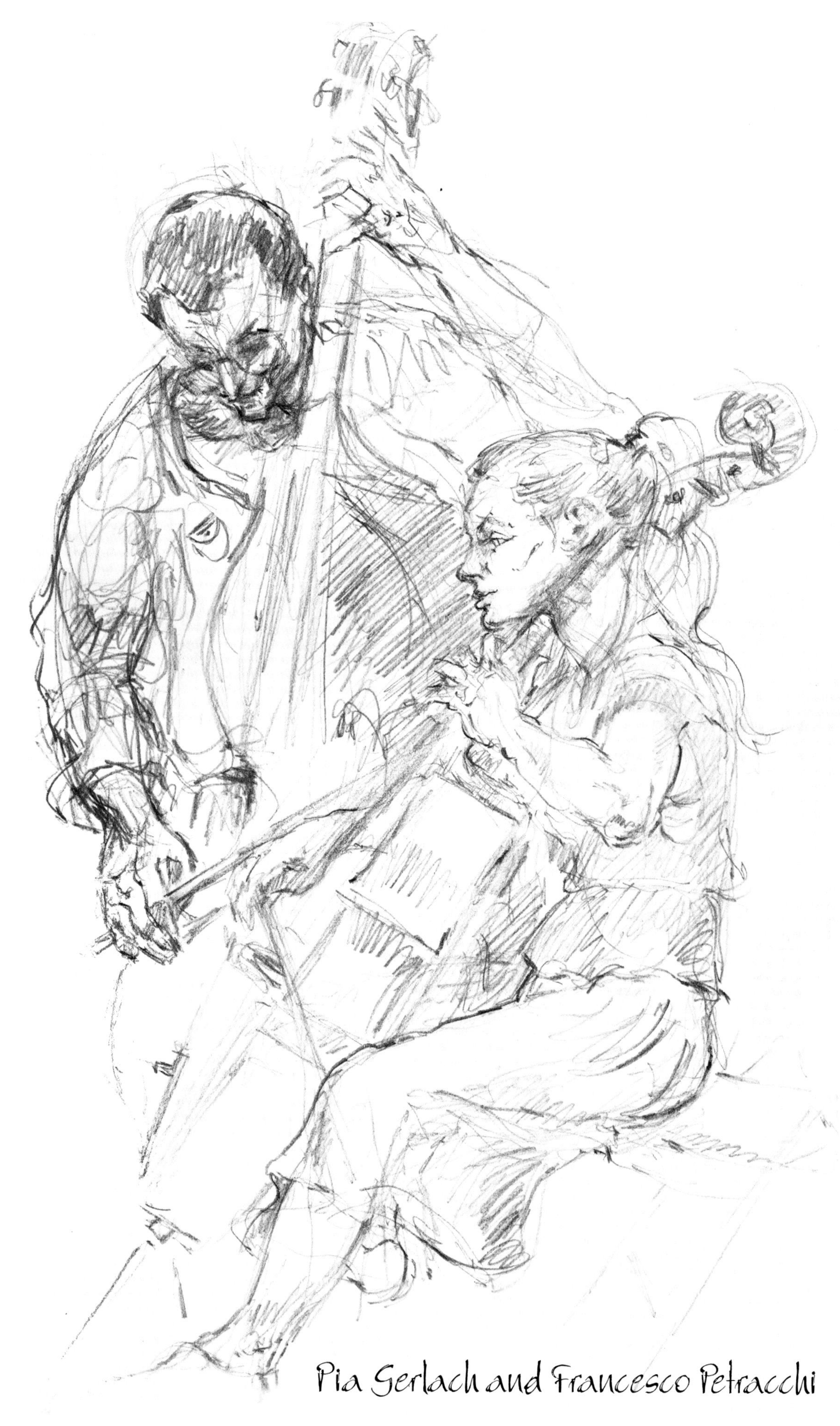

Pia Gerlach and Francesco Petracchi

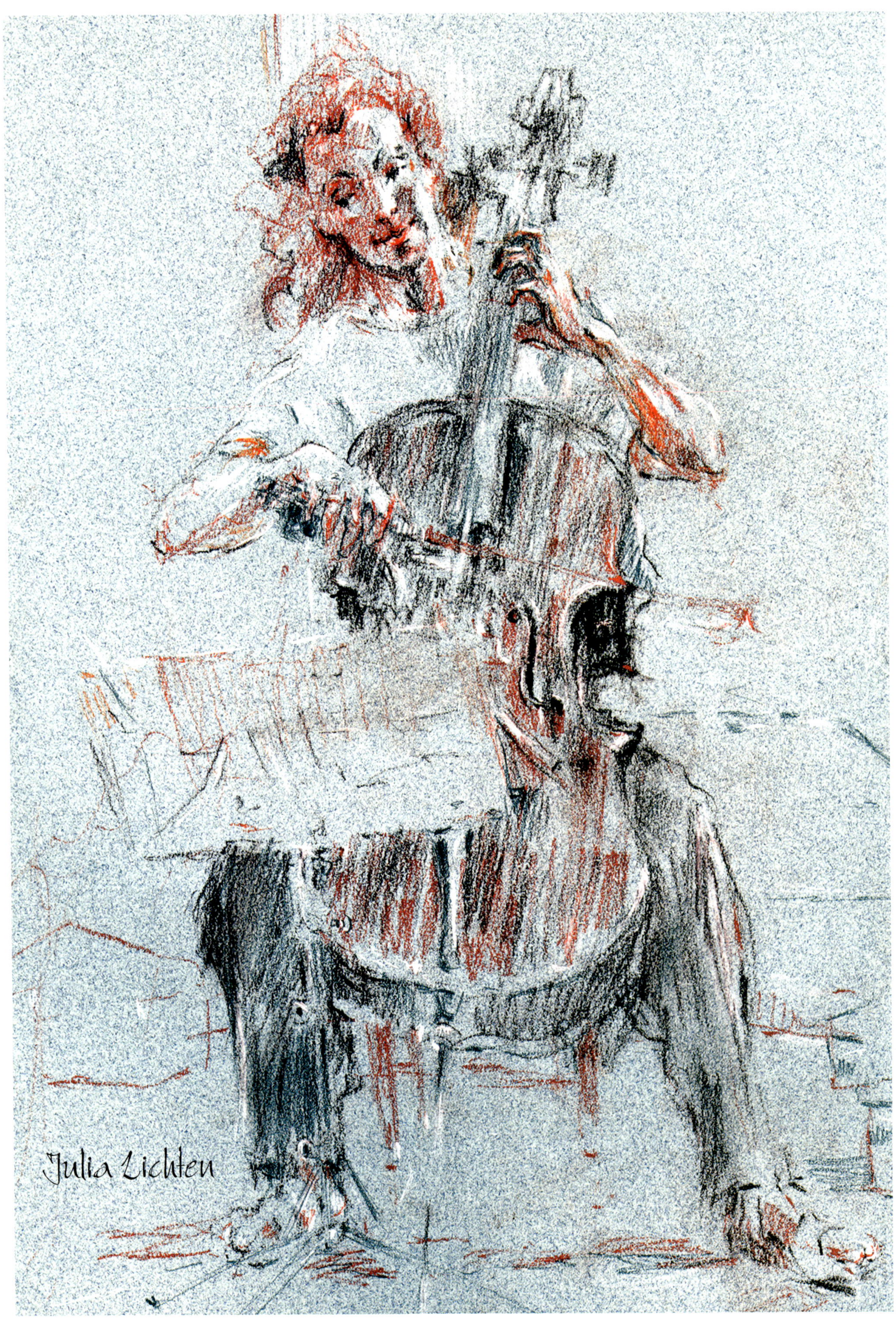
Julia Lichten

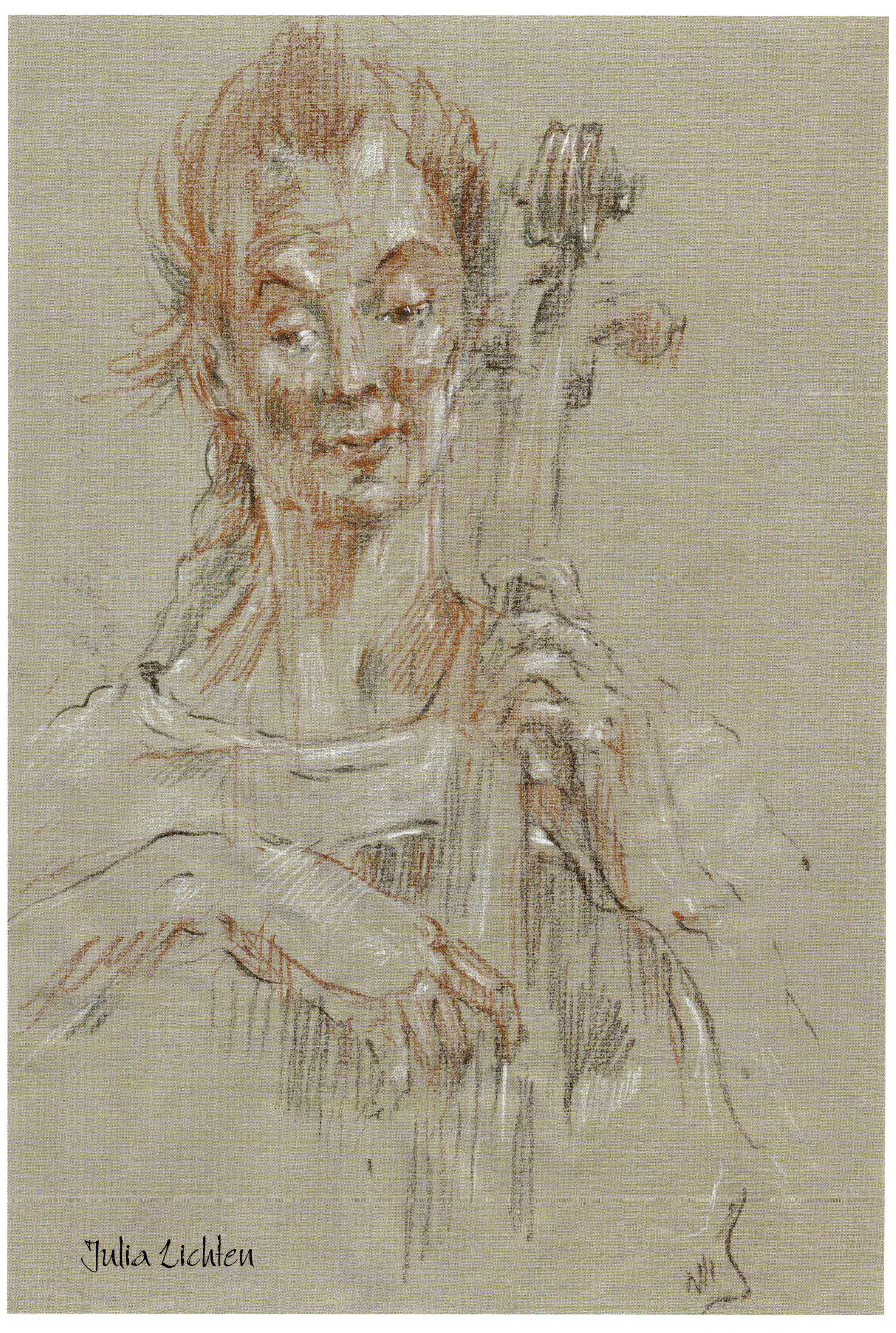
Julia Lichten

Norbert Brainin, First Violin of the Amadeus String Quartet,
rehearsing with Julia Lichten

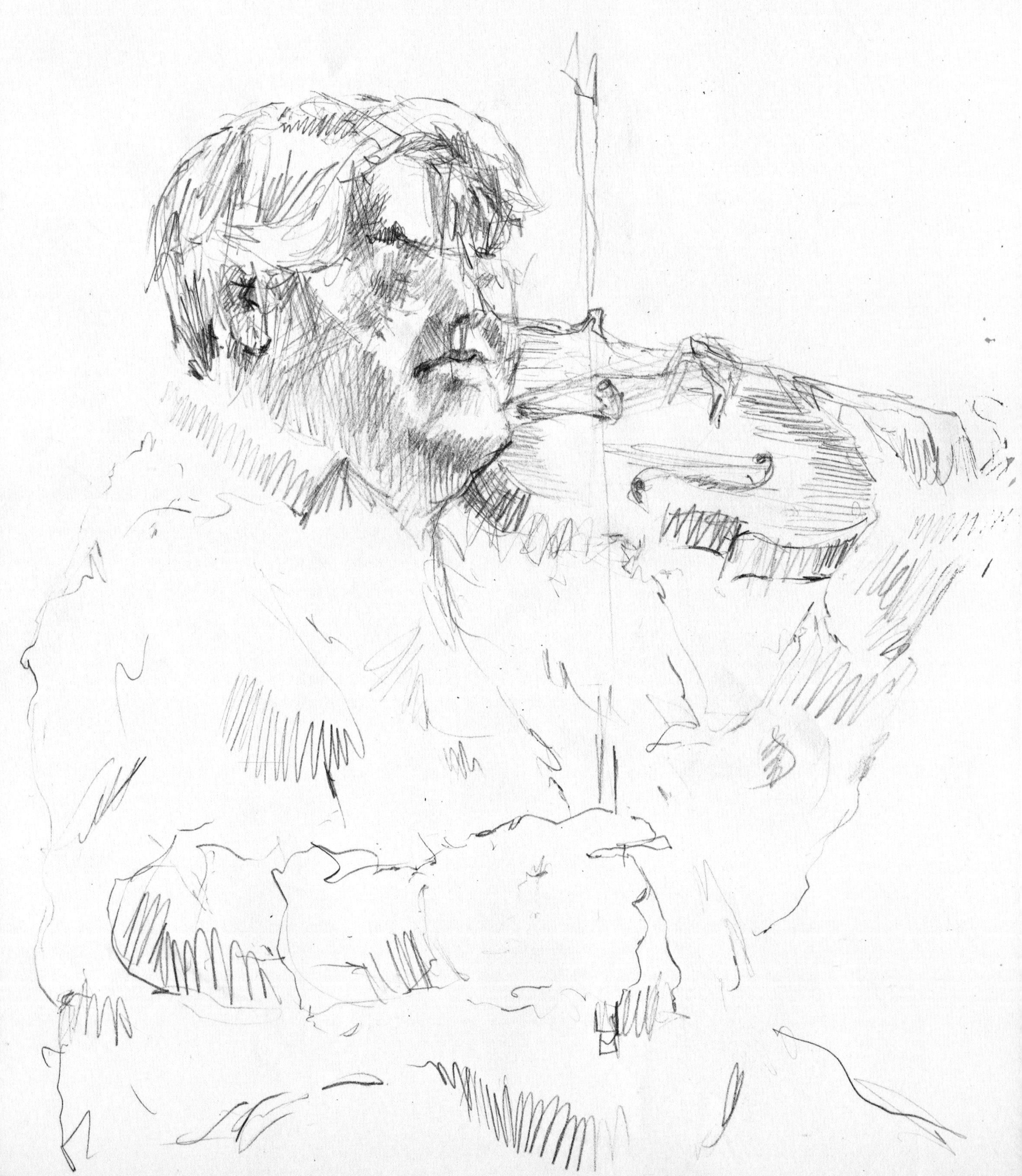

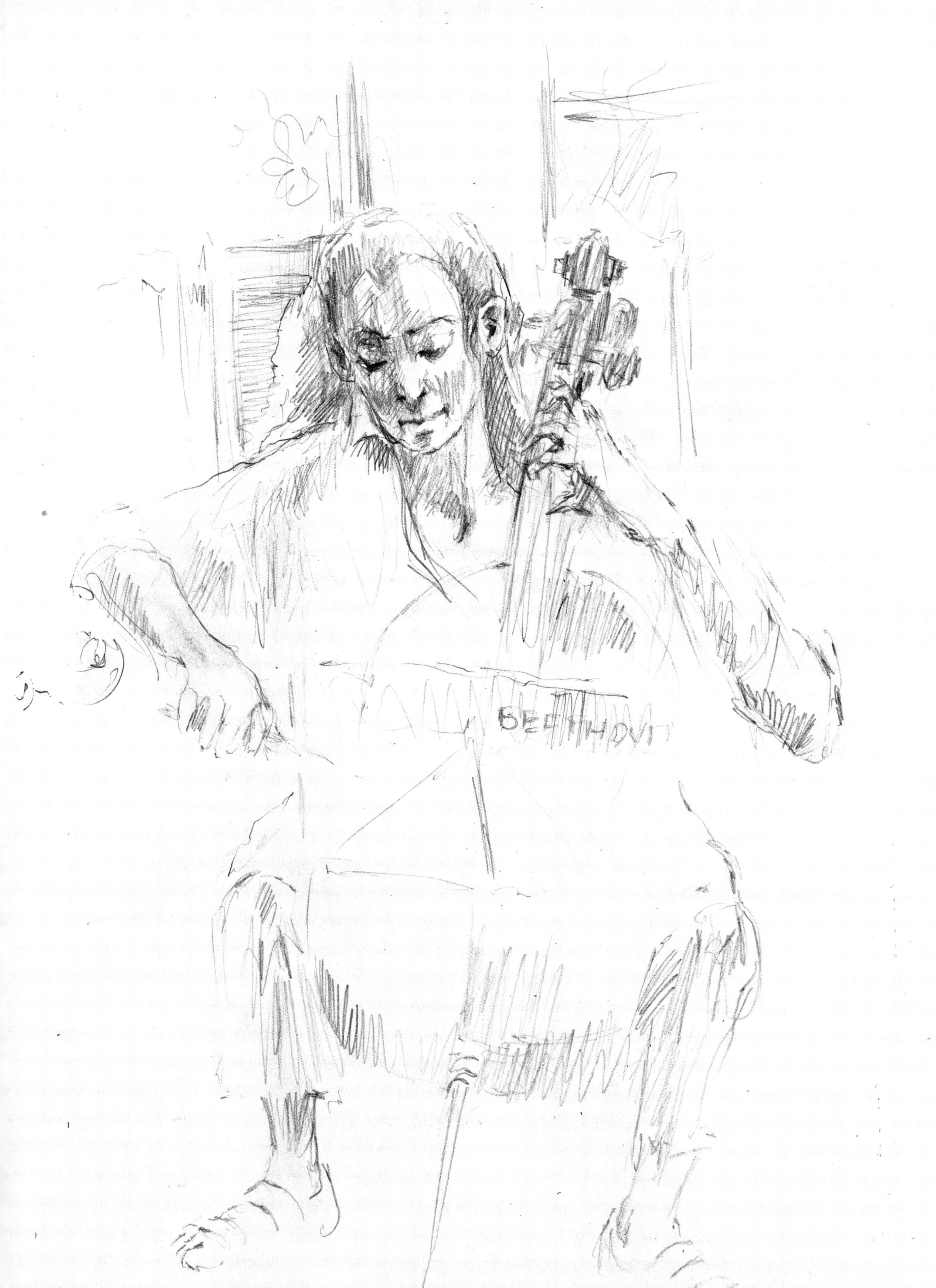

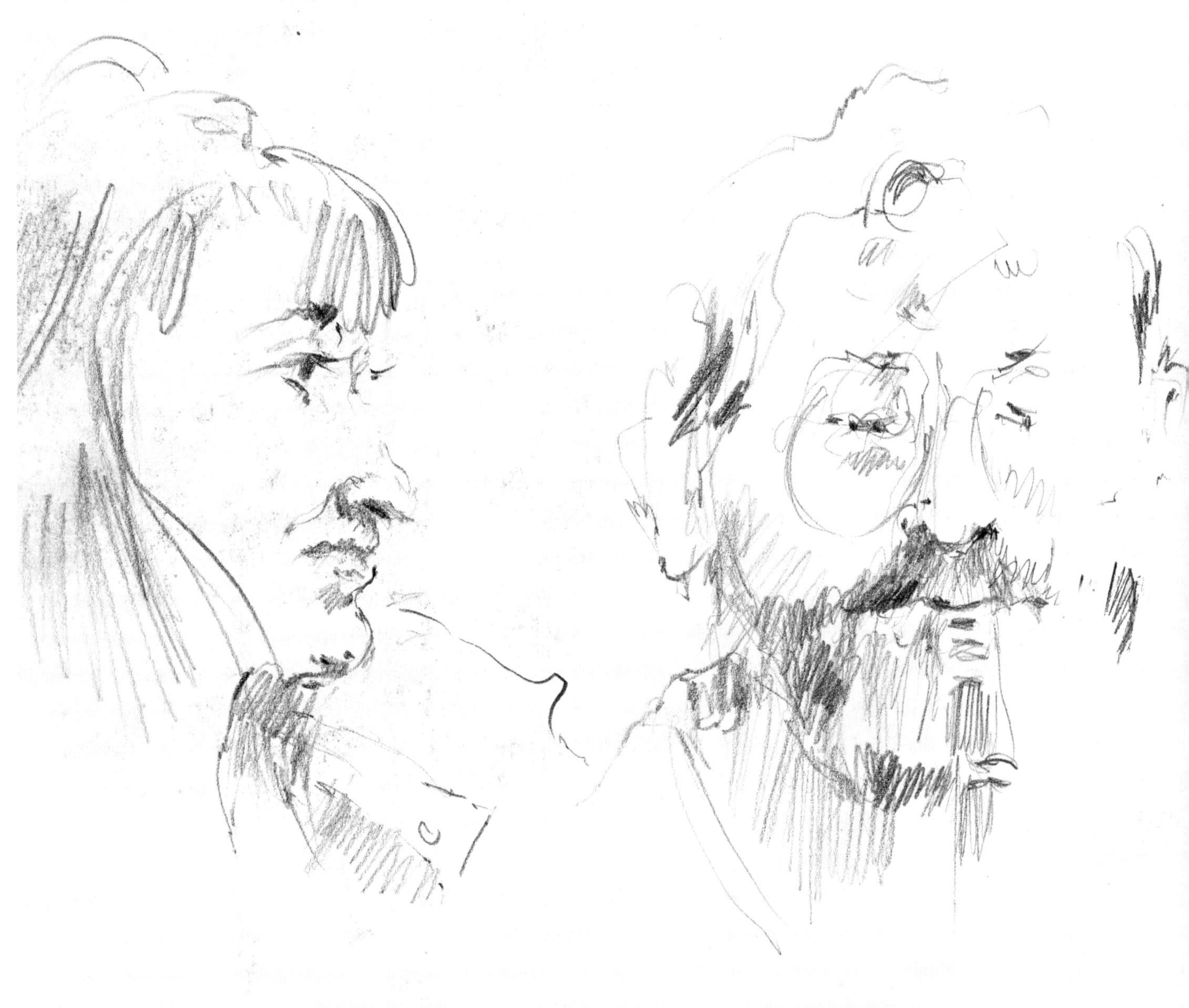
ANI KAVAFIAN
DAVID SHIFRIN

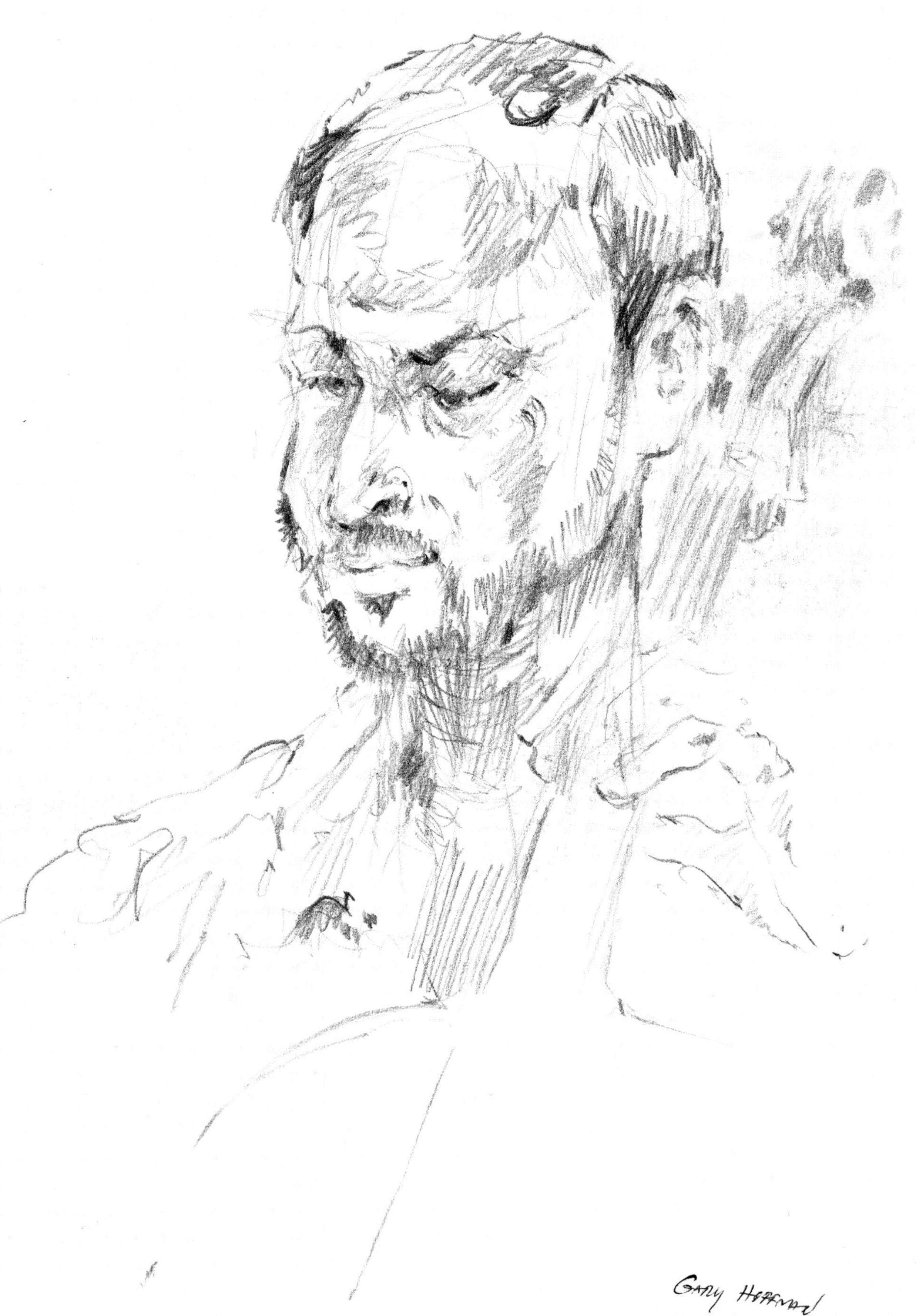
GARY HOFFMAN

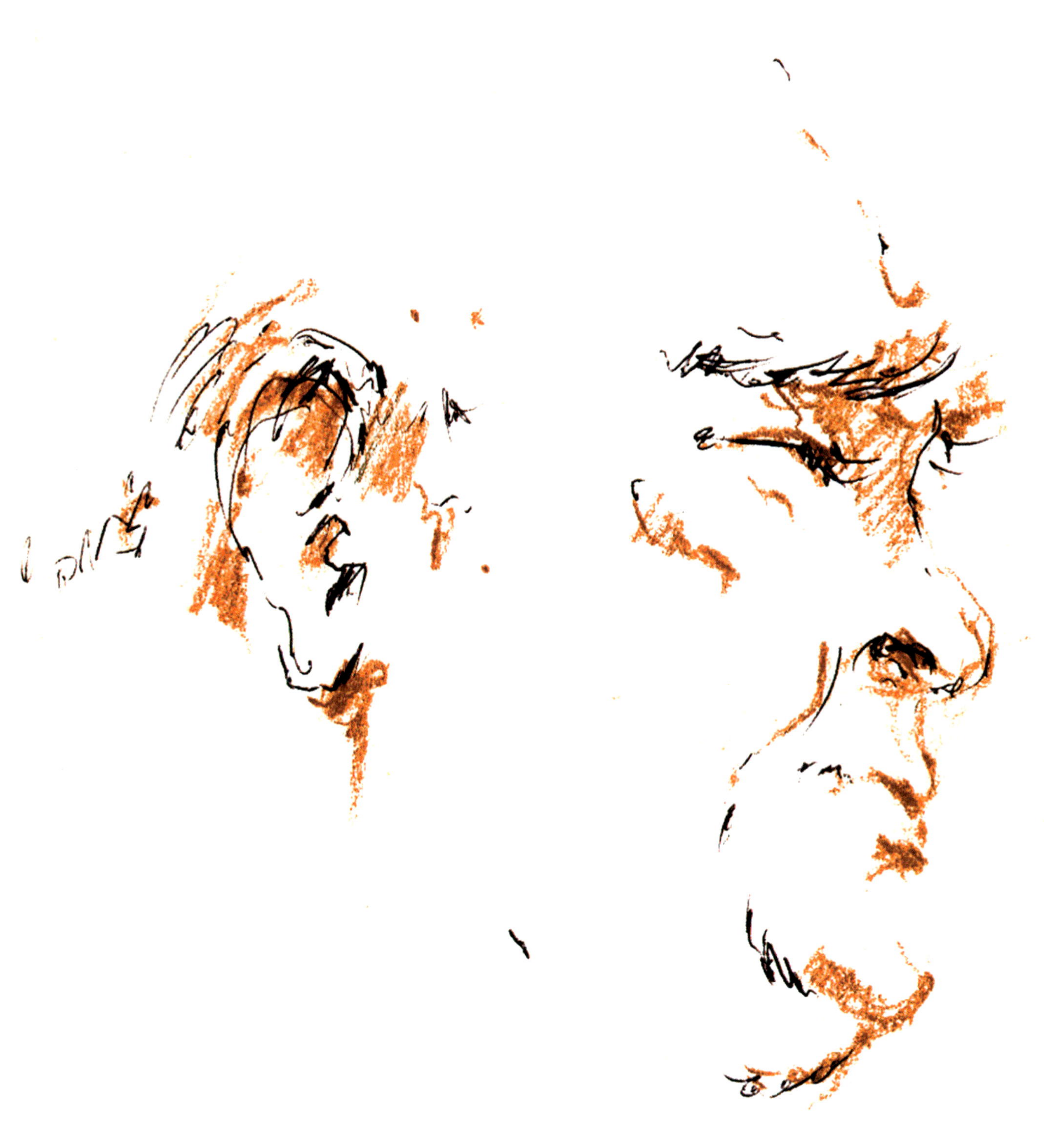

Joseph Silverstein, violinist

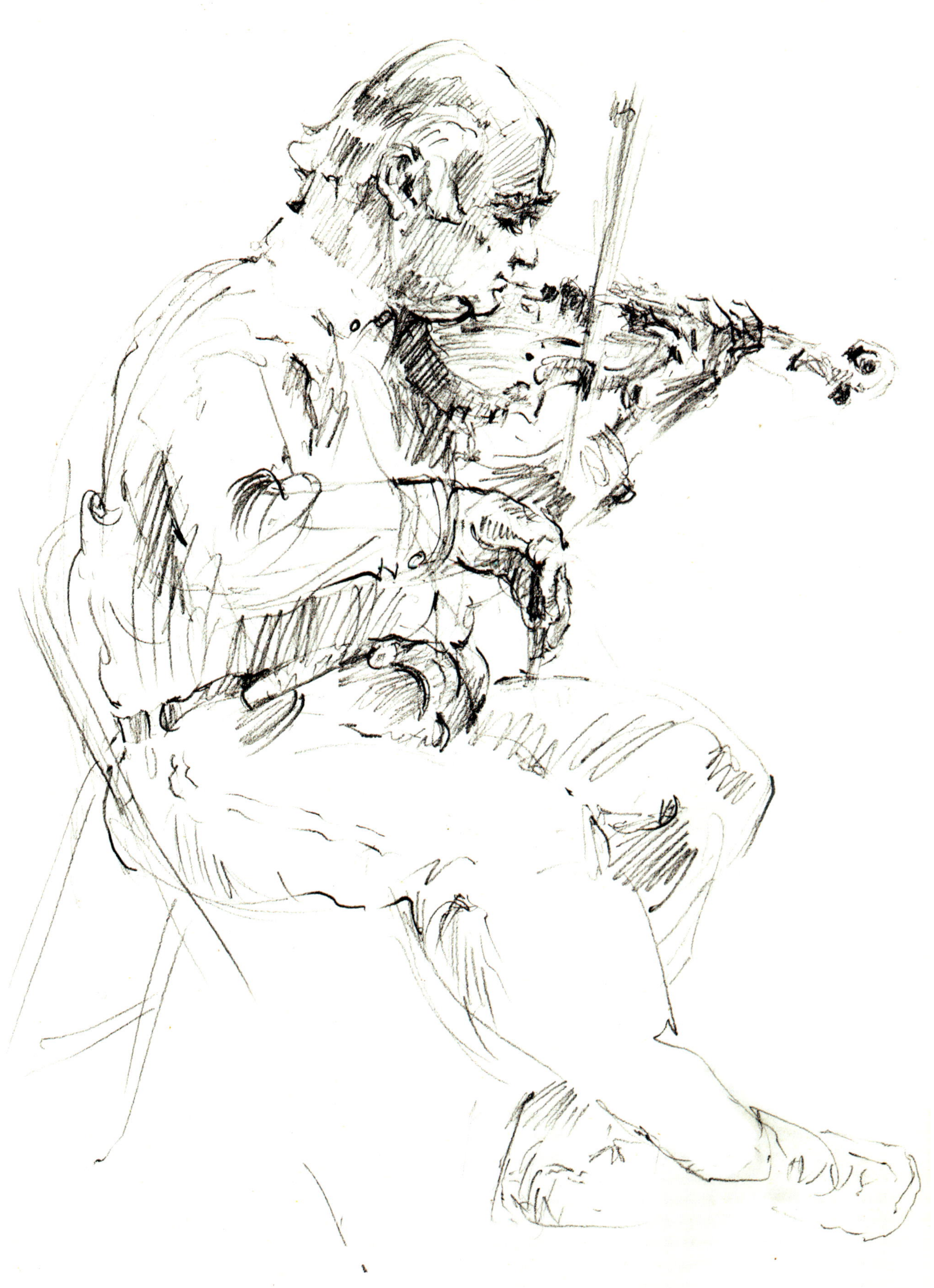

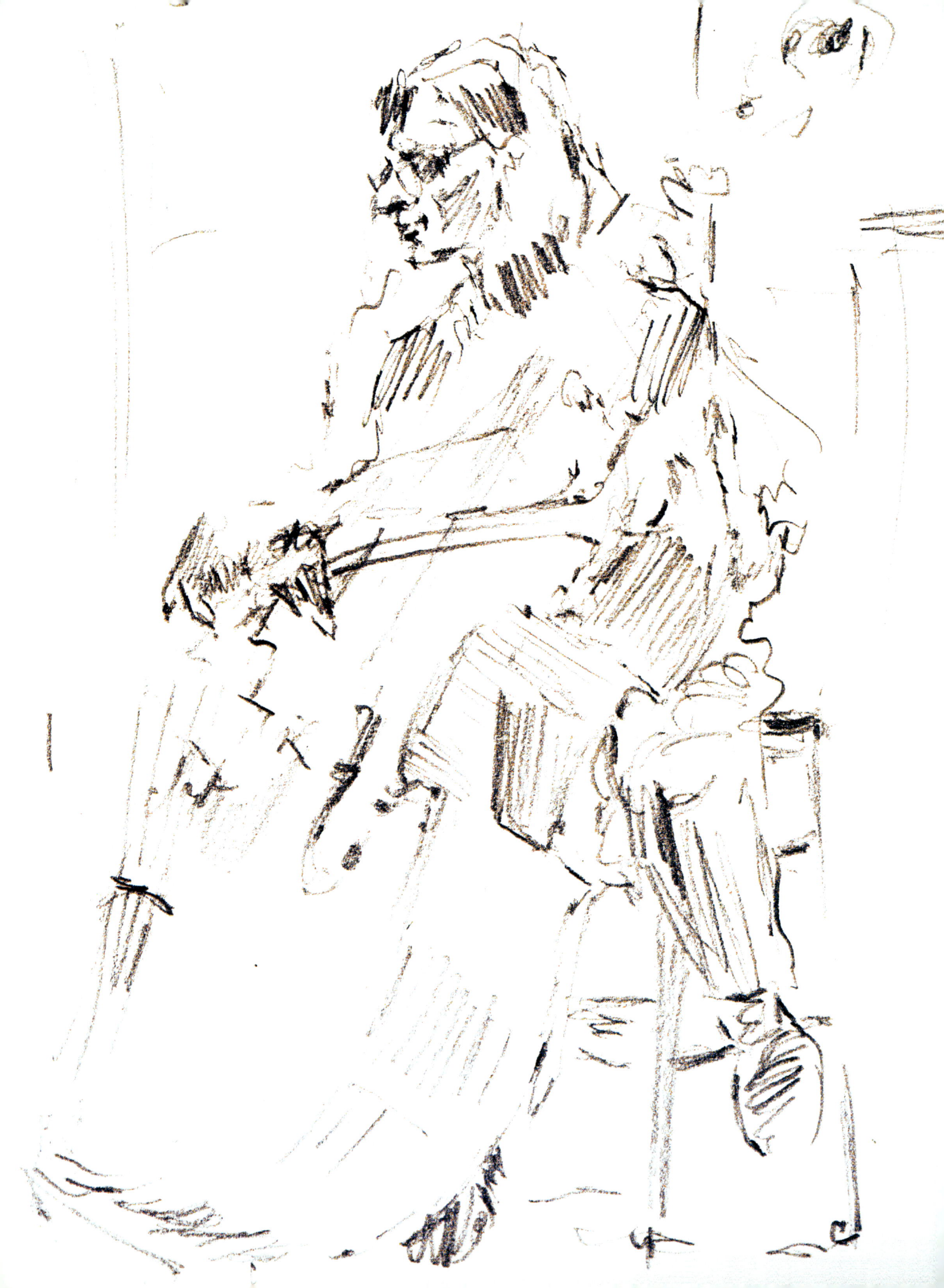

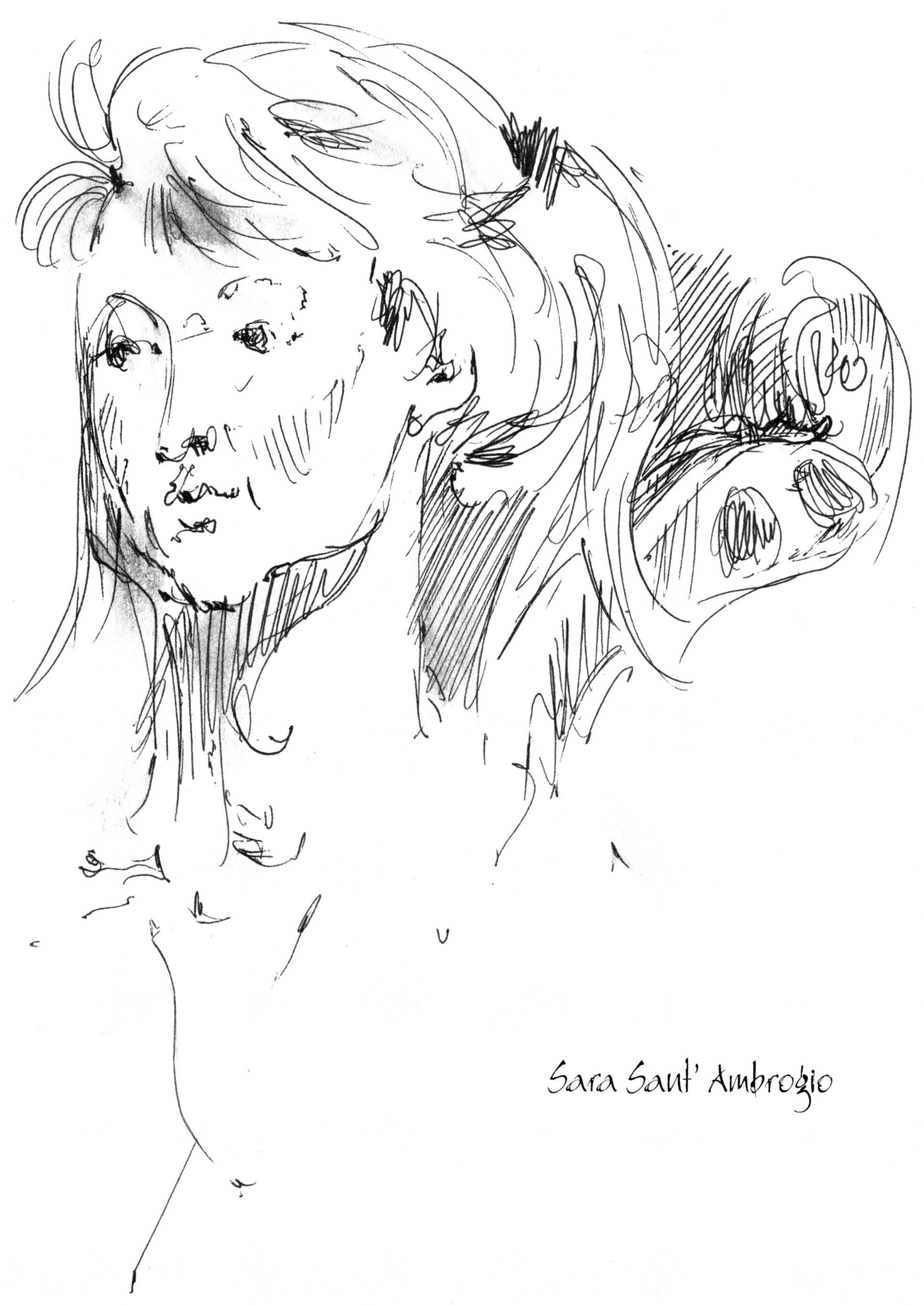

Sara Sant' Ambrogio

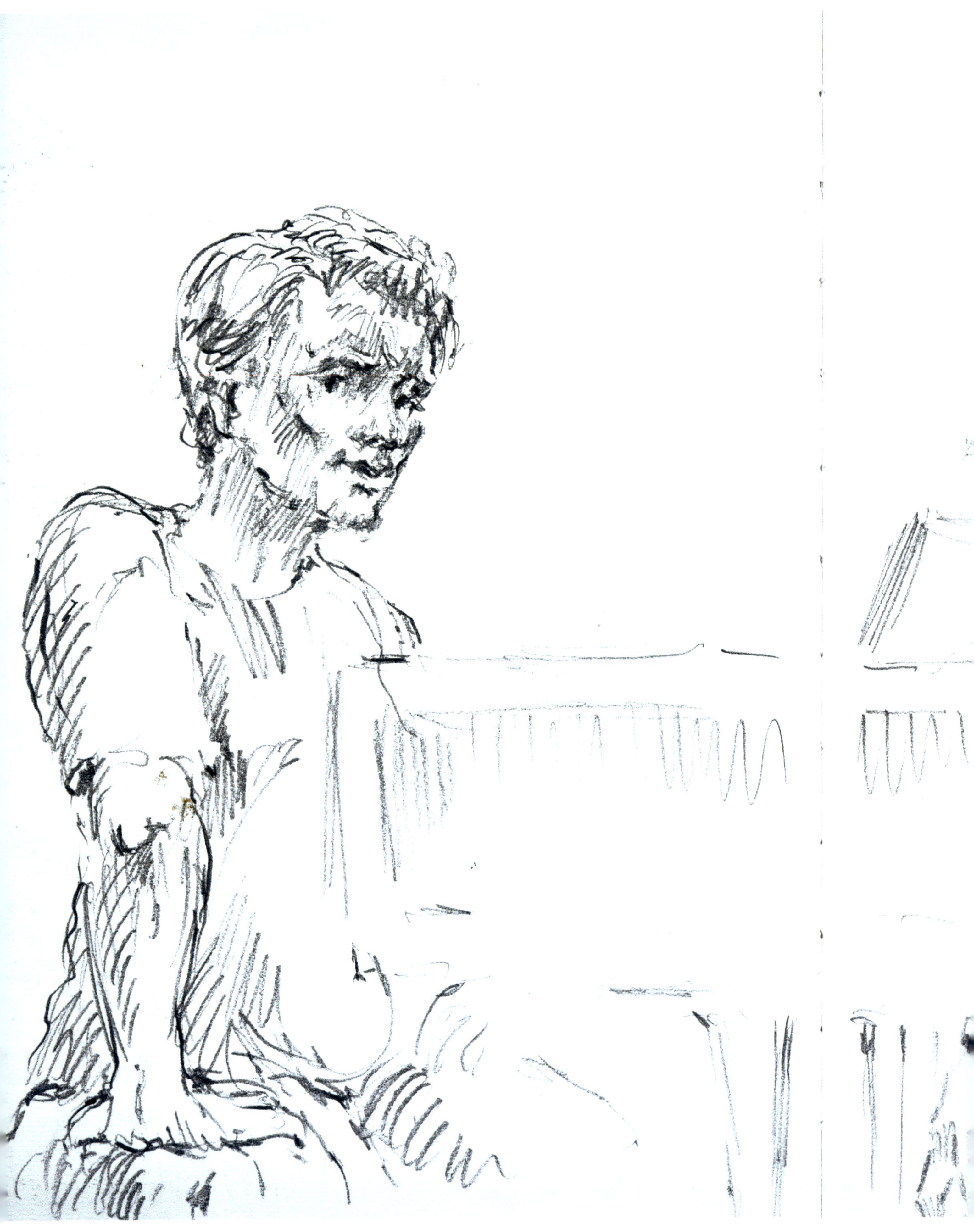

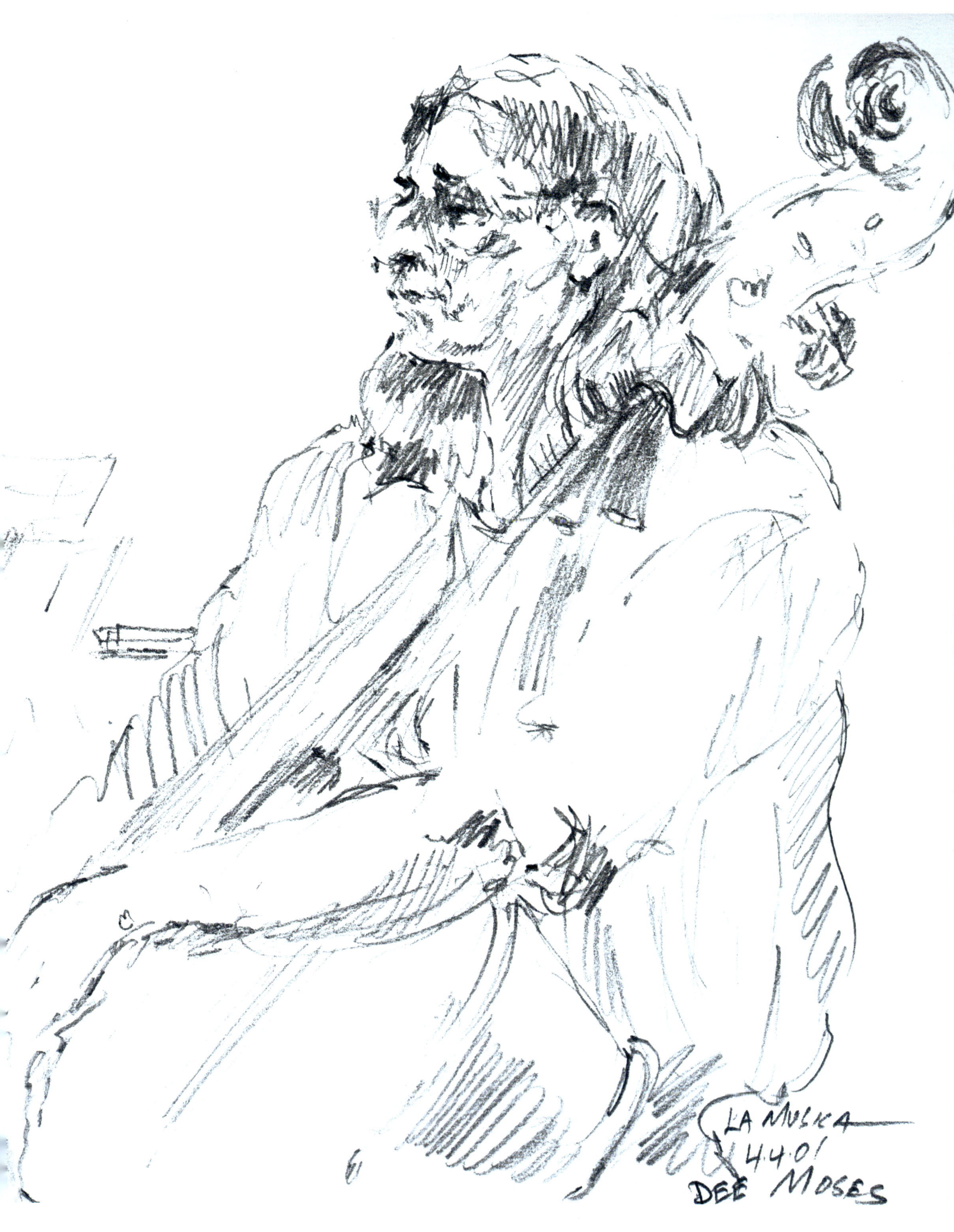
LA MUSKA
4.4.01
DEE MOSES

"Sol's likenesses are striking, but to see what is really meaningful about his La Musica portraits, have a look at his sketch of Bruno in 1996: that is a Happy Man!"

– Daniel Avshalomov, violist

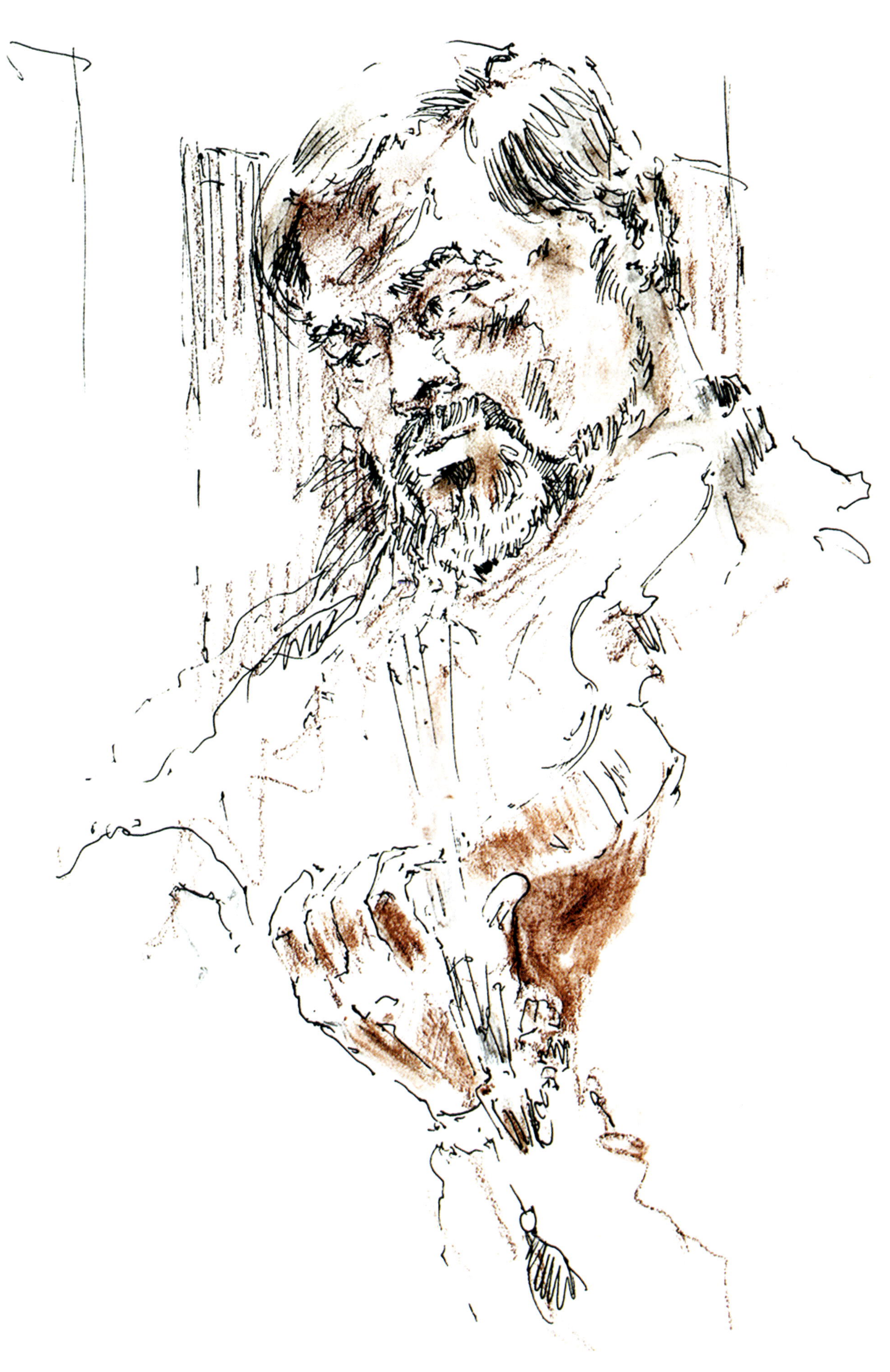

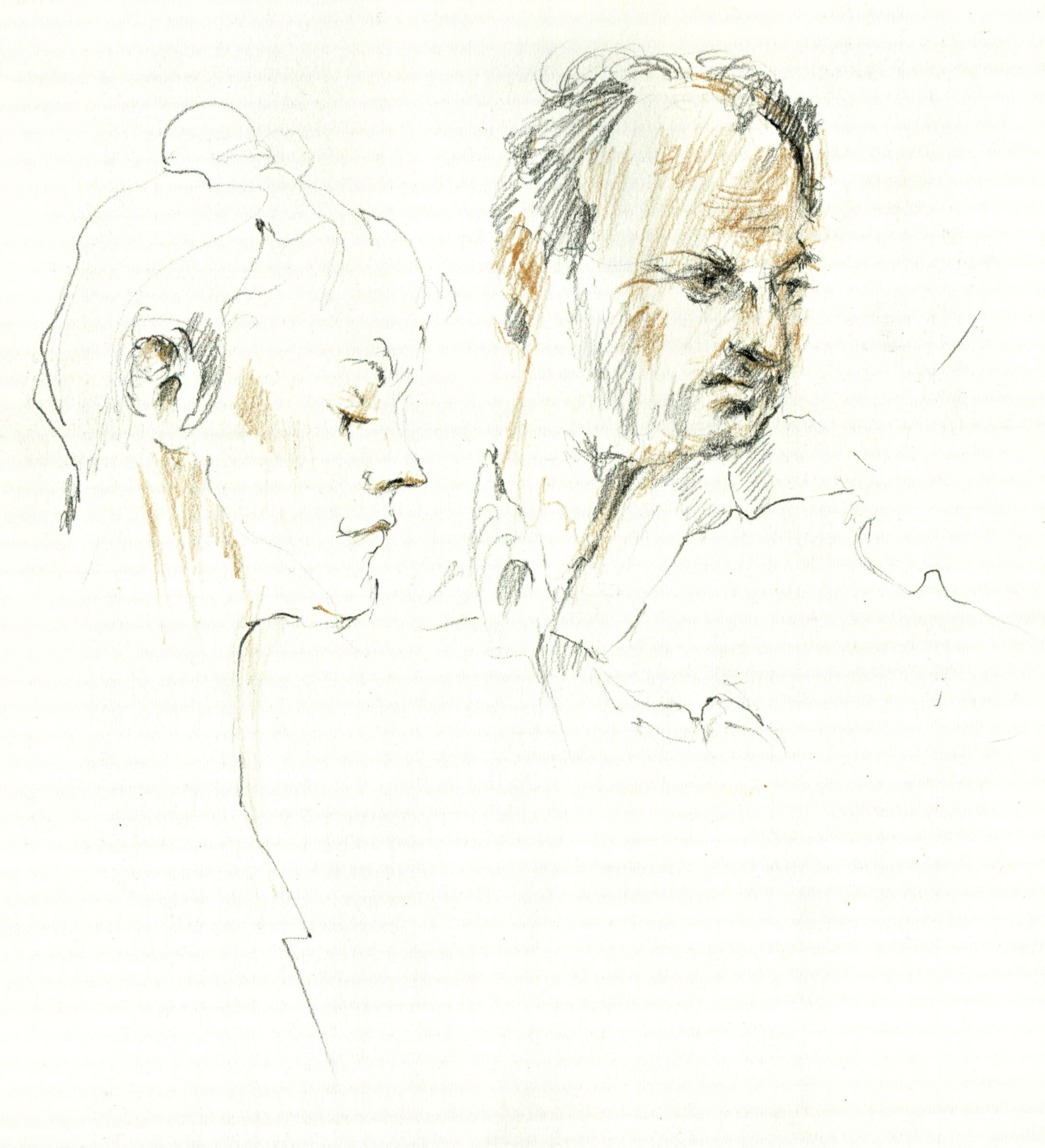

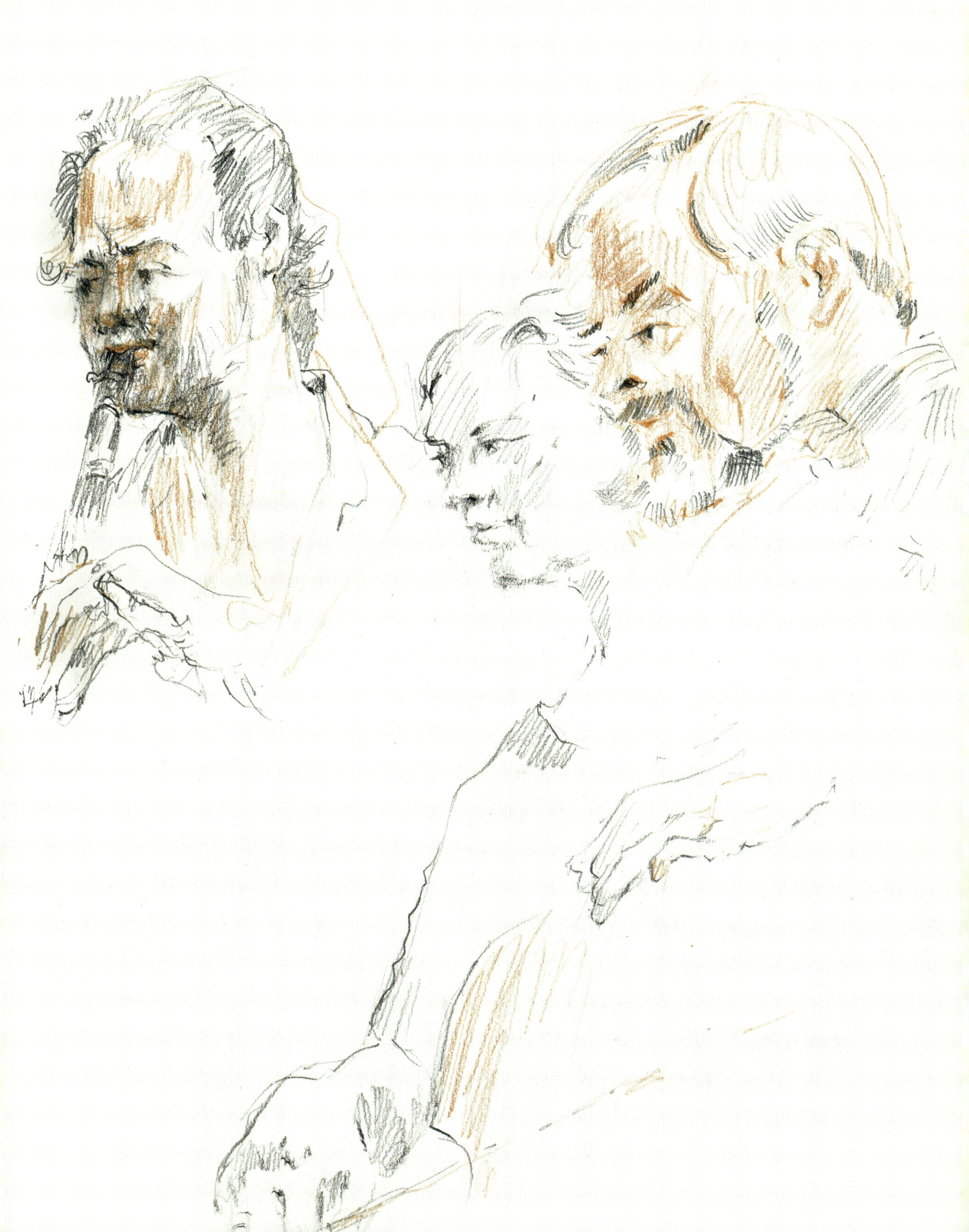

Daniel Avshalomov is one of the world's preeminent viola soloists. He is also a noted author, raconteur and has written all the notes for the La Musica Festival since its inception in 1987. He is a member of The American String Quartet and a highly regarded teacher on the faculty of Manhattan and Aspen Schools of Music. Daniel is also known for his outstanding abilities as a cook. For recreation he is a mountain climber, and he is probably the handsomest violist that has ever lived.

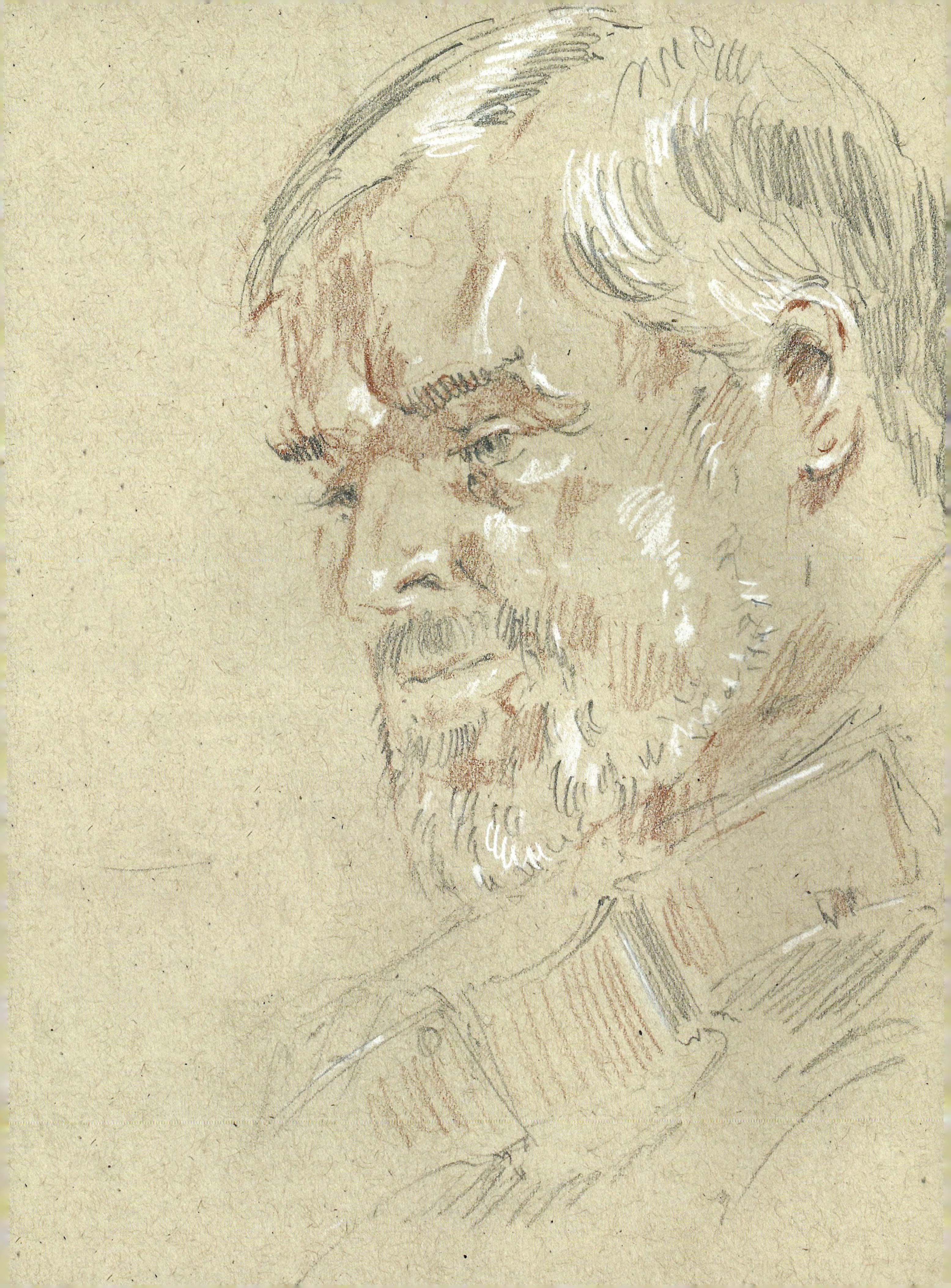

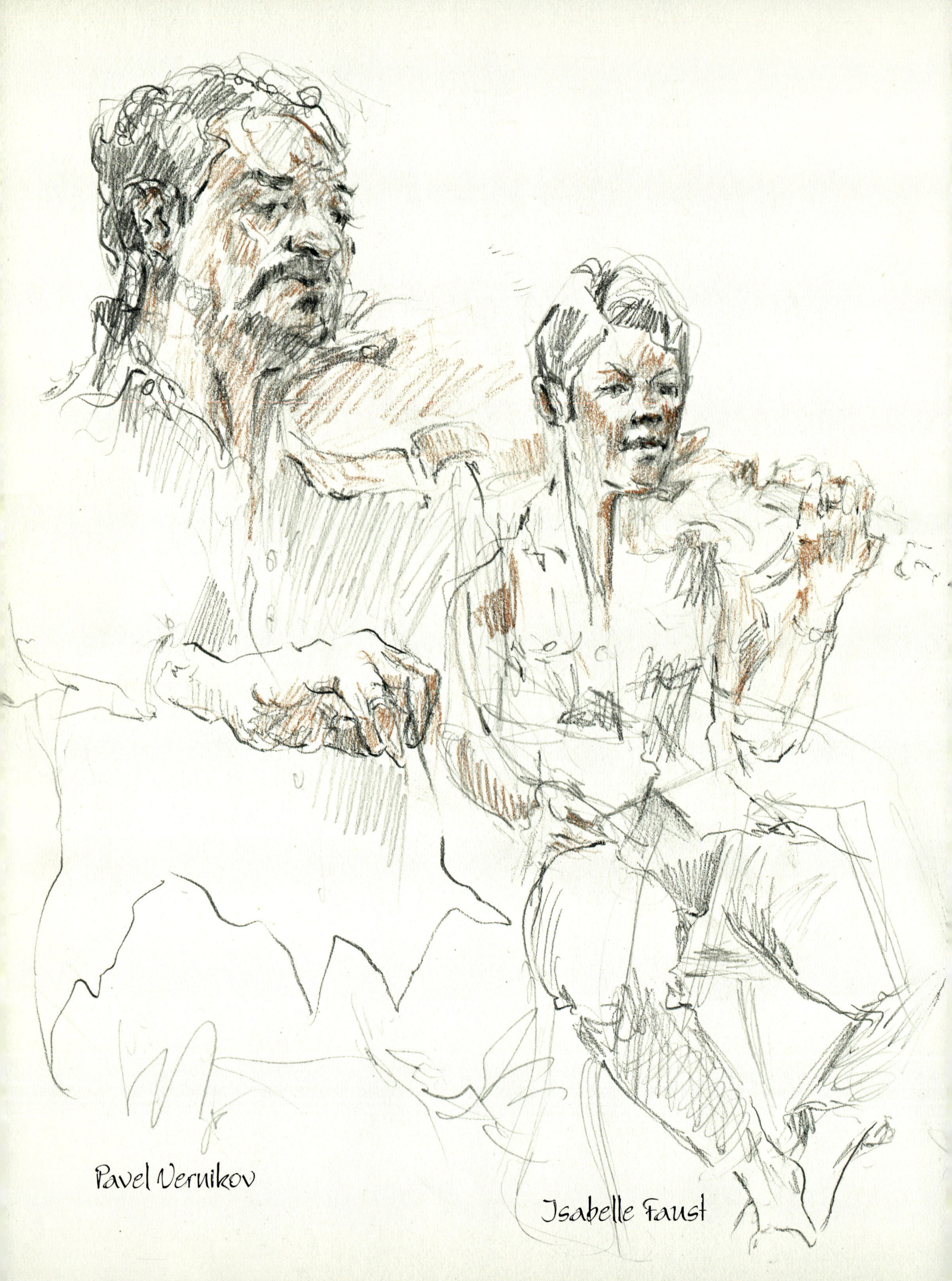
Pavel Vernikov
Isabelle Faust

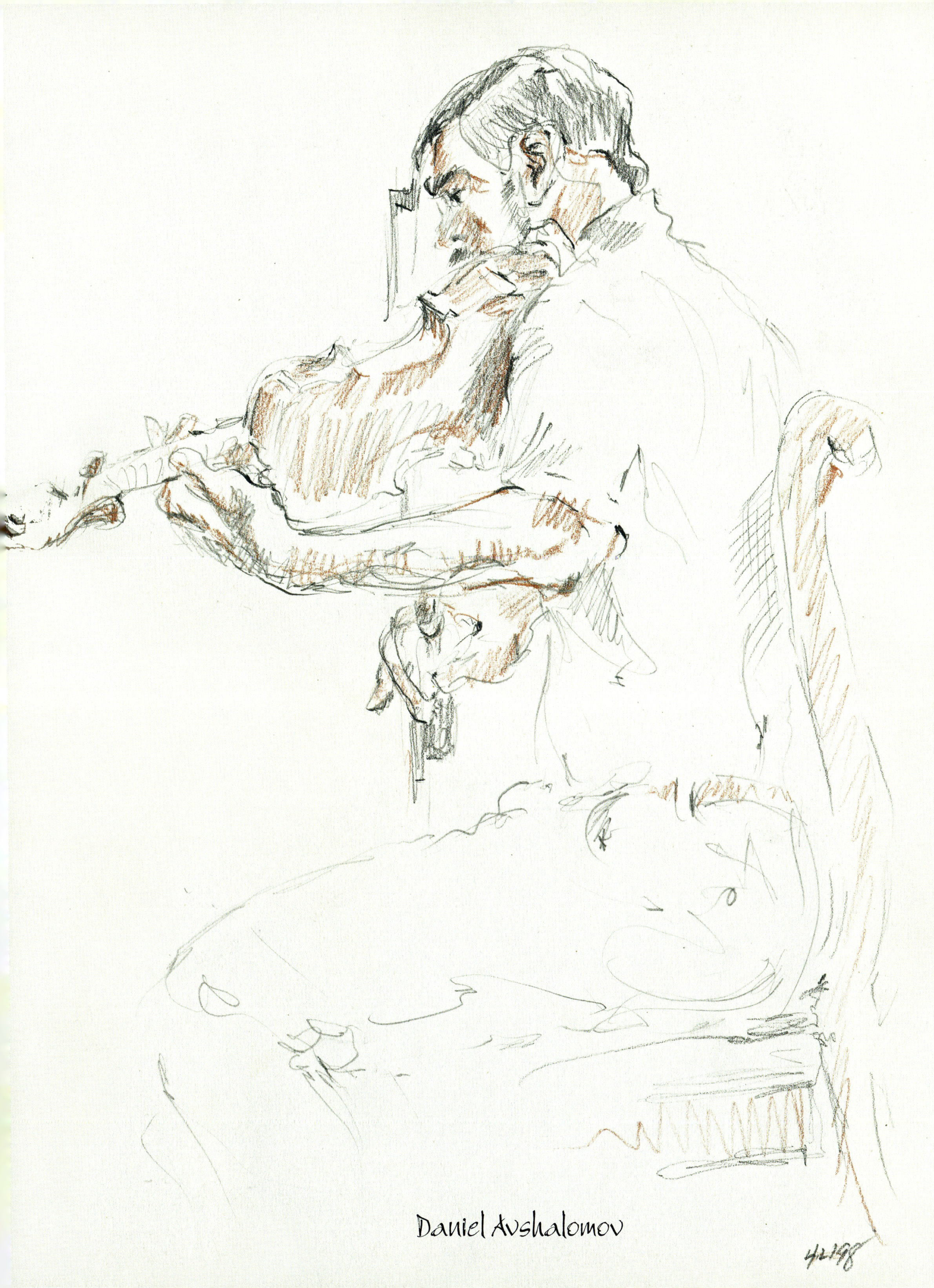

Daniel Avshalomov

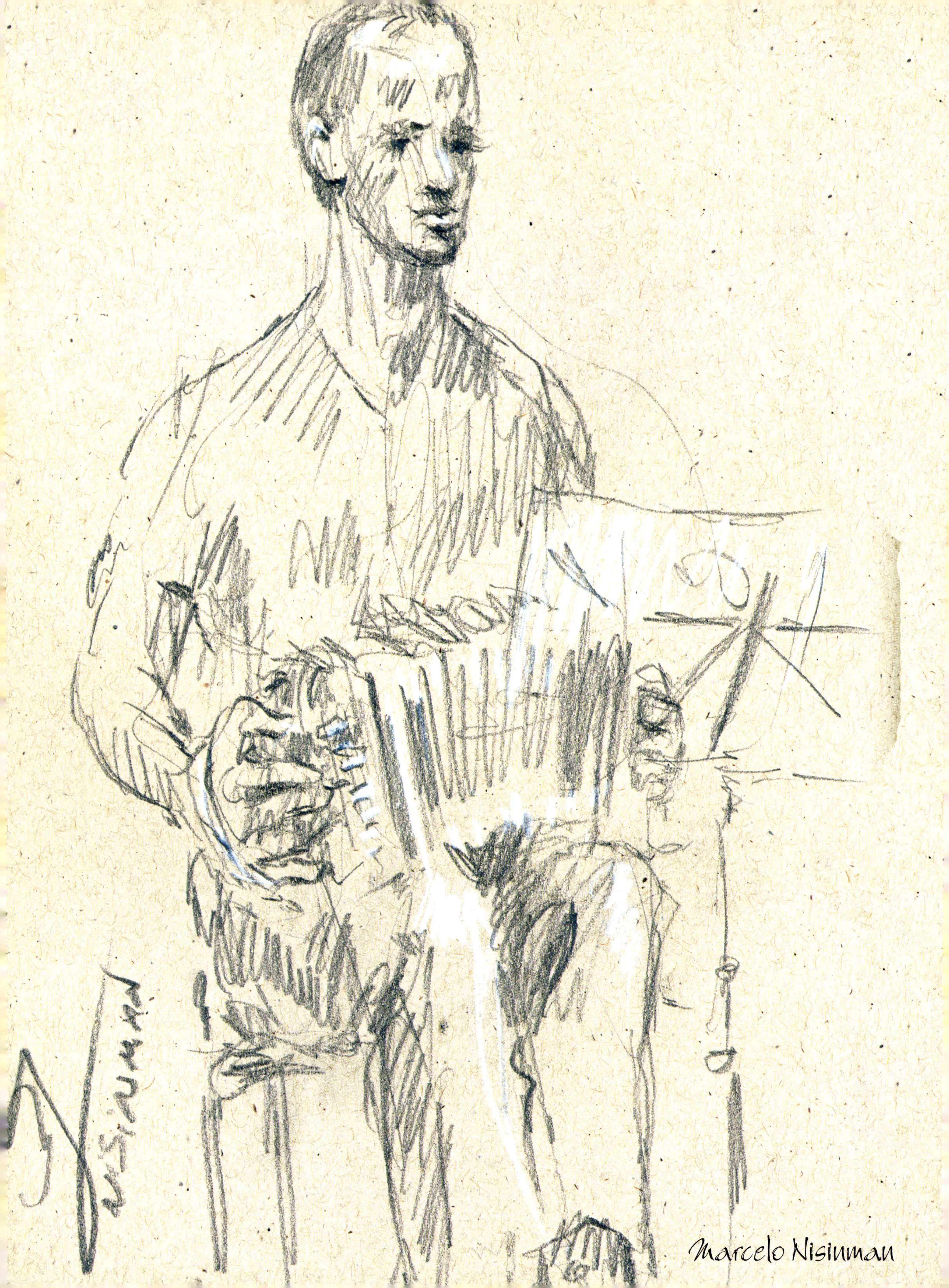
Marcelo Nisinman

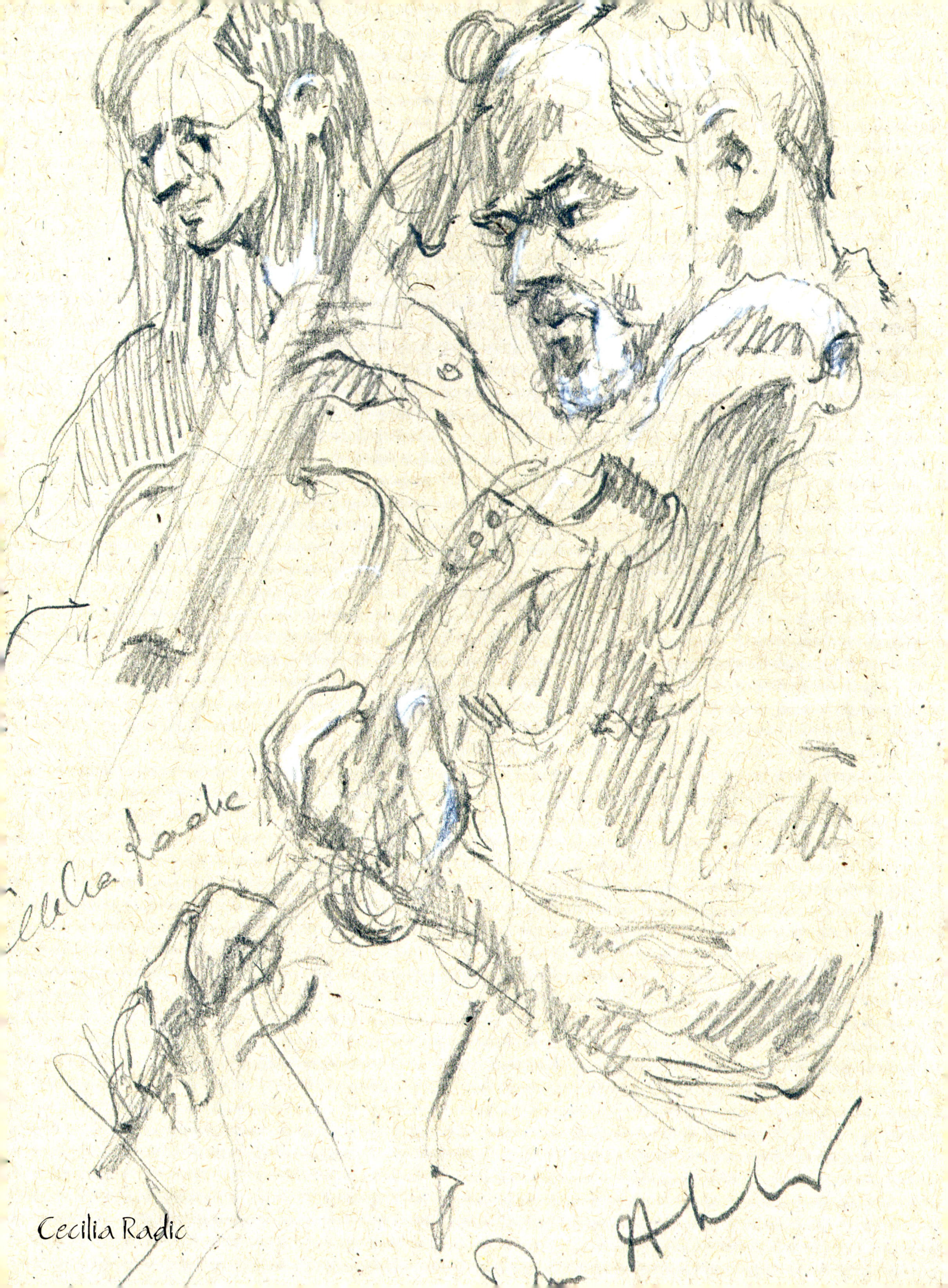
Cecilia Radic

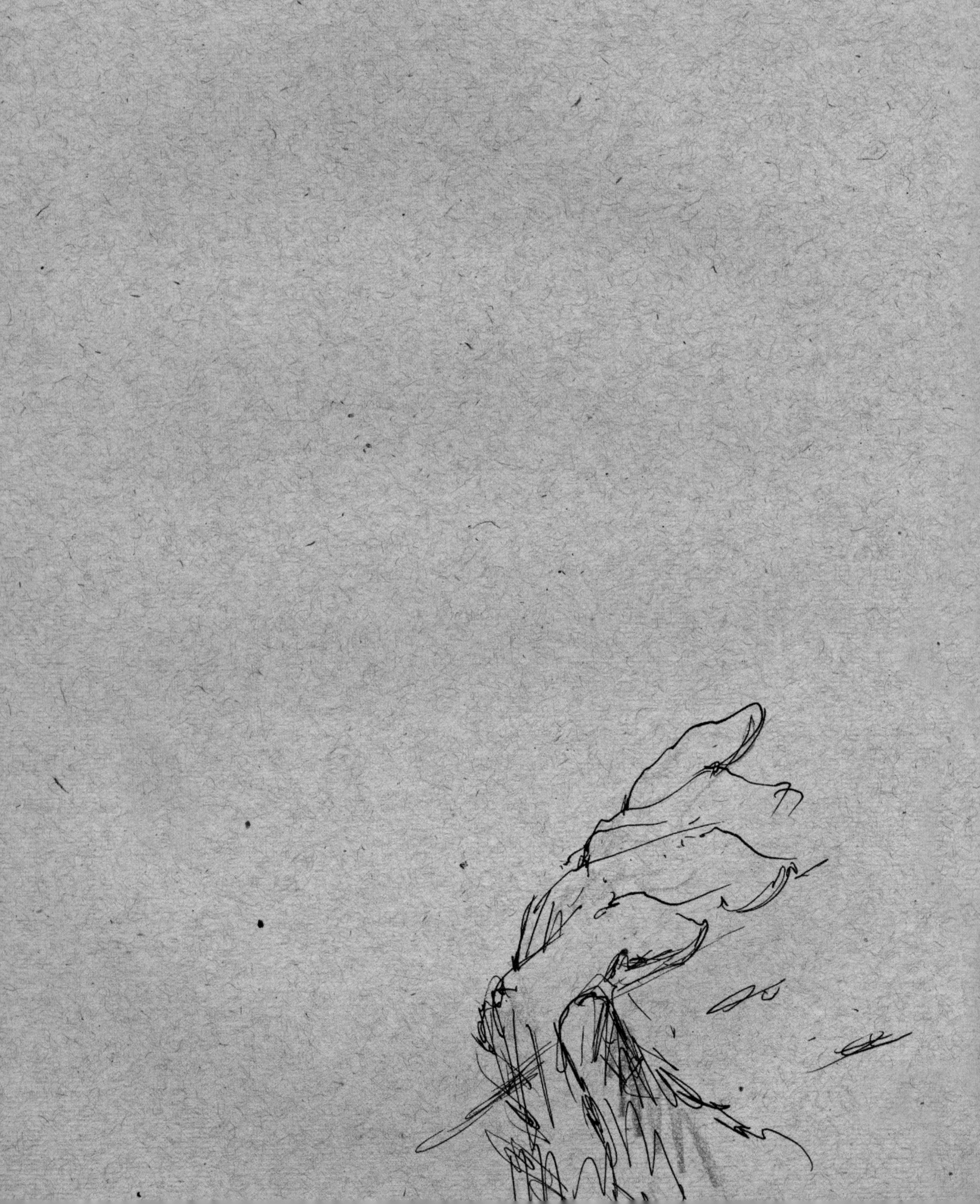

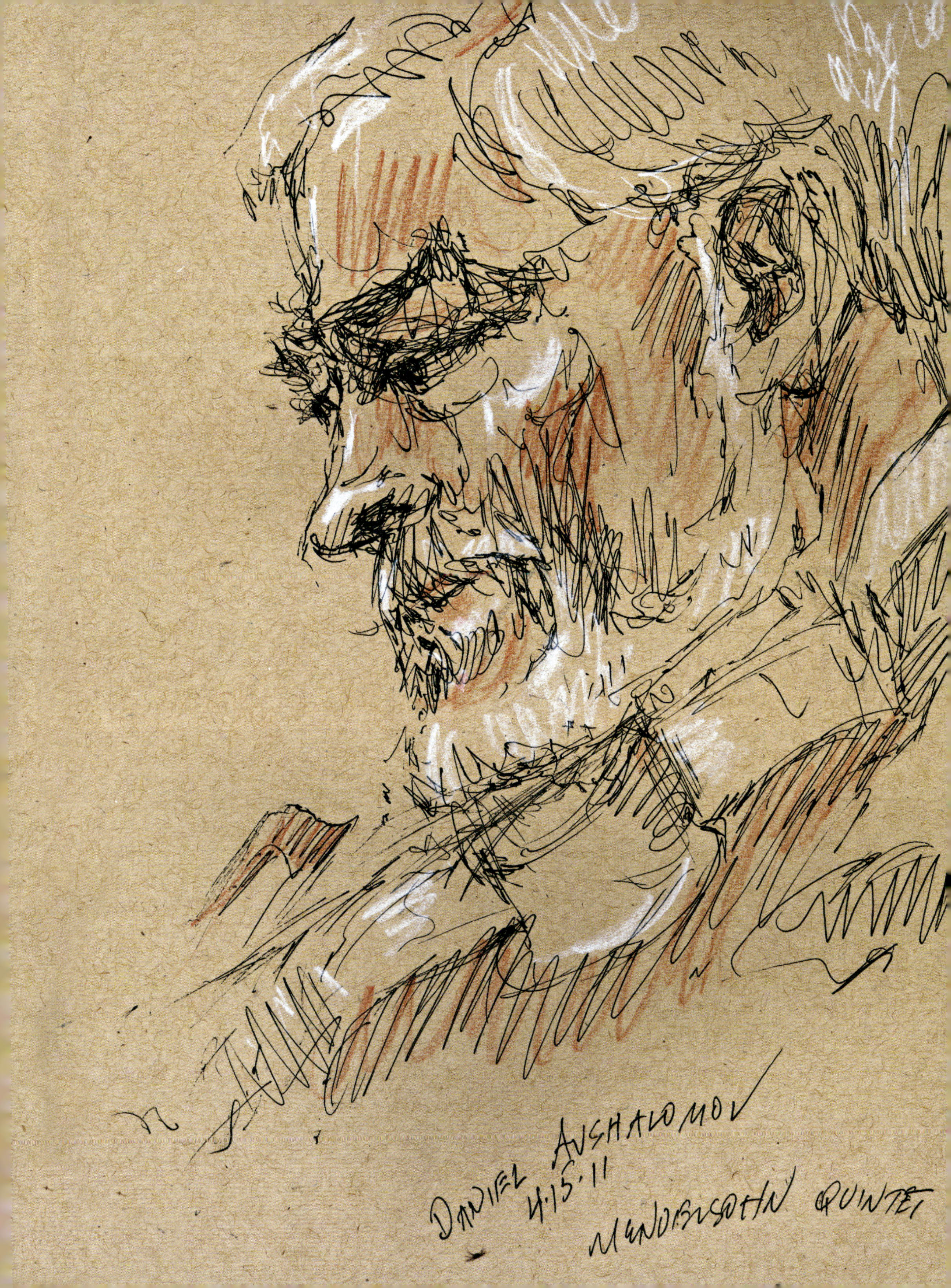
DANIEL AVSHALOMOV
4·15·11
MENDELSSOHN QUINTET

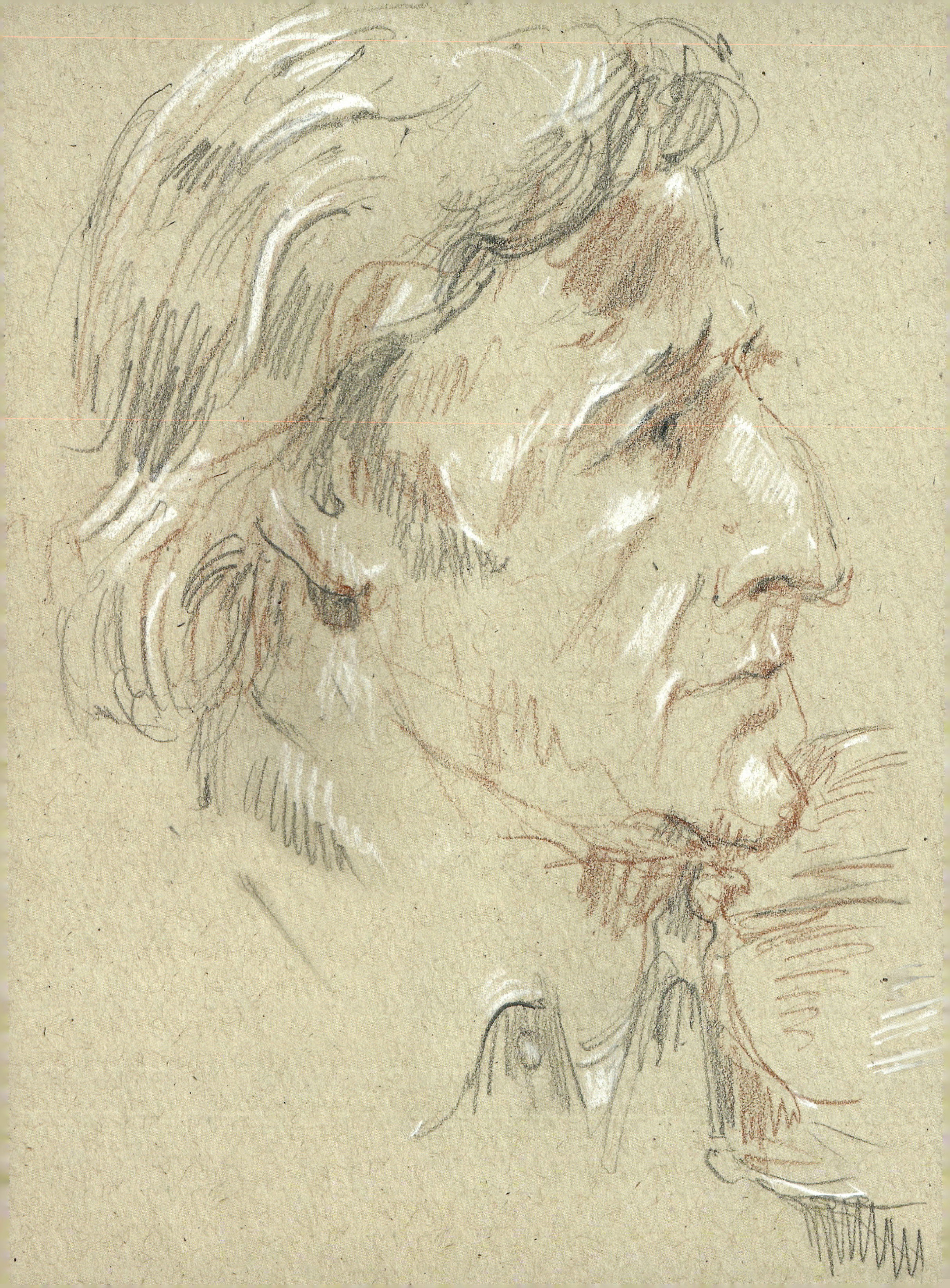

Federico Agostini is both a soloist and Concert Master of the famed "I Musici." He is also the Founder of the d' Amici String Quartet. He has been a long standing artist at La Musica and is on the faculty of the Eastman School of Music.

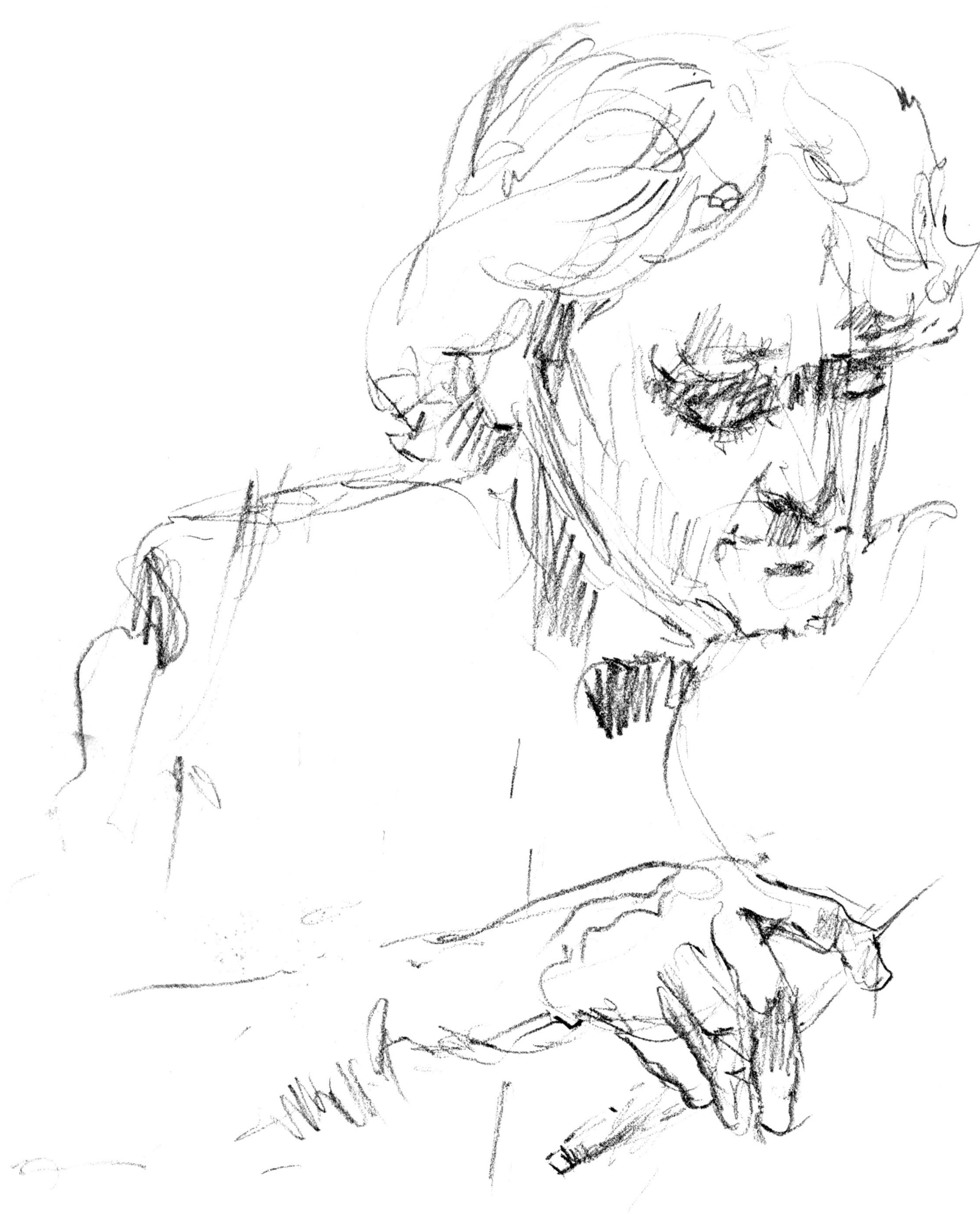

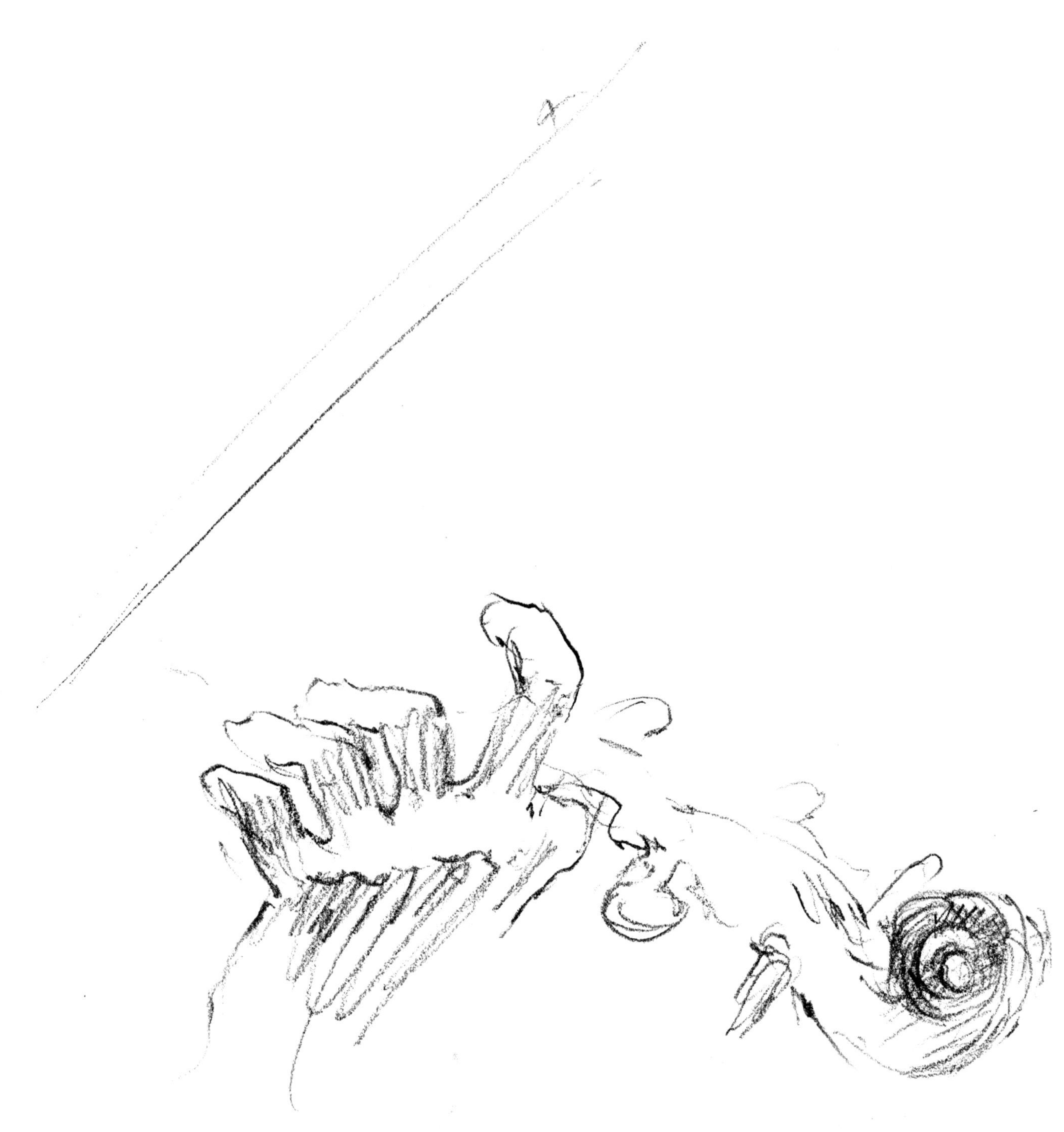

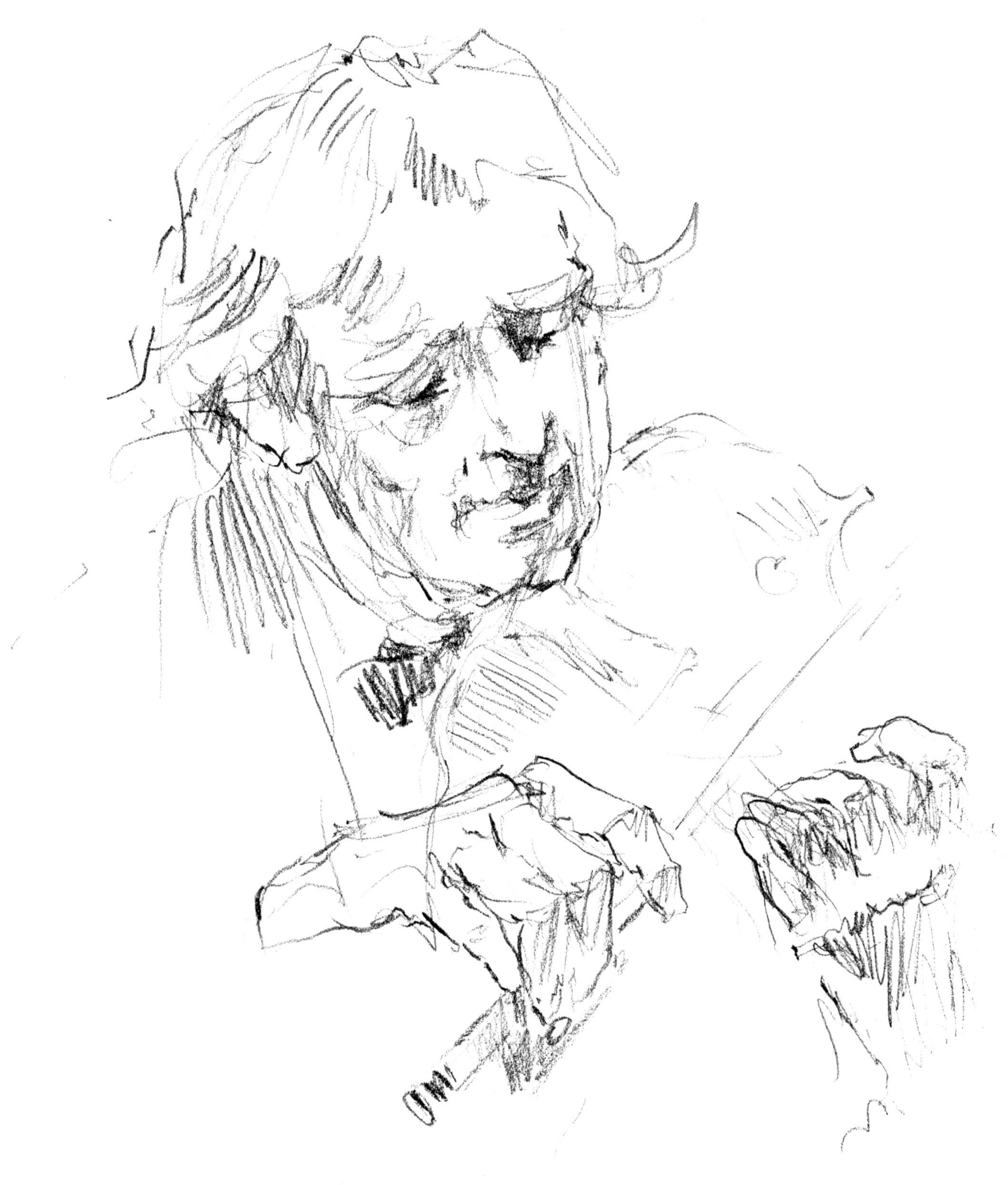

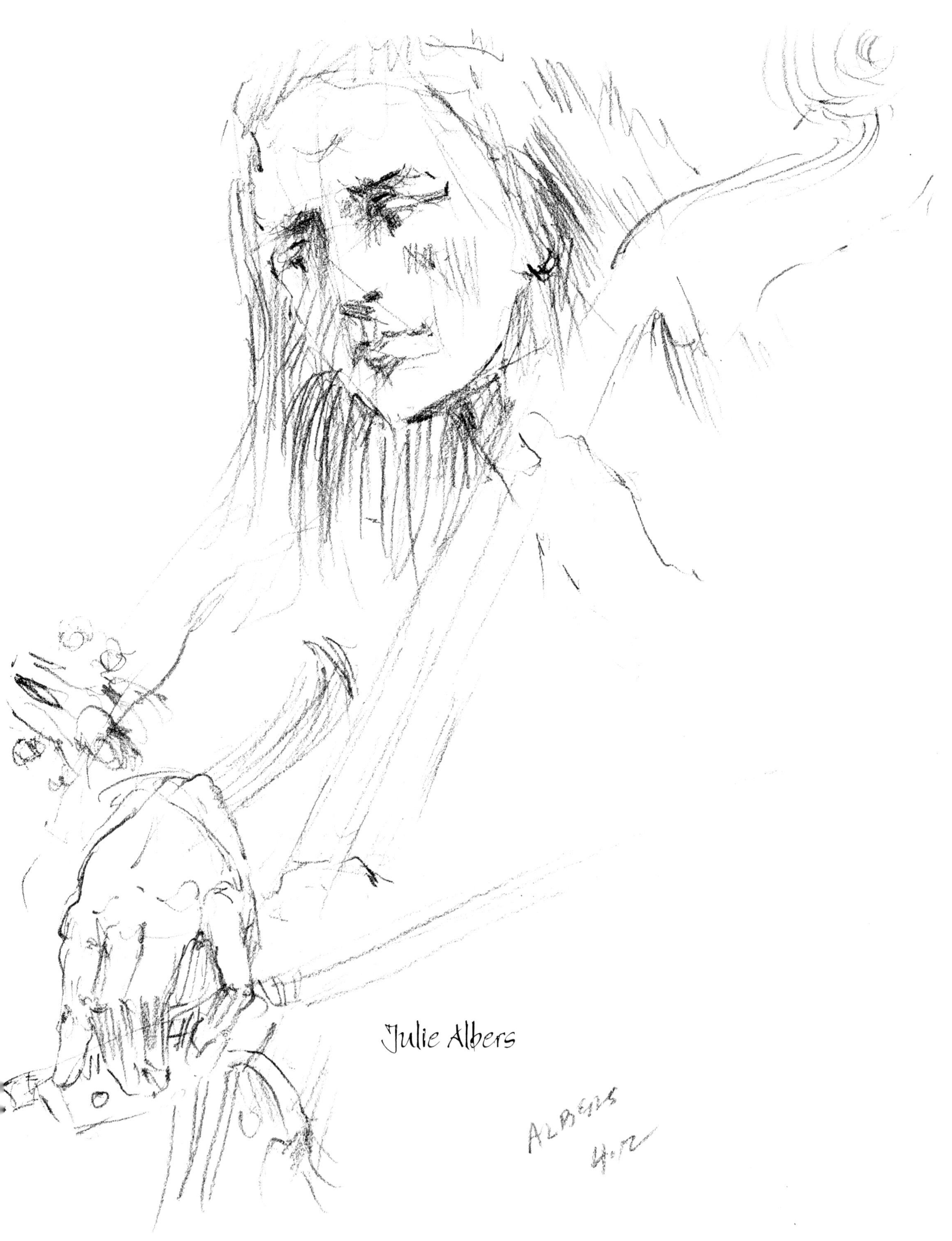

Julie Albers

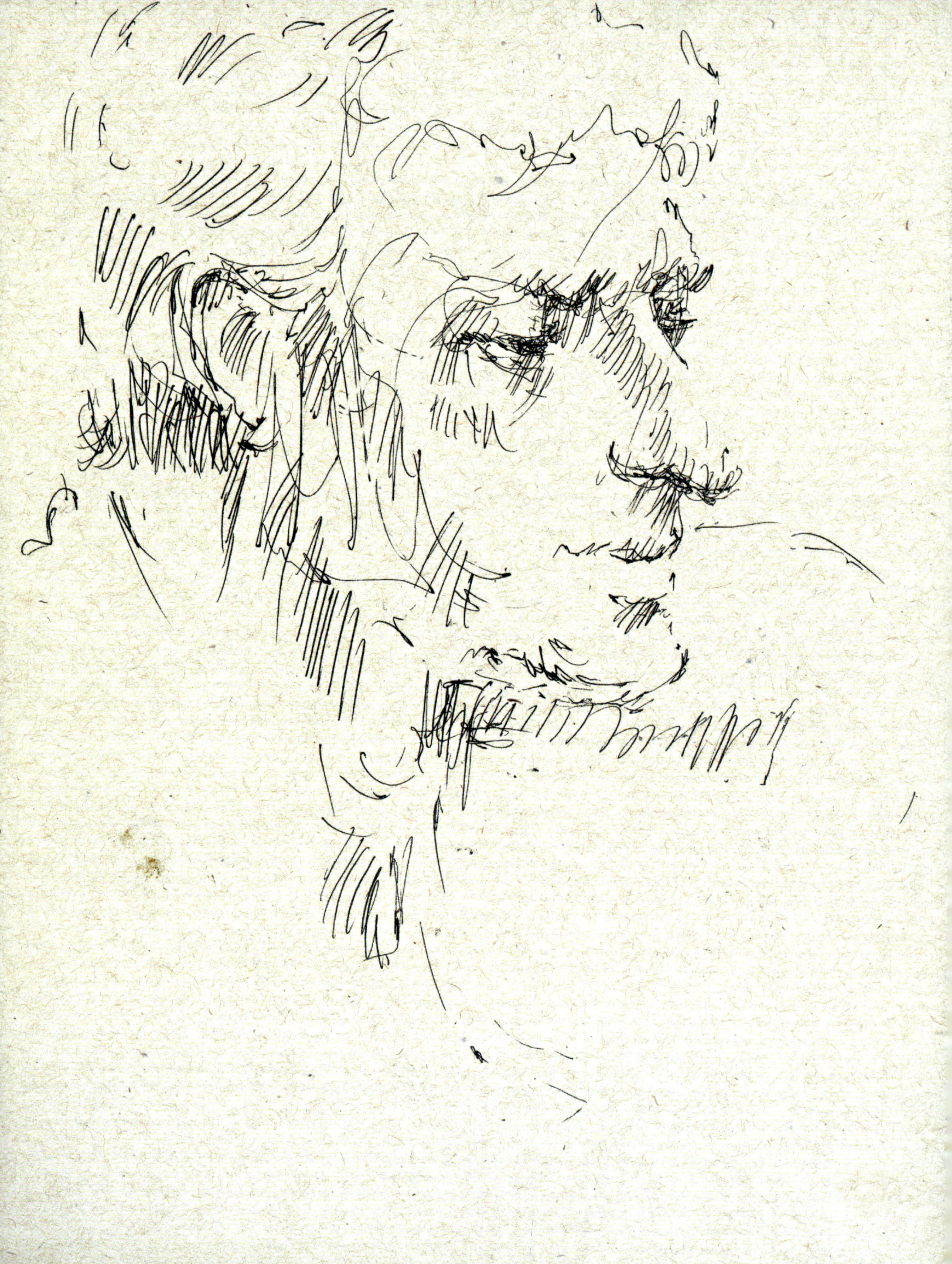

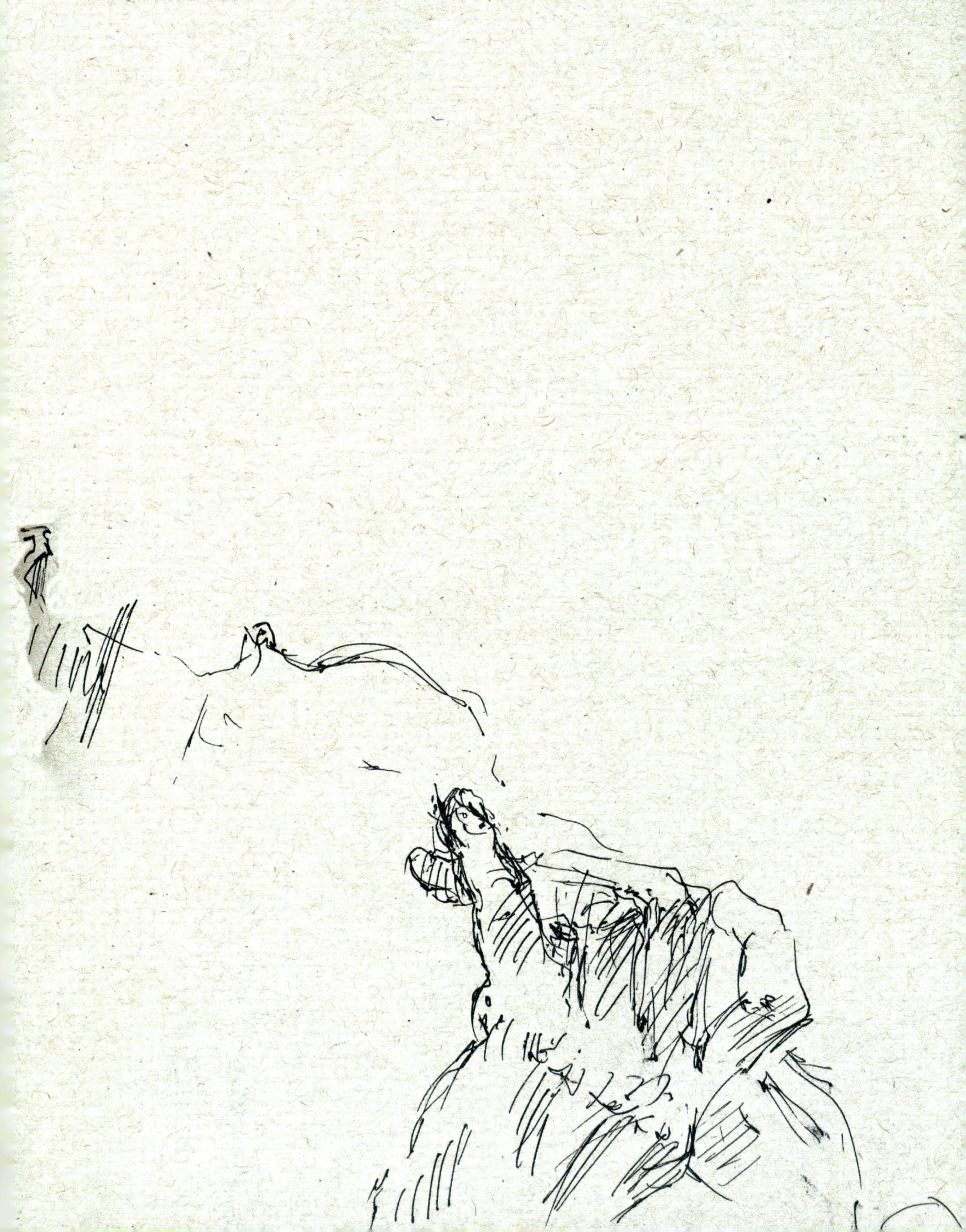

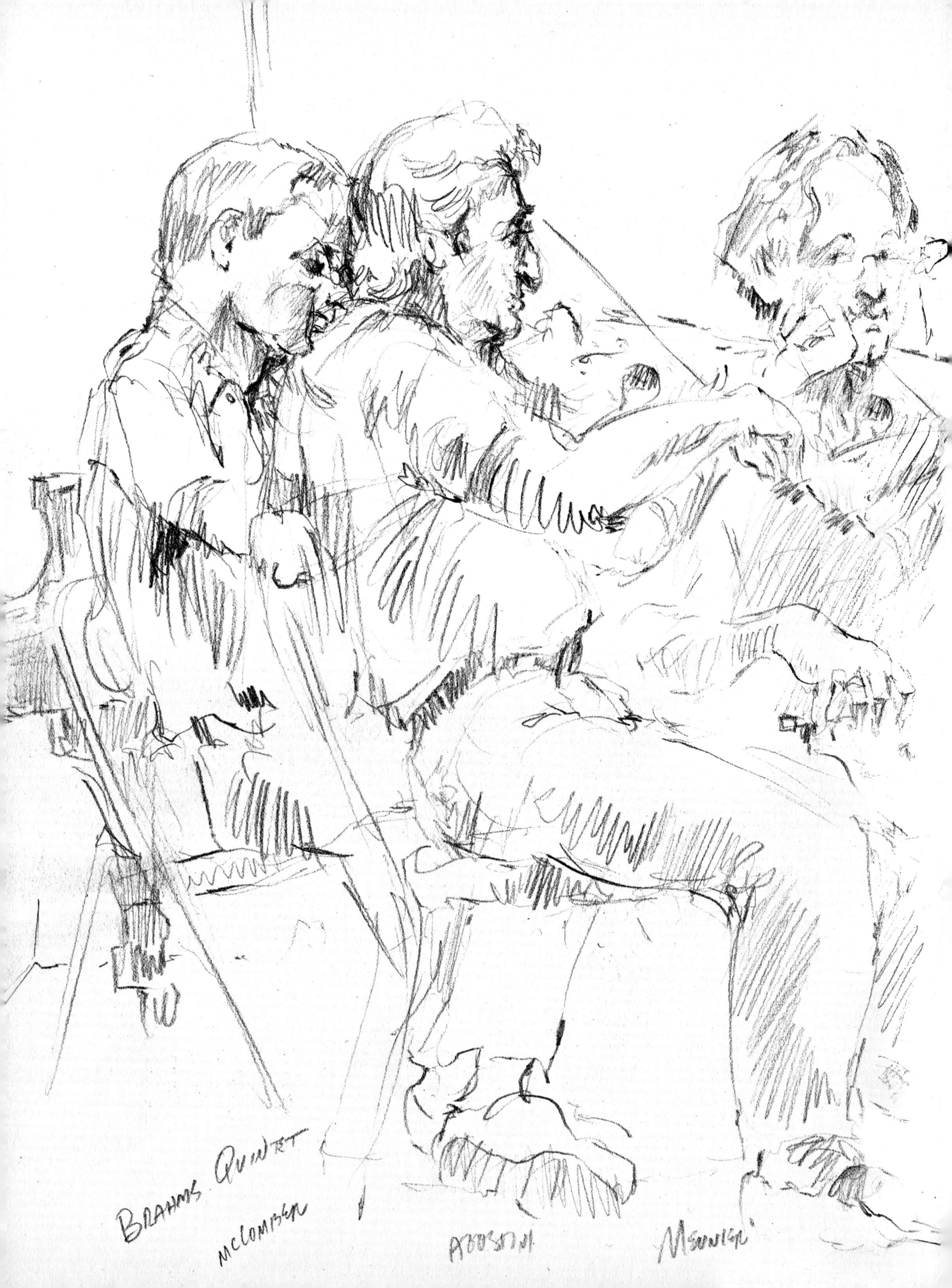
BRAHMS QUINTET
MCLOMBER

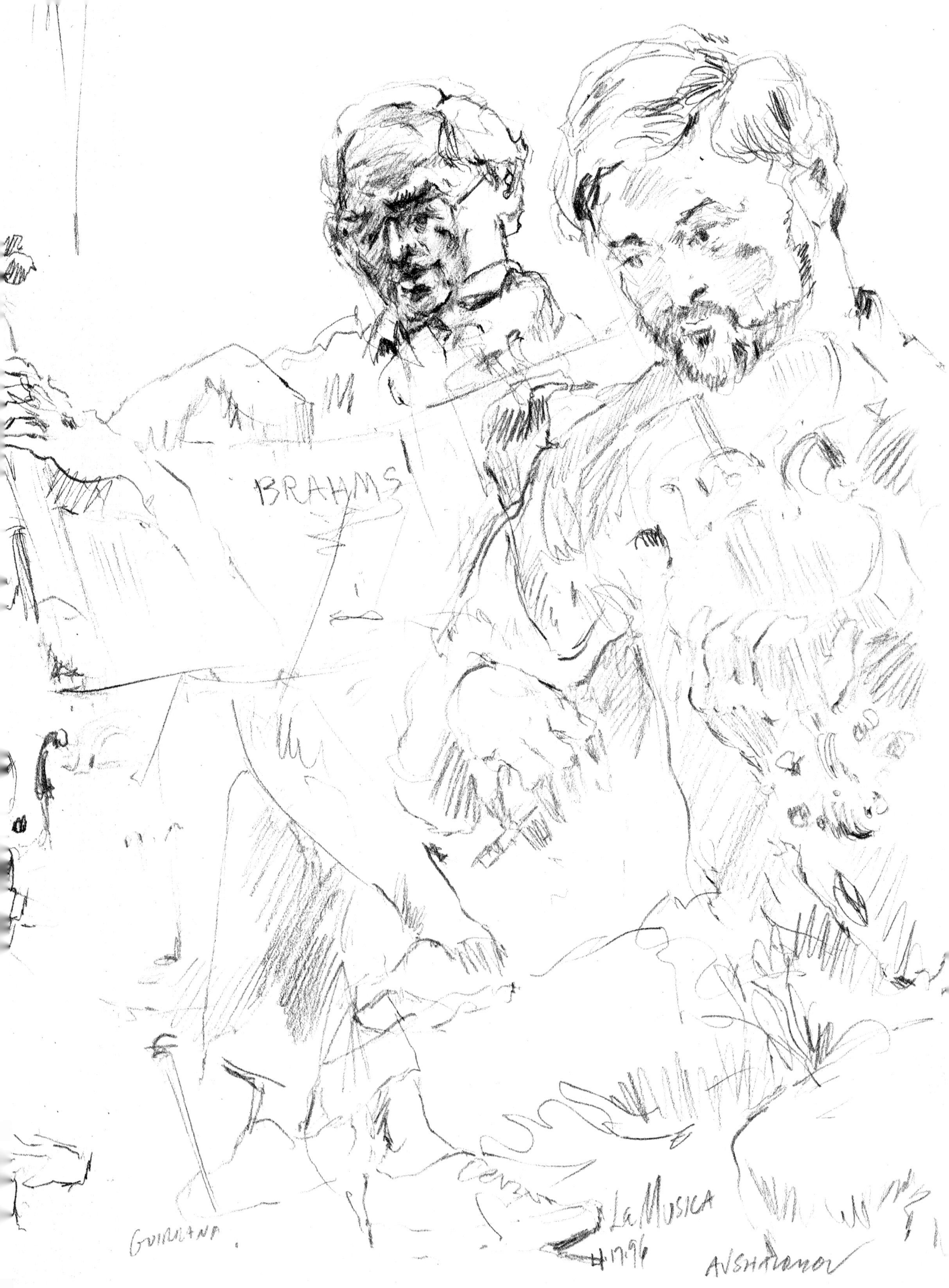
BRAHMS
La Musica
4.17.96

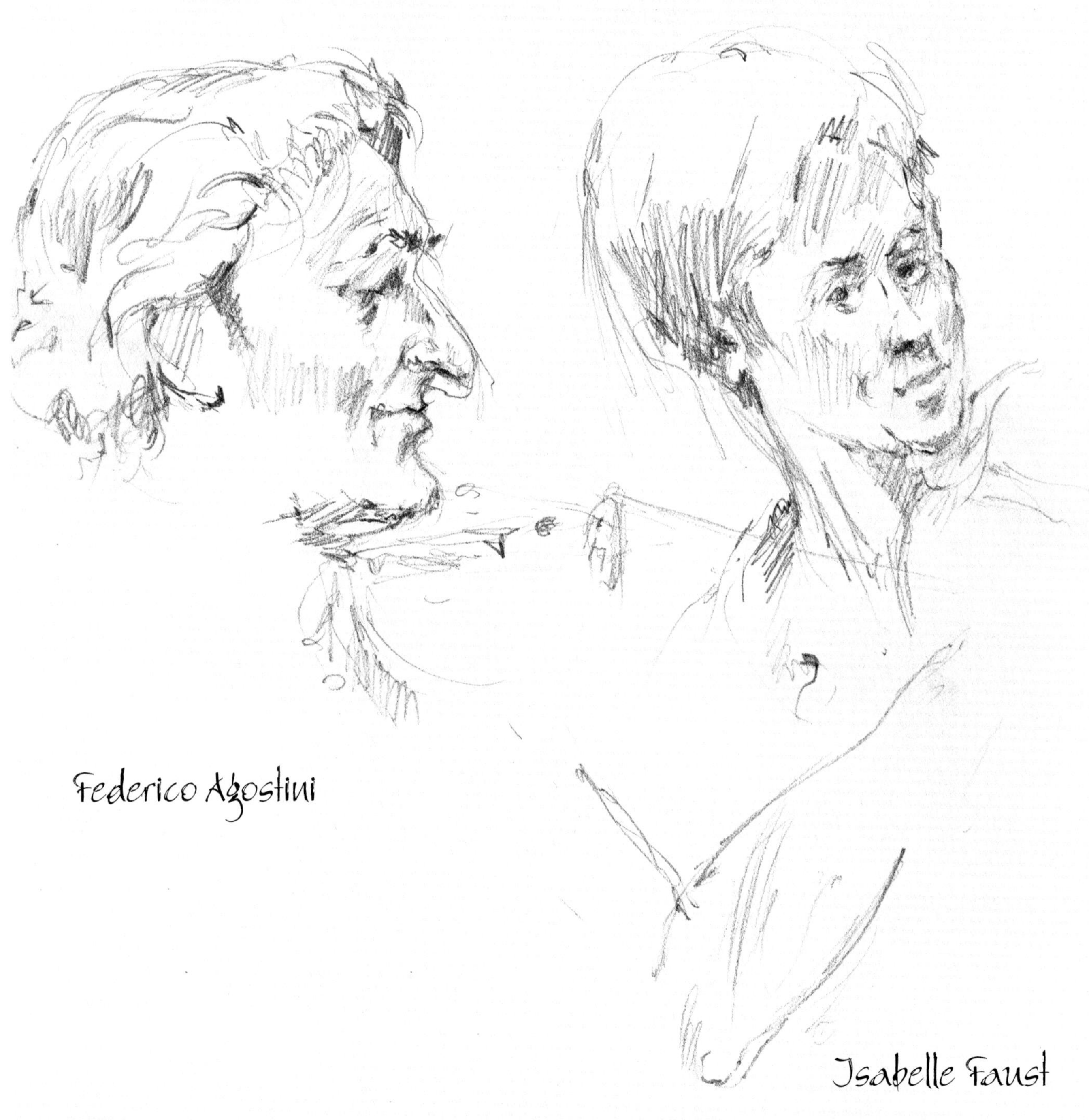

Trout Quintet
This might be called Trout á la Meuniére

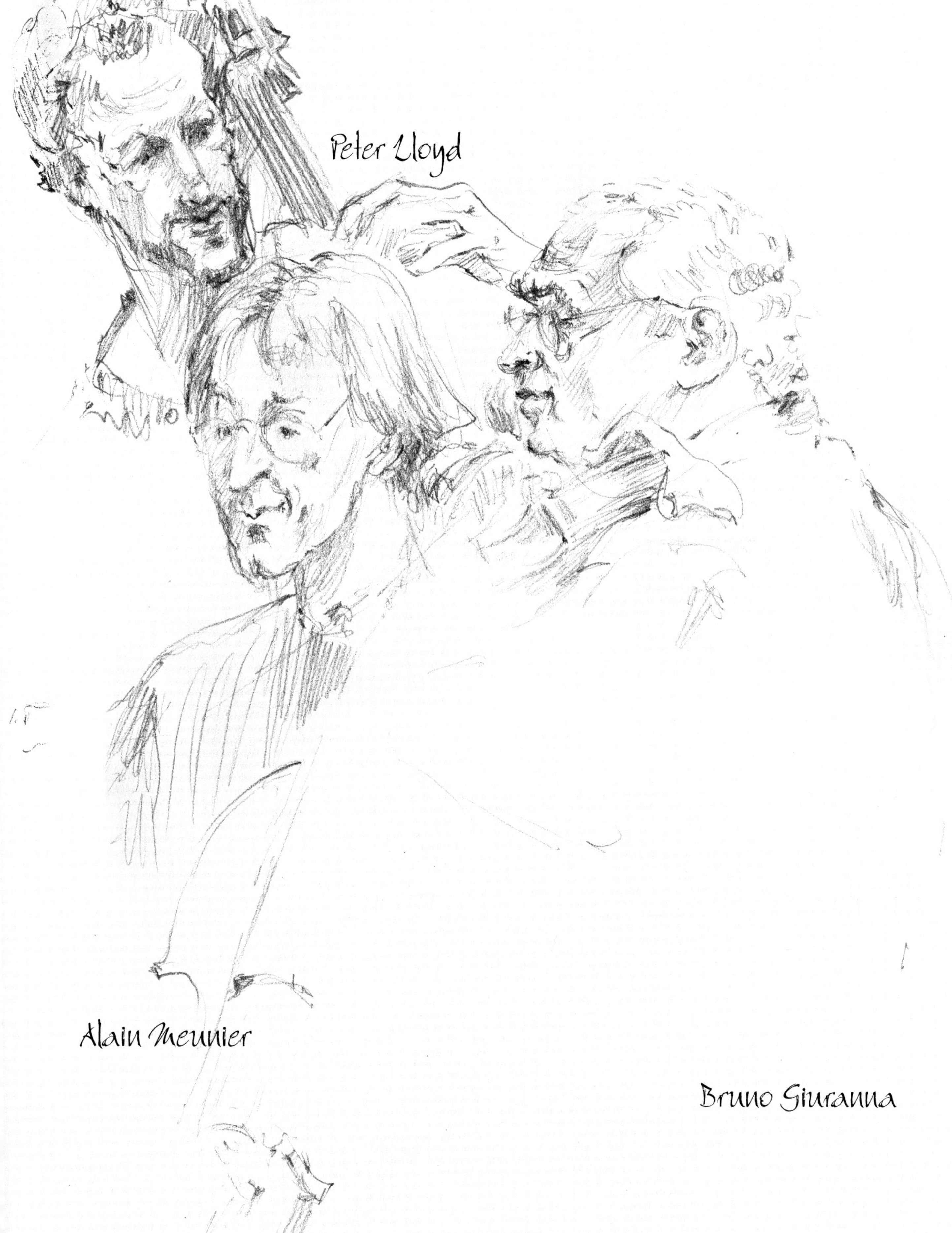
Peter Lloyd
Alain Meunier
Bruno Giuranna

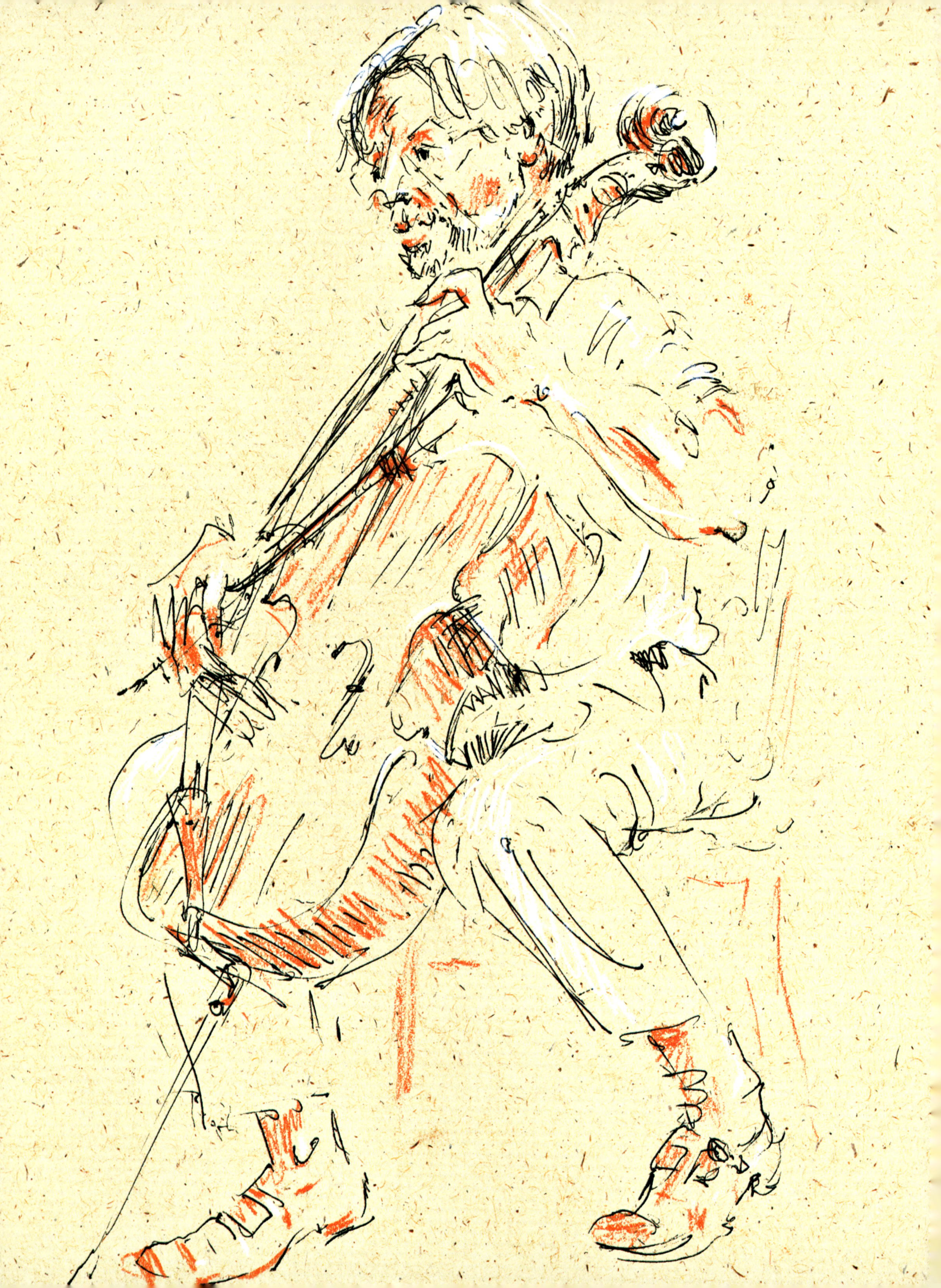

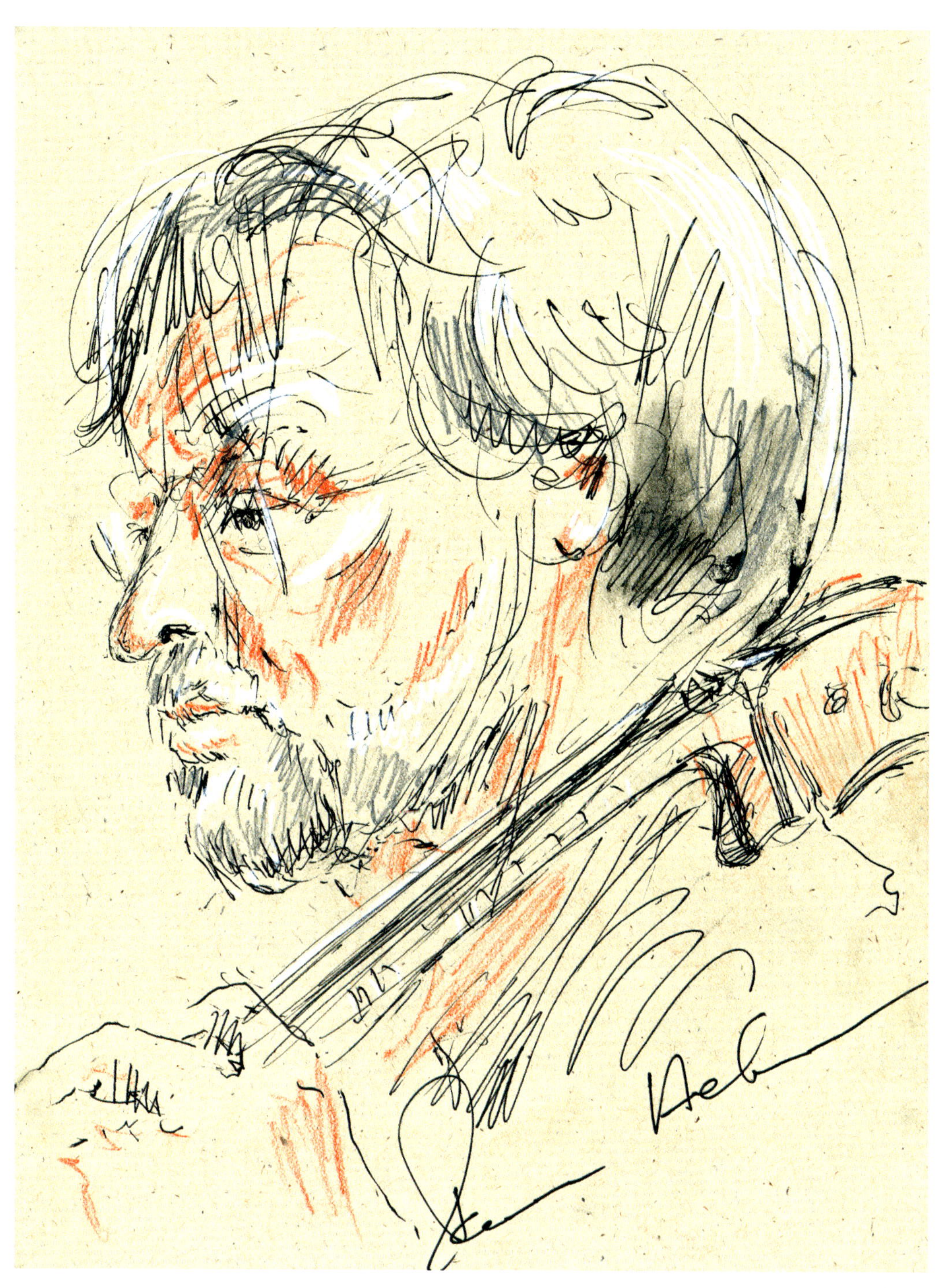

Frans Helmerson, cellist

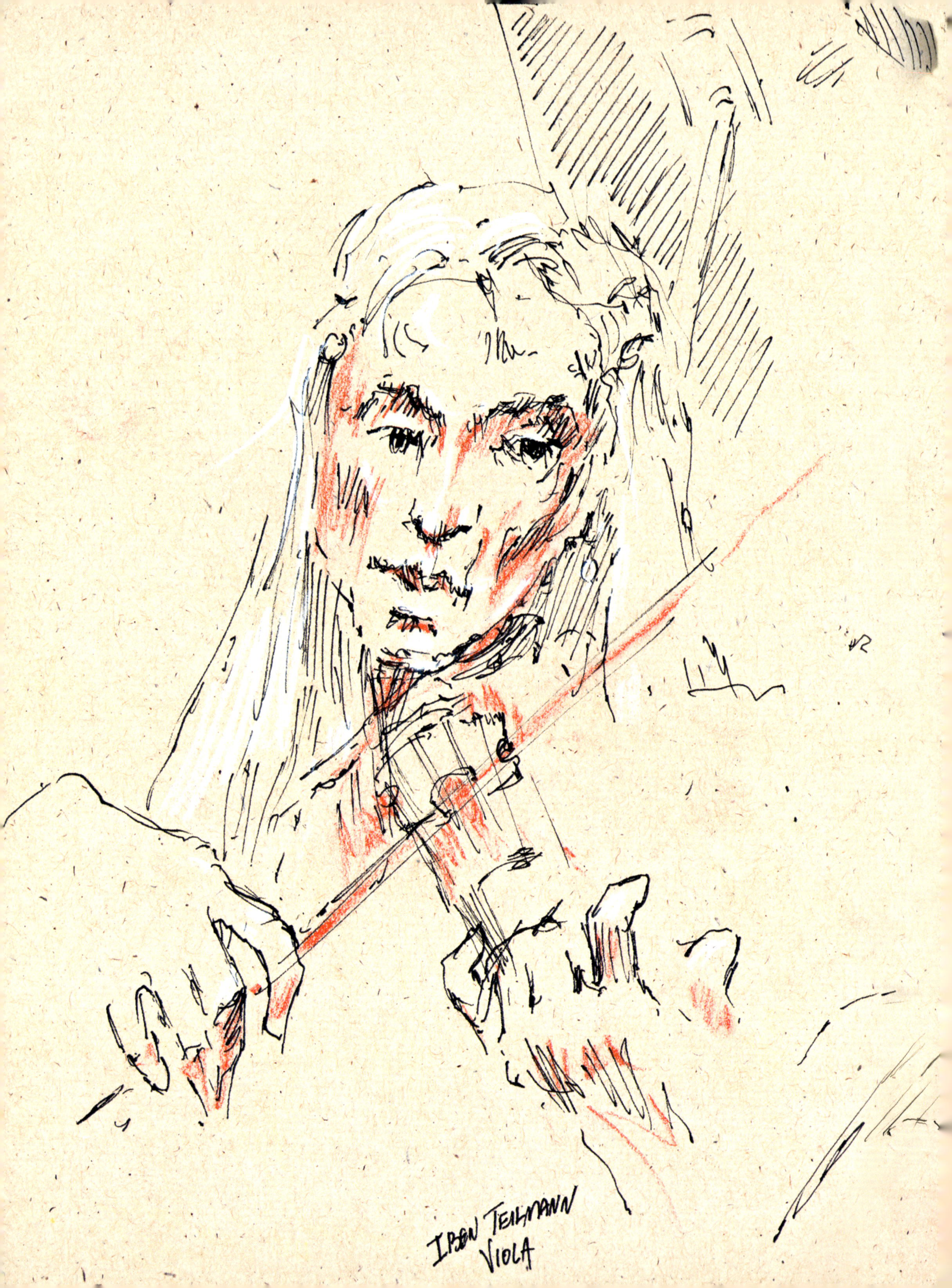
IBEN TEILMANN
VIOLA

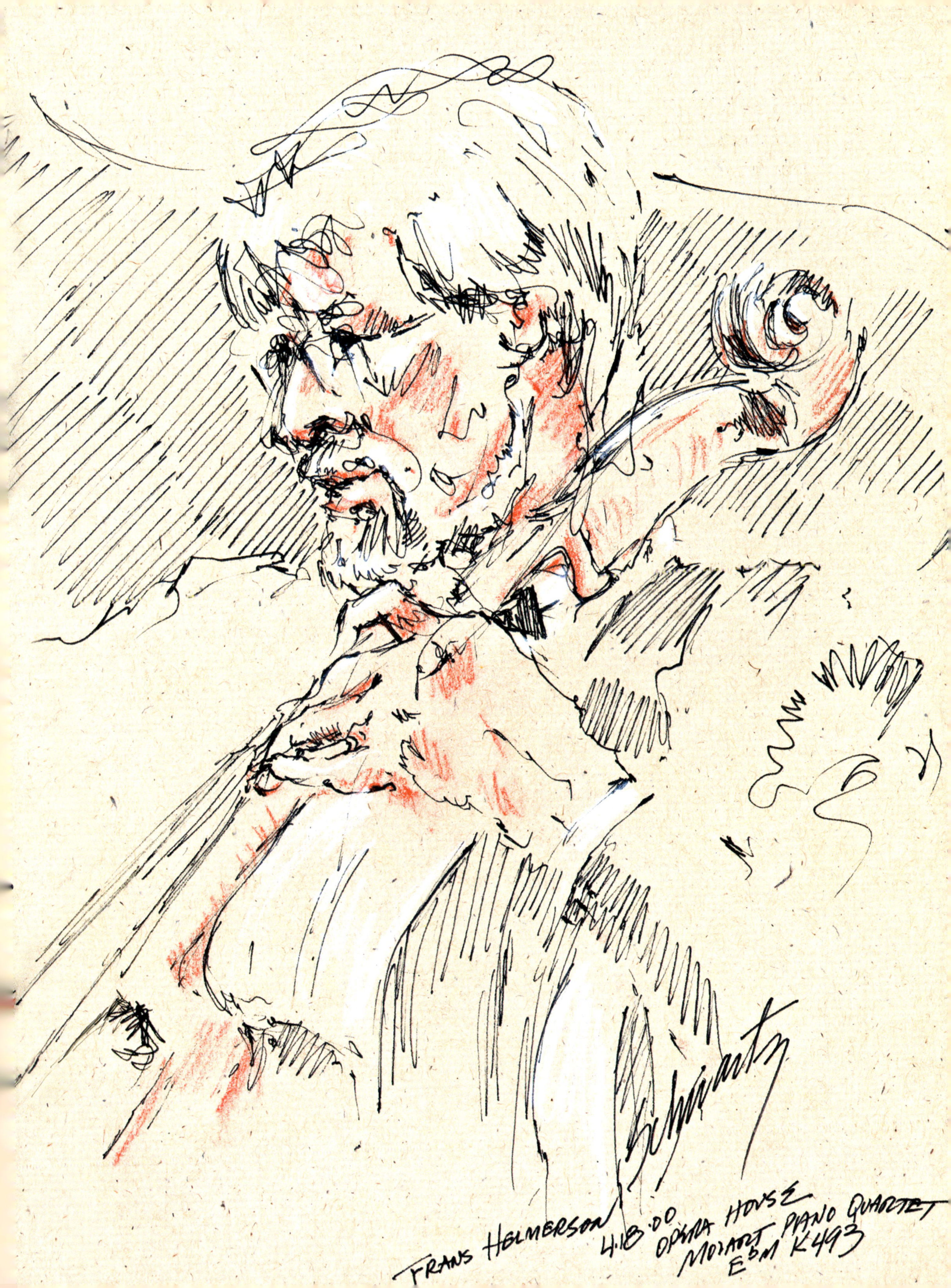
Schwartz
FRANS HELMERSON
4.18.00
OPERA HOUSE
MOZART PIANO QUARTET
E♭M K493

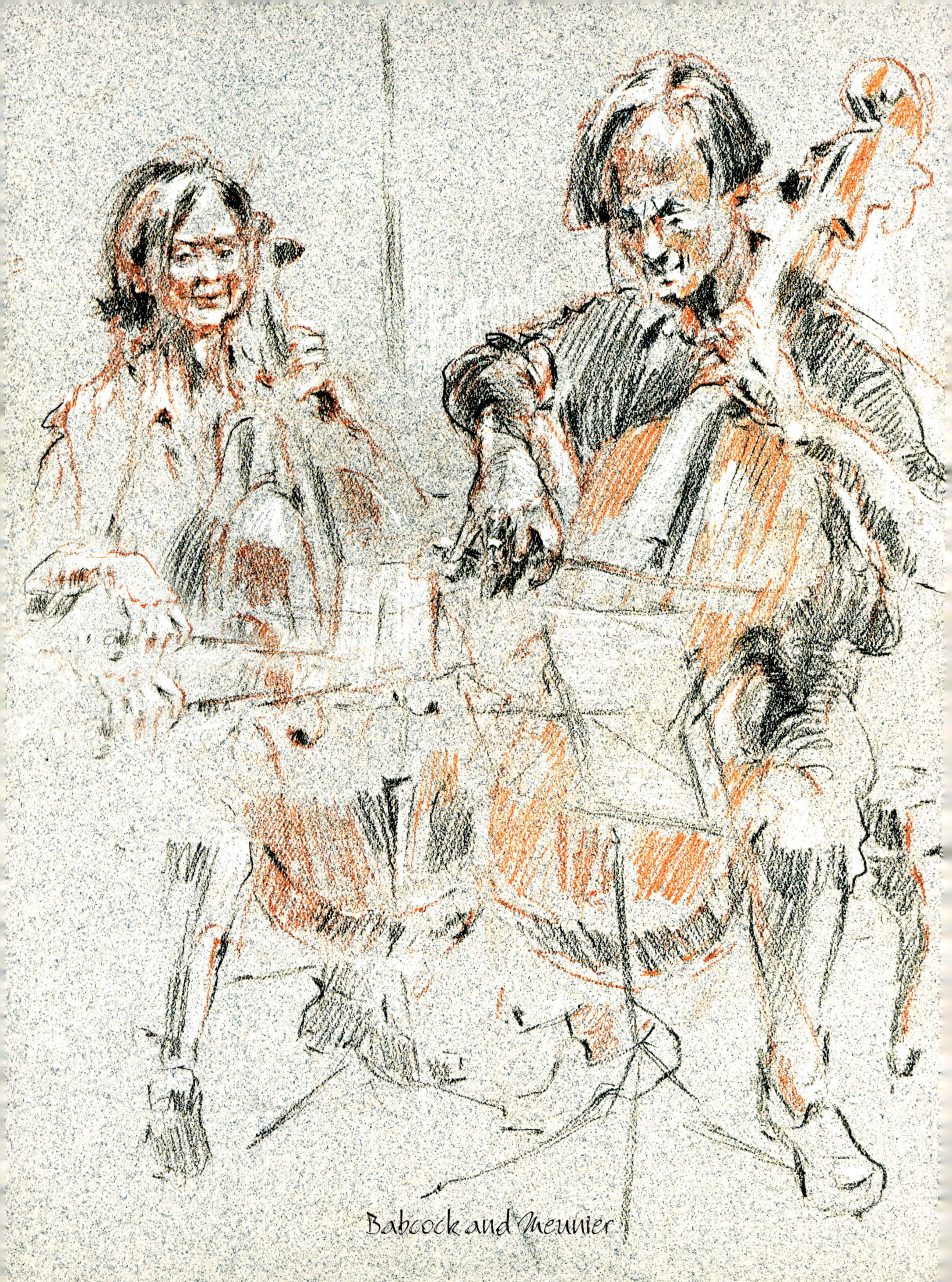

Babcock and Meunier

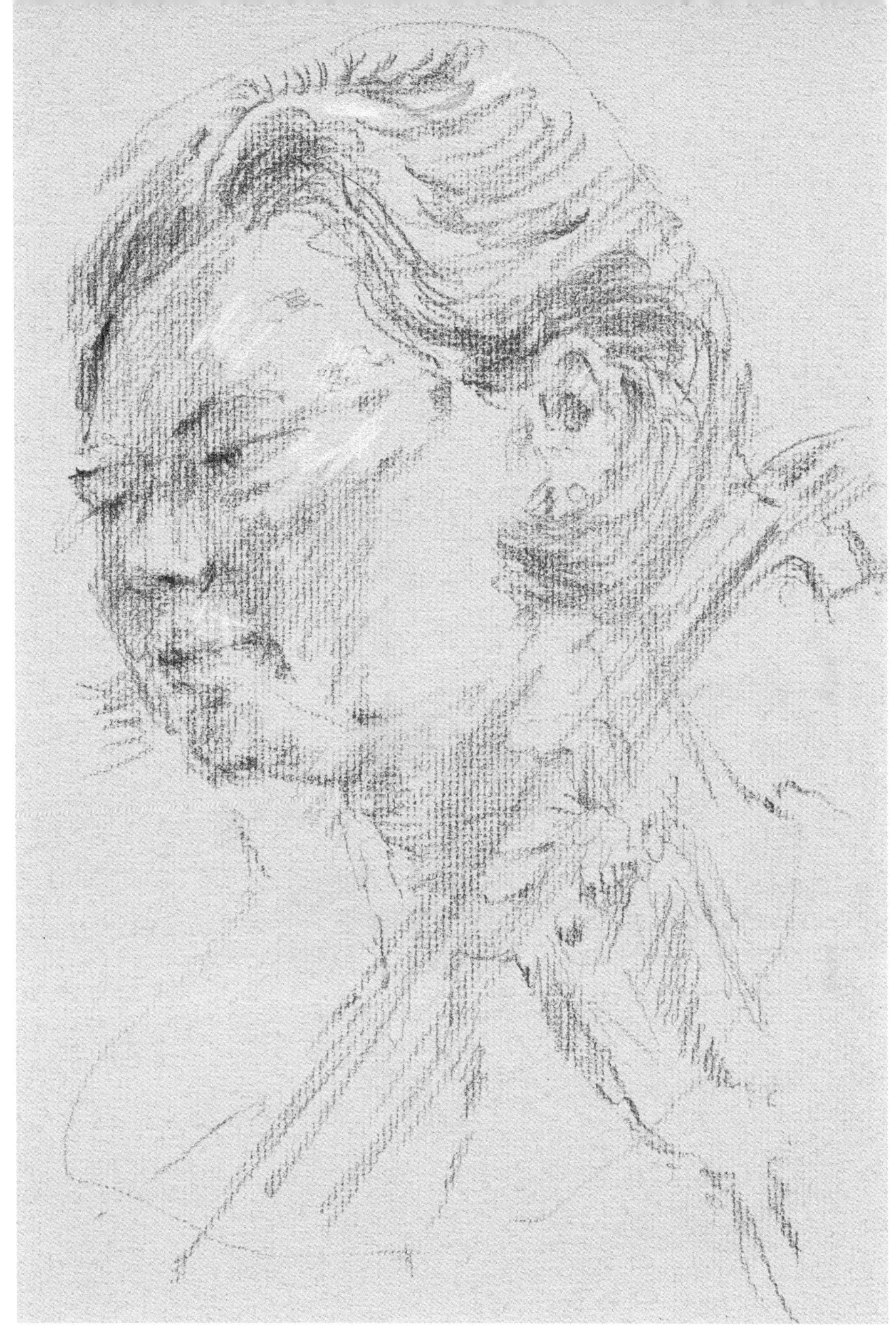

Martha Babcock, cellist, Boston Symphony Orchestra

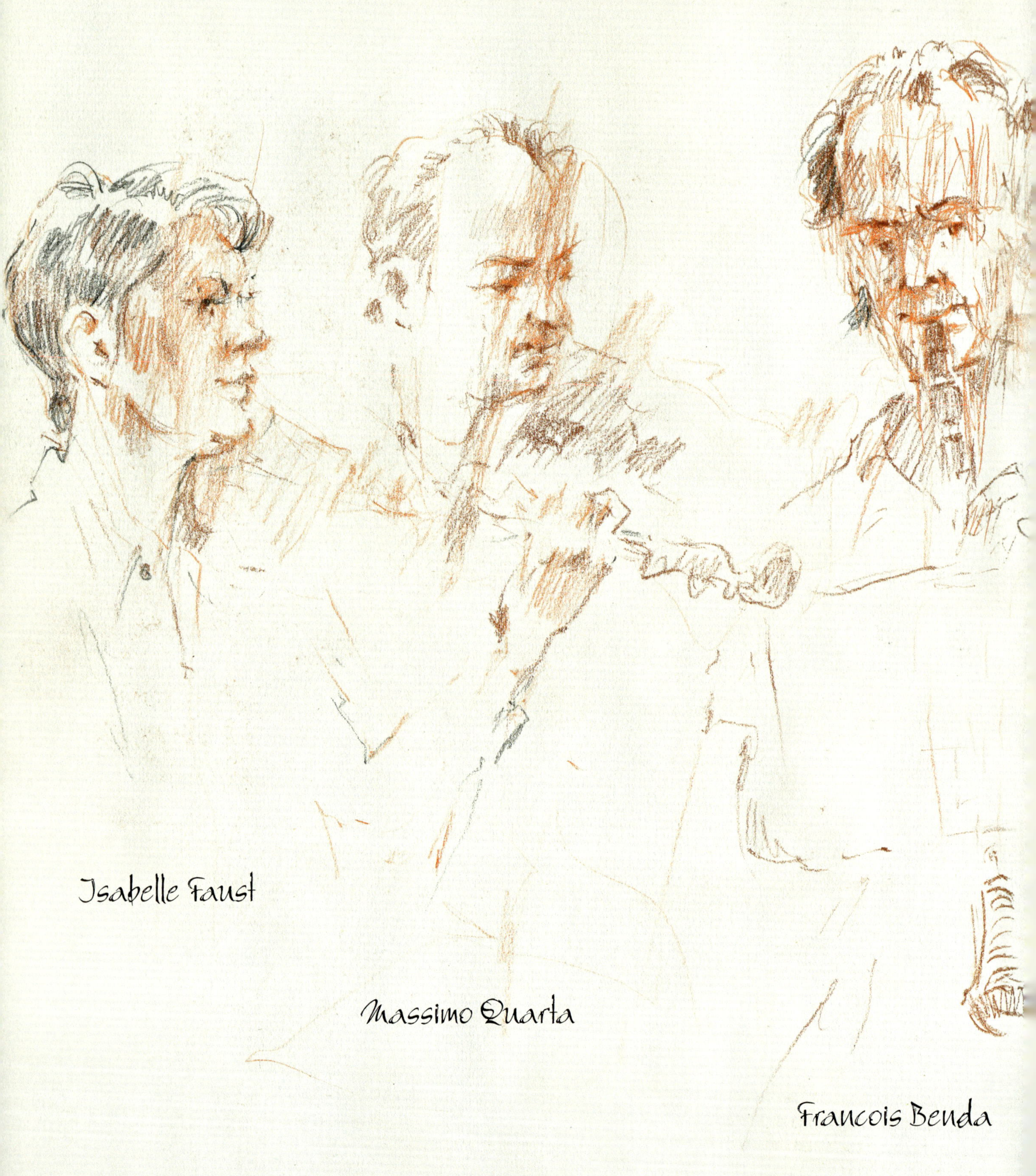

Isabelle Faust

Massimo Quarta

Francois Benda

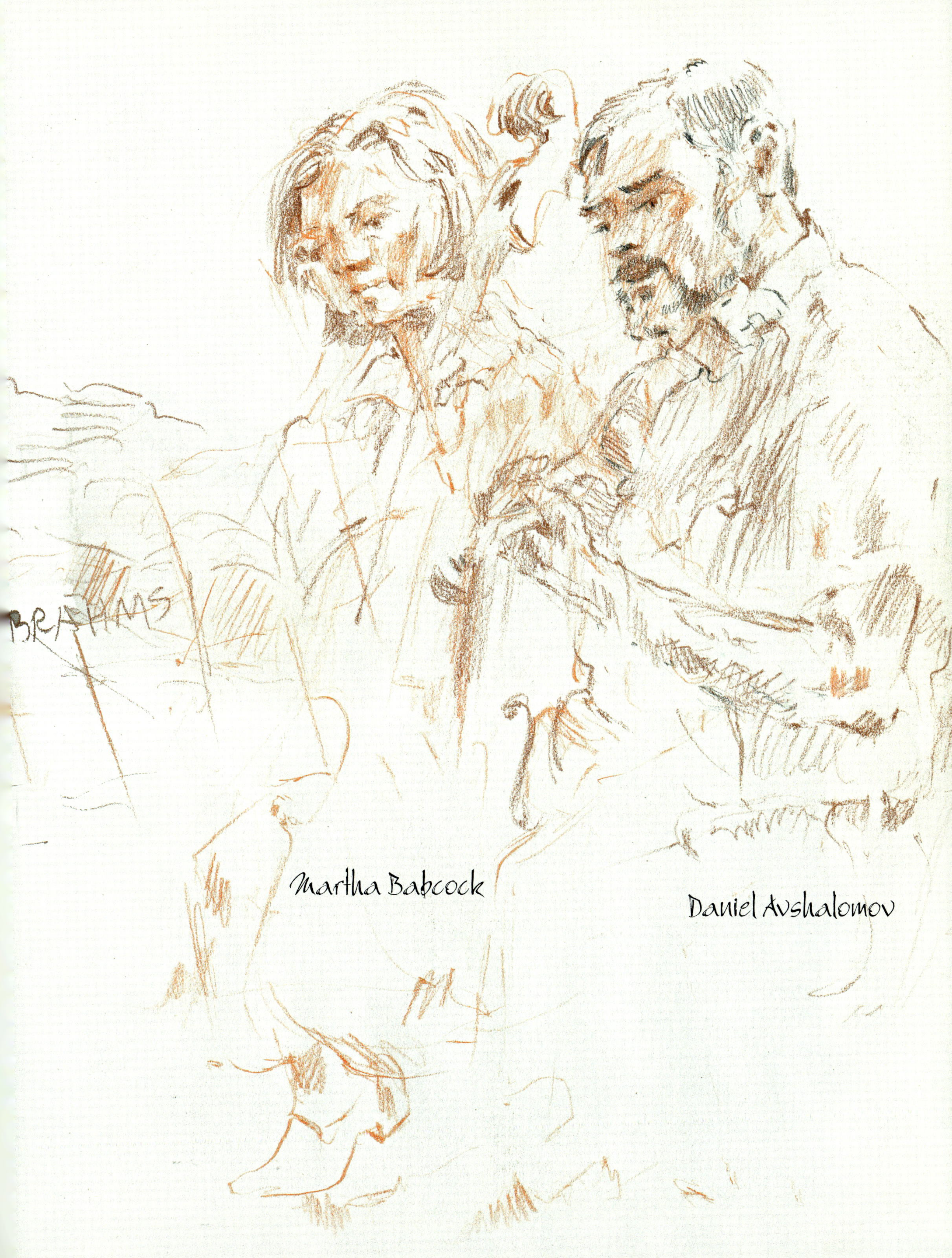
BRAHMS
Martha Babcock
Daniel Avshalomov

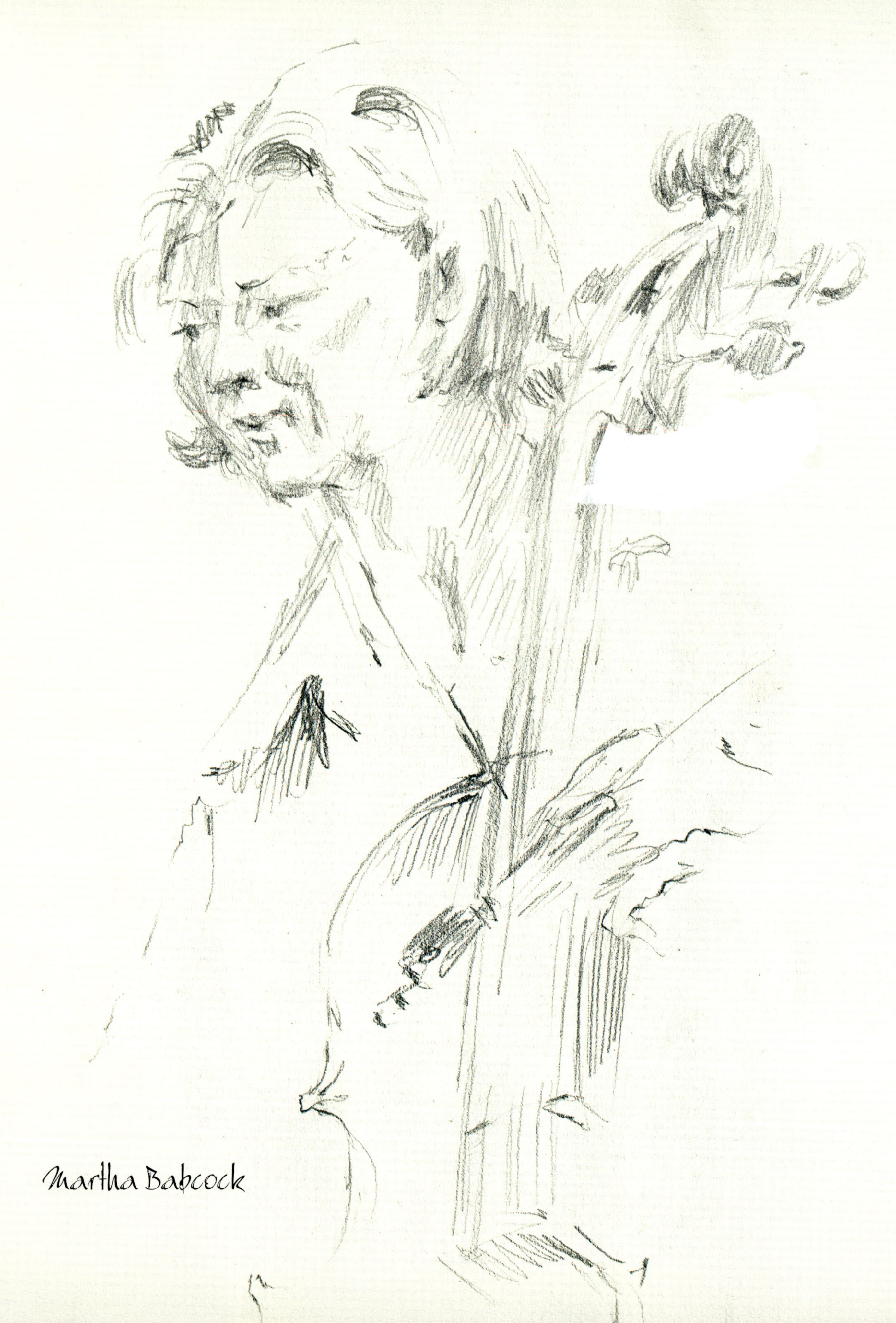
Martha Babcock

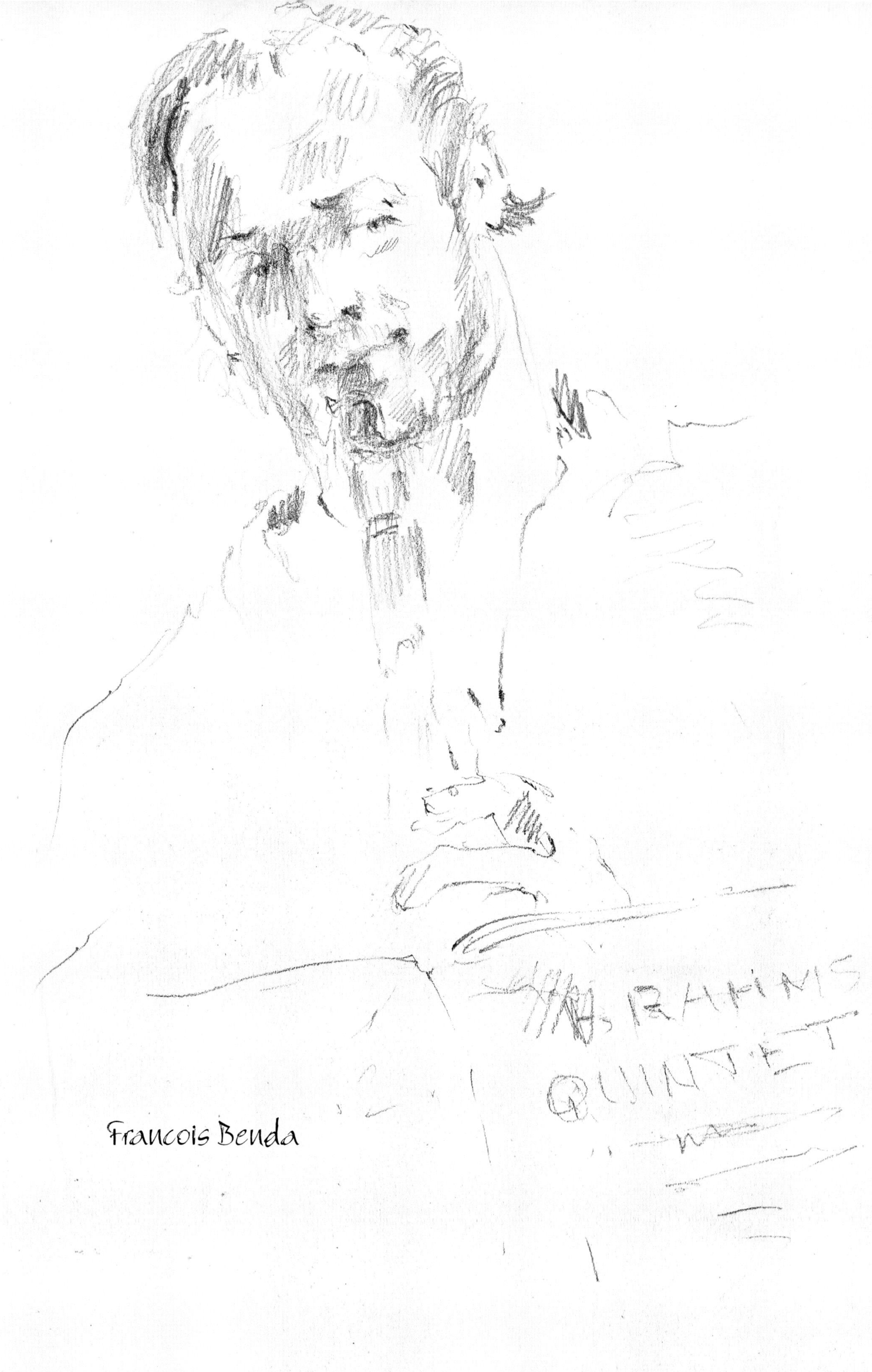

Francois Benda

Cynthia Phelps, Principal Violist, New York Philharmonic

Cynthia Phelps
4.10.02

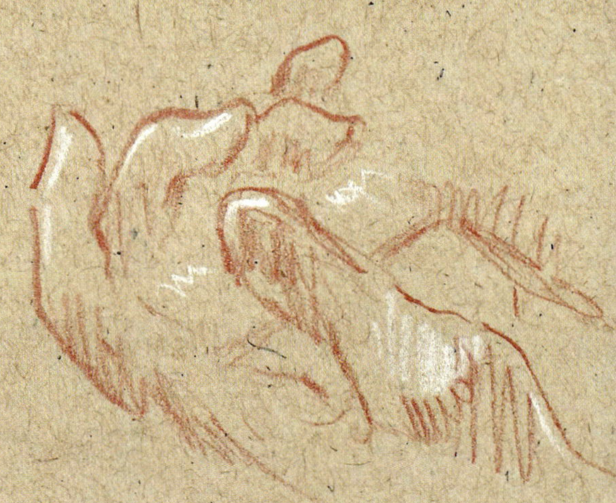

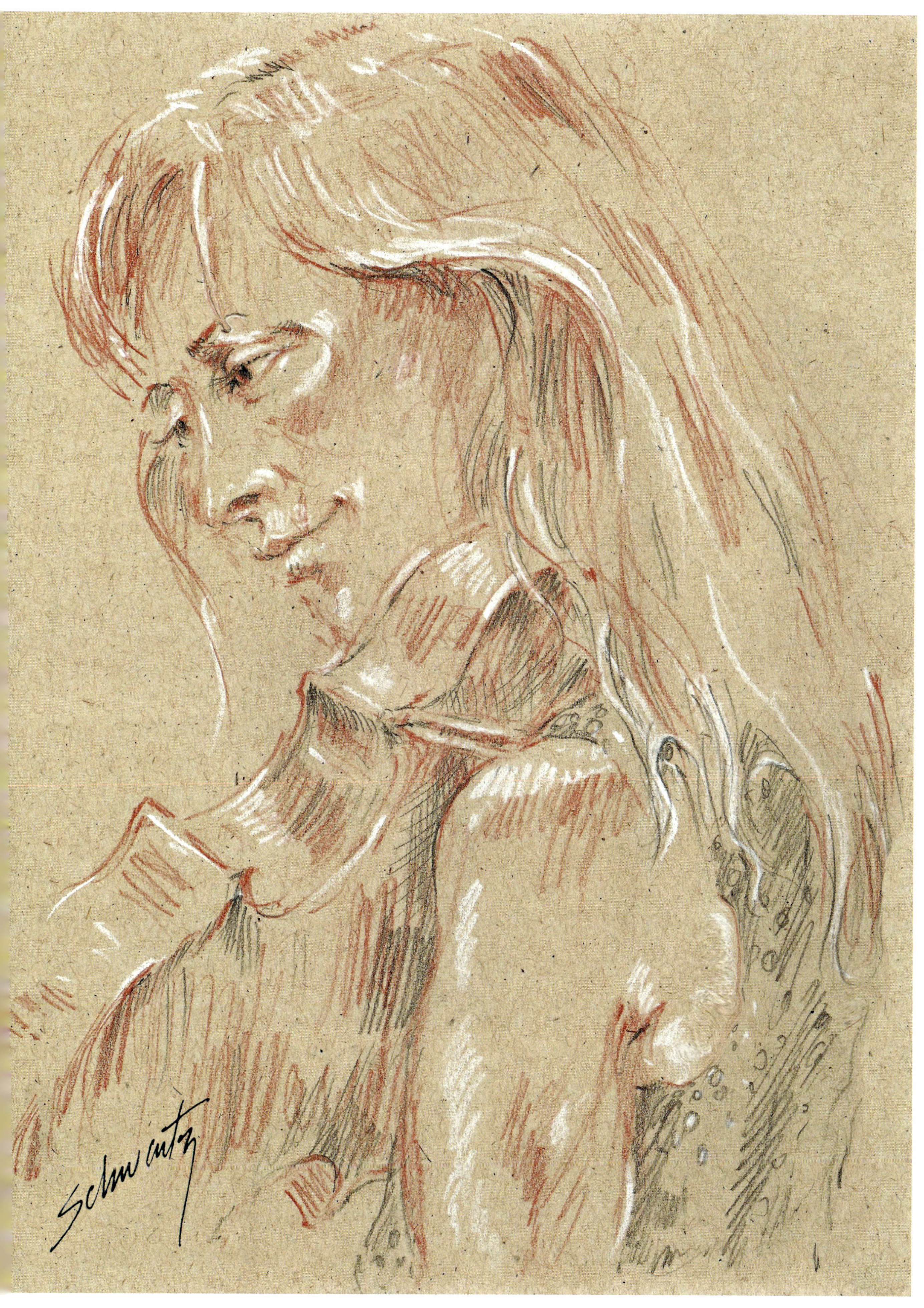
Schwartz

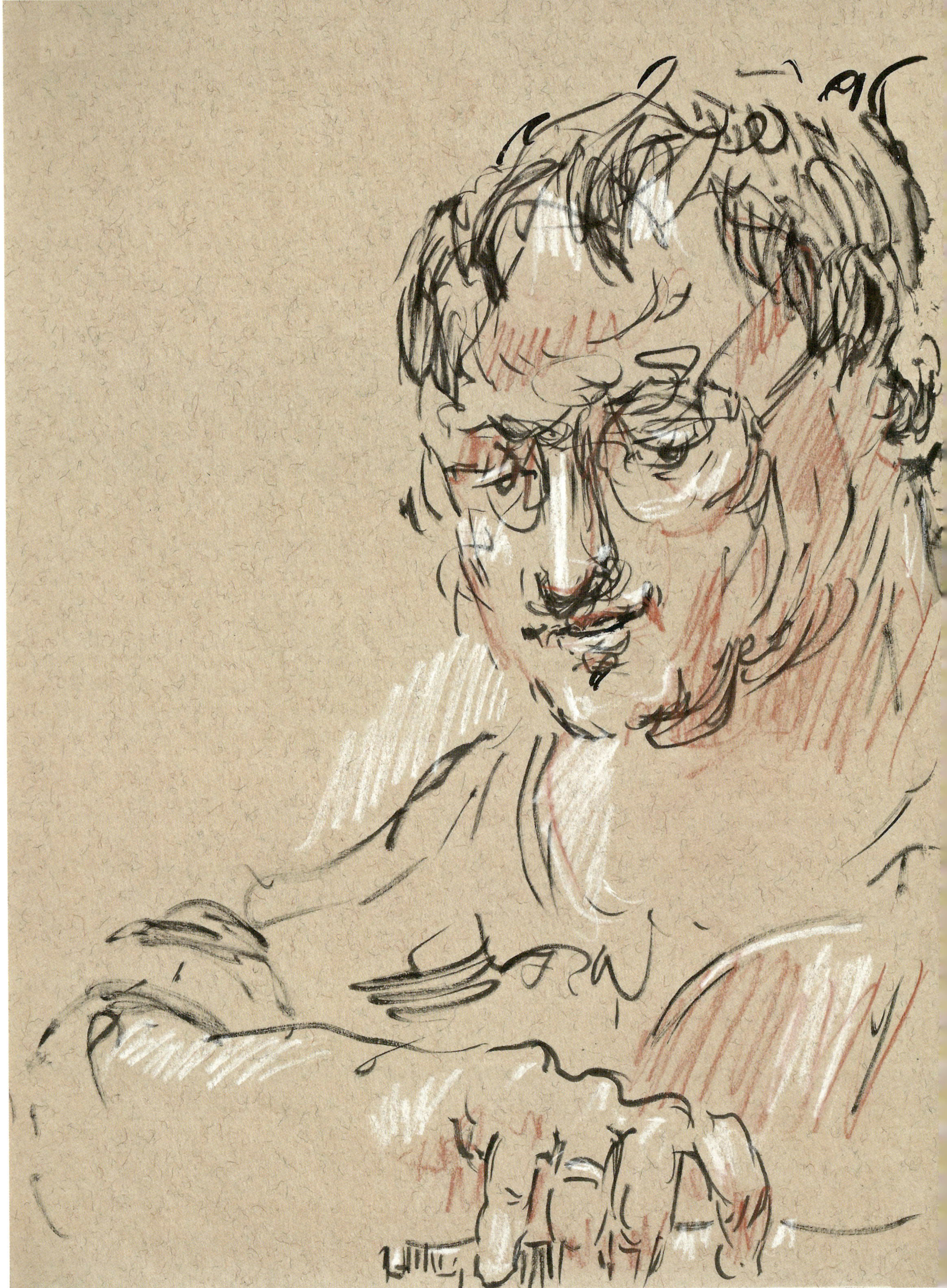

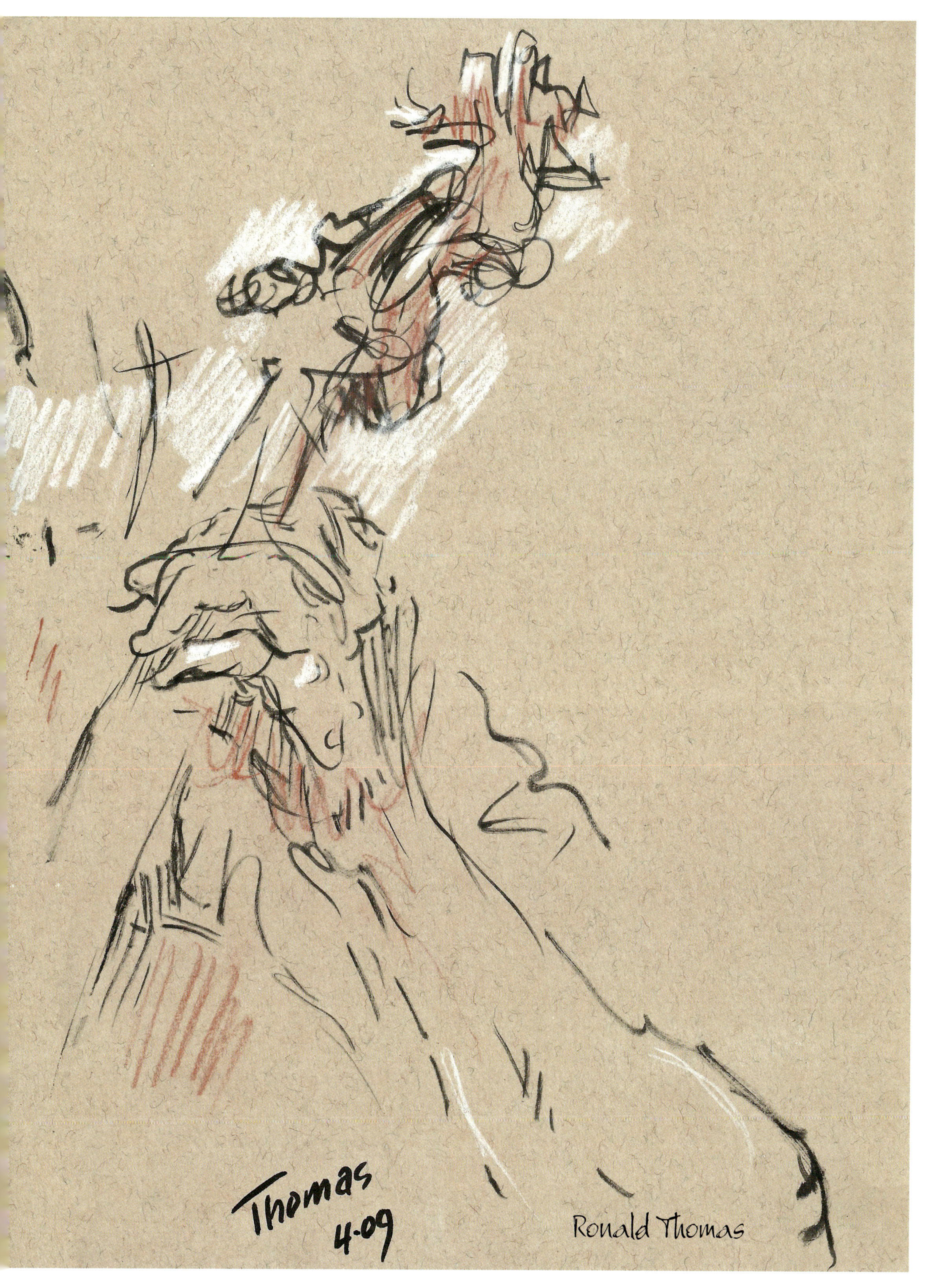

Ronald Thomas

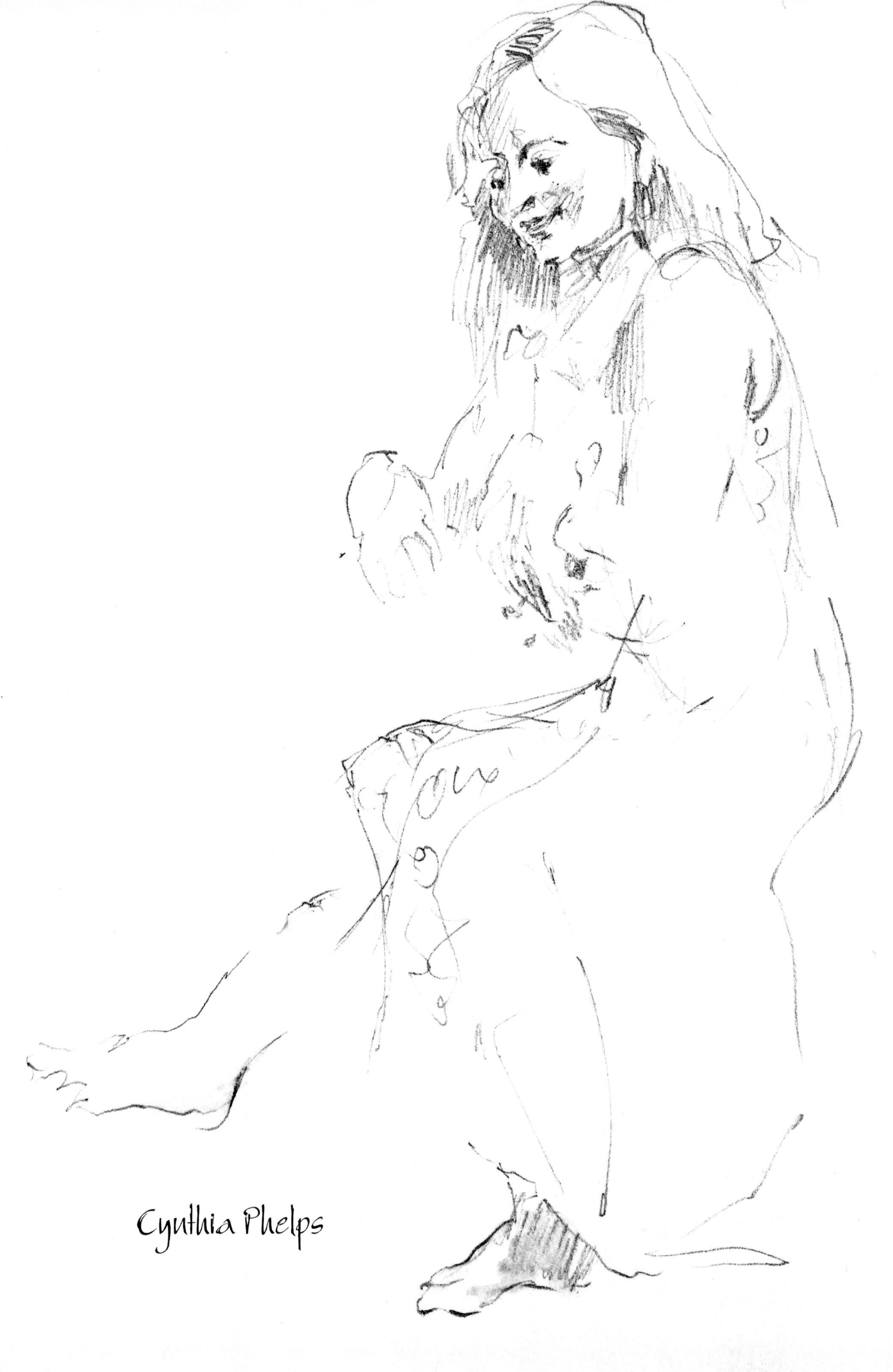
Cynthia Phelps

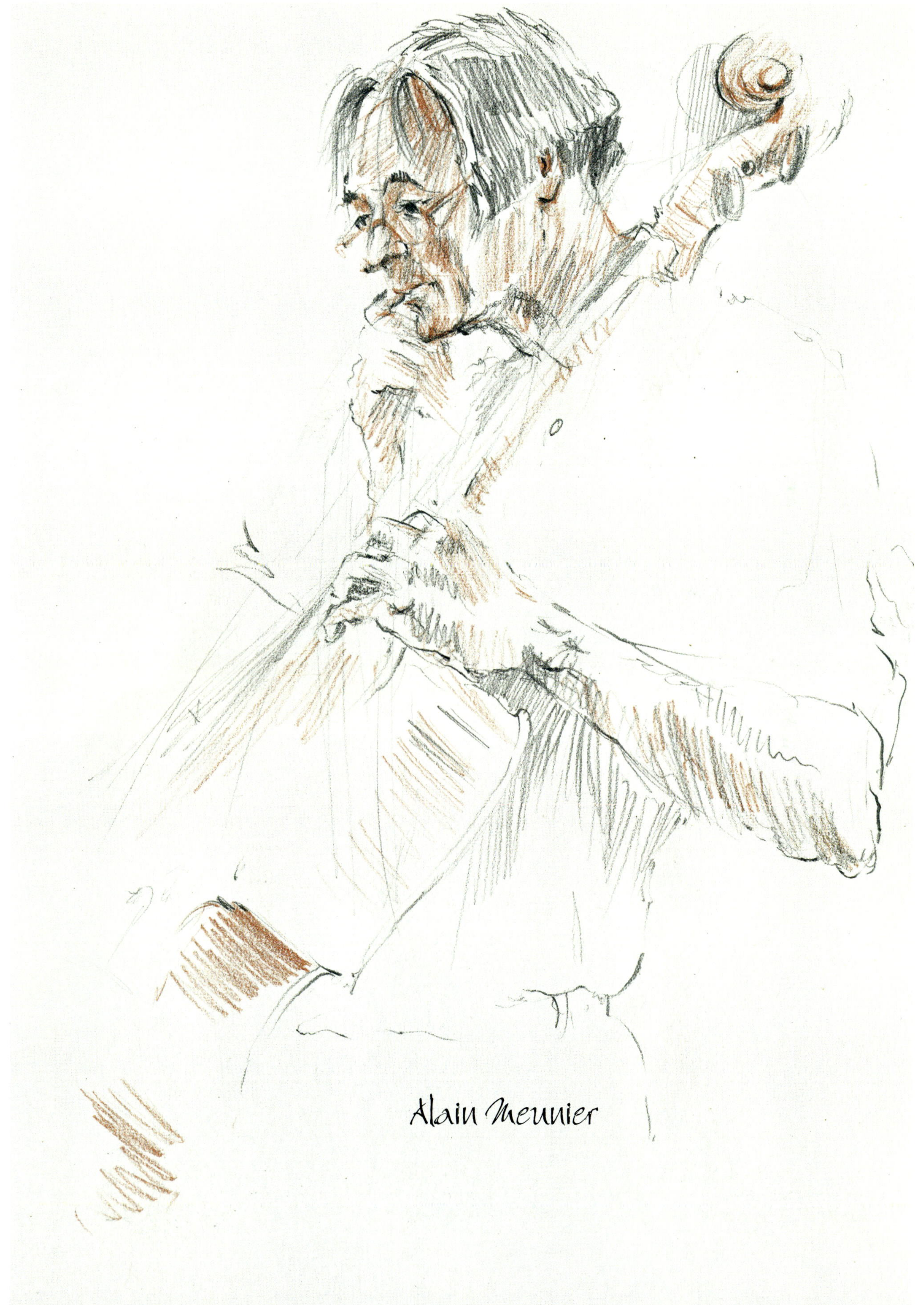
Alain Meunier

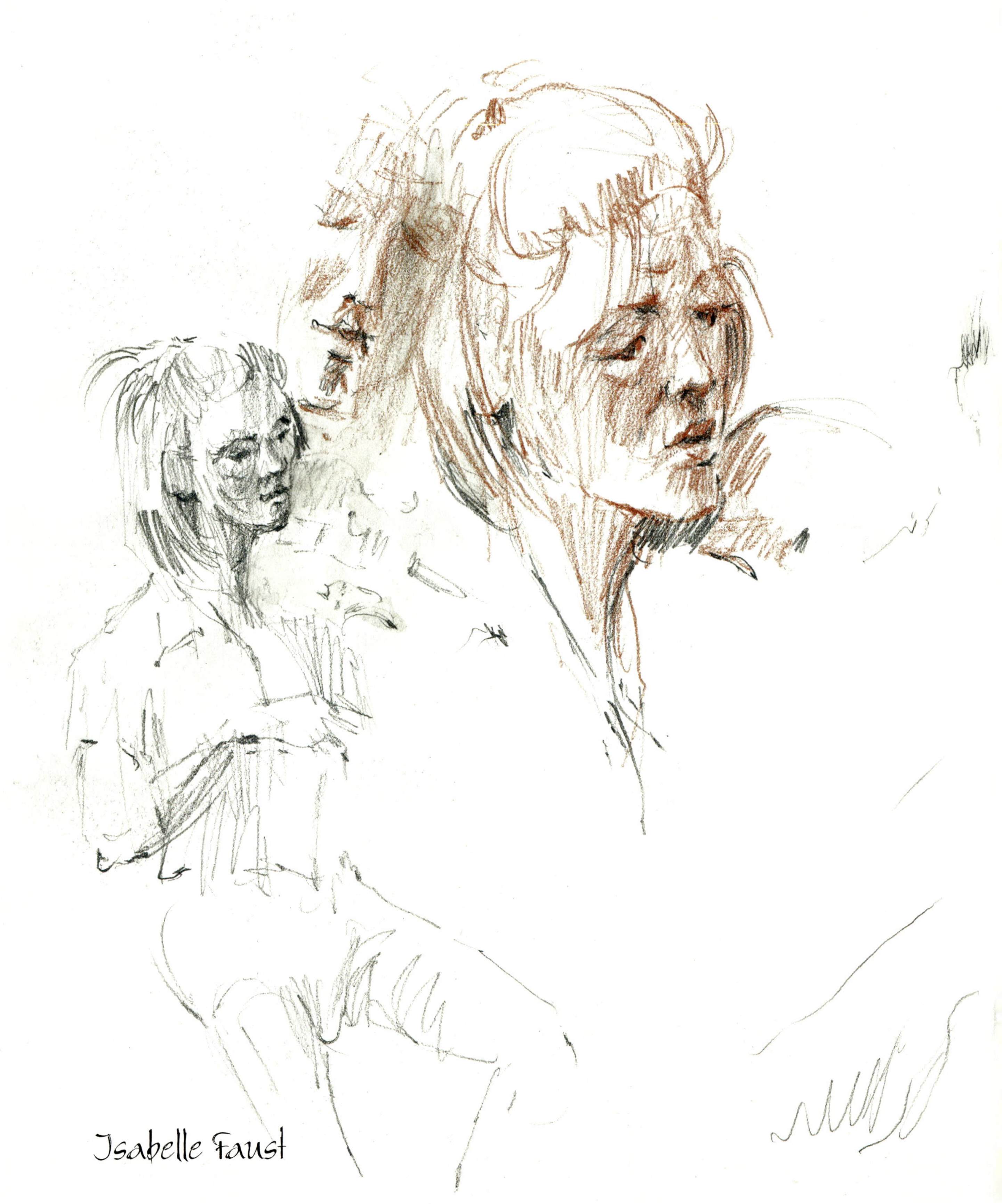

Isabelle Faust

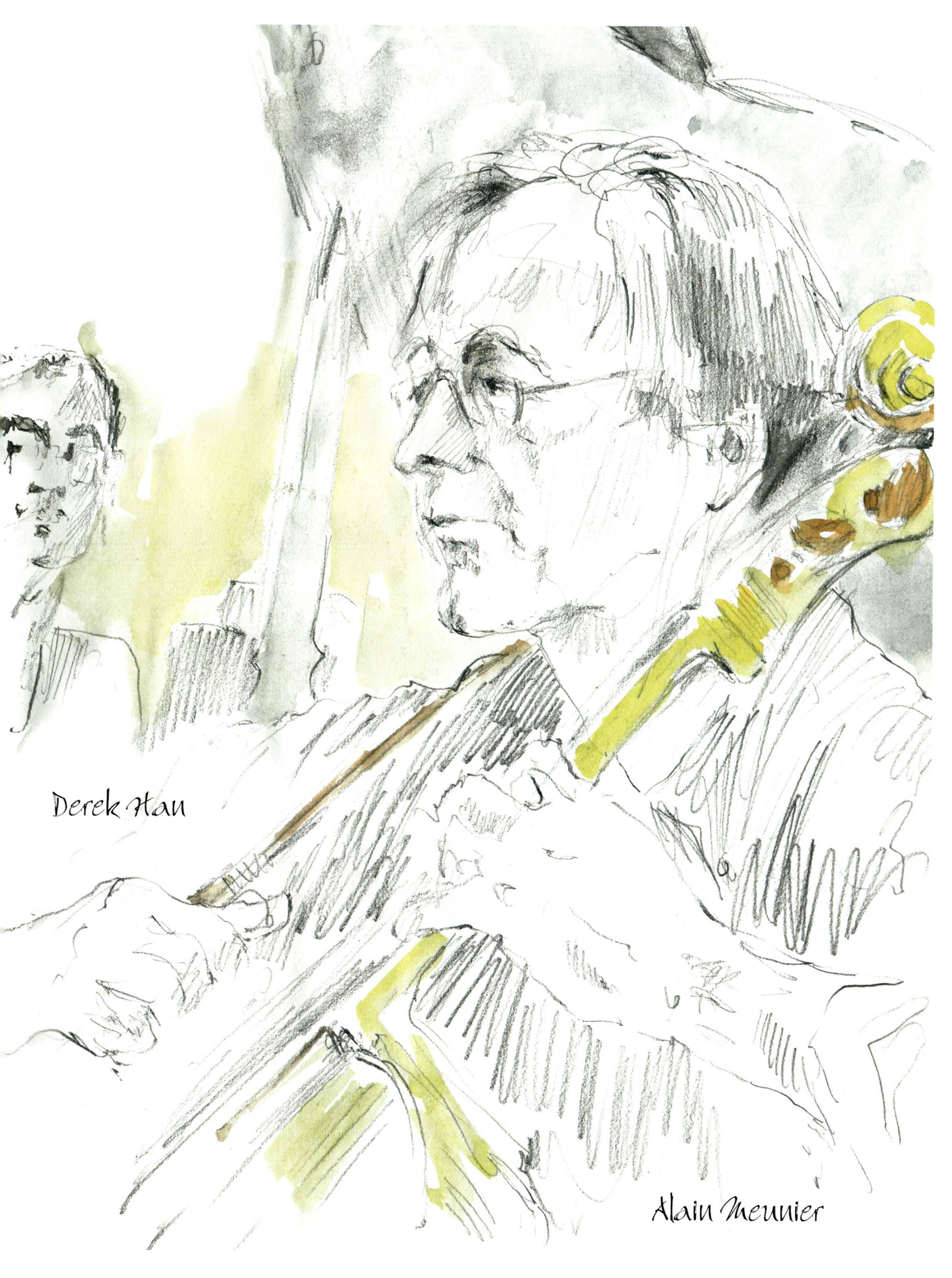
Derek Han
Alain Meunier

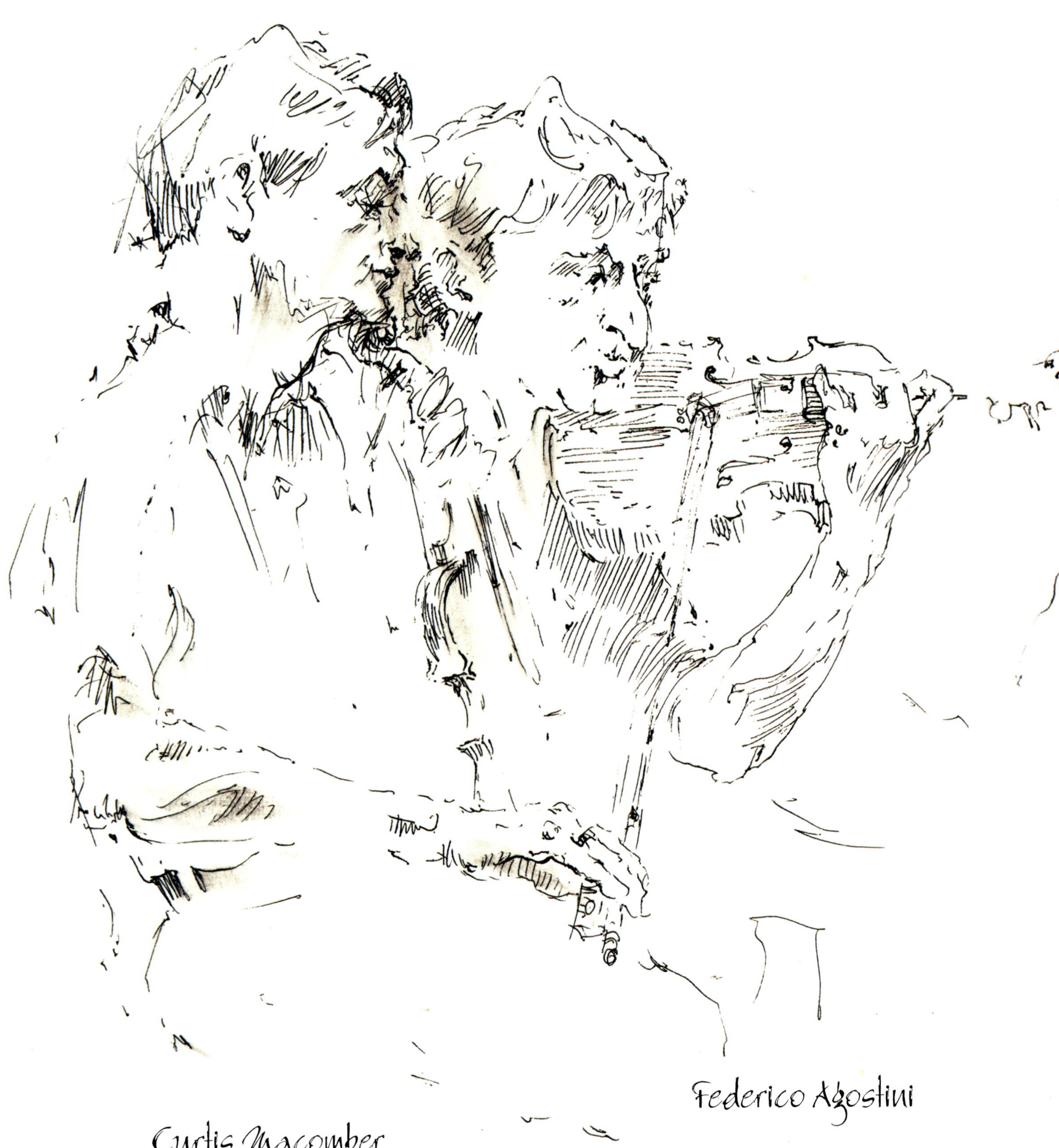
Federico Agostini
Curtis Macomber

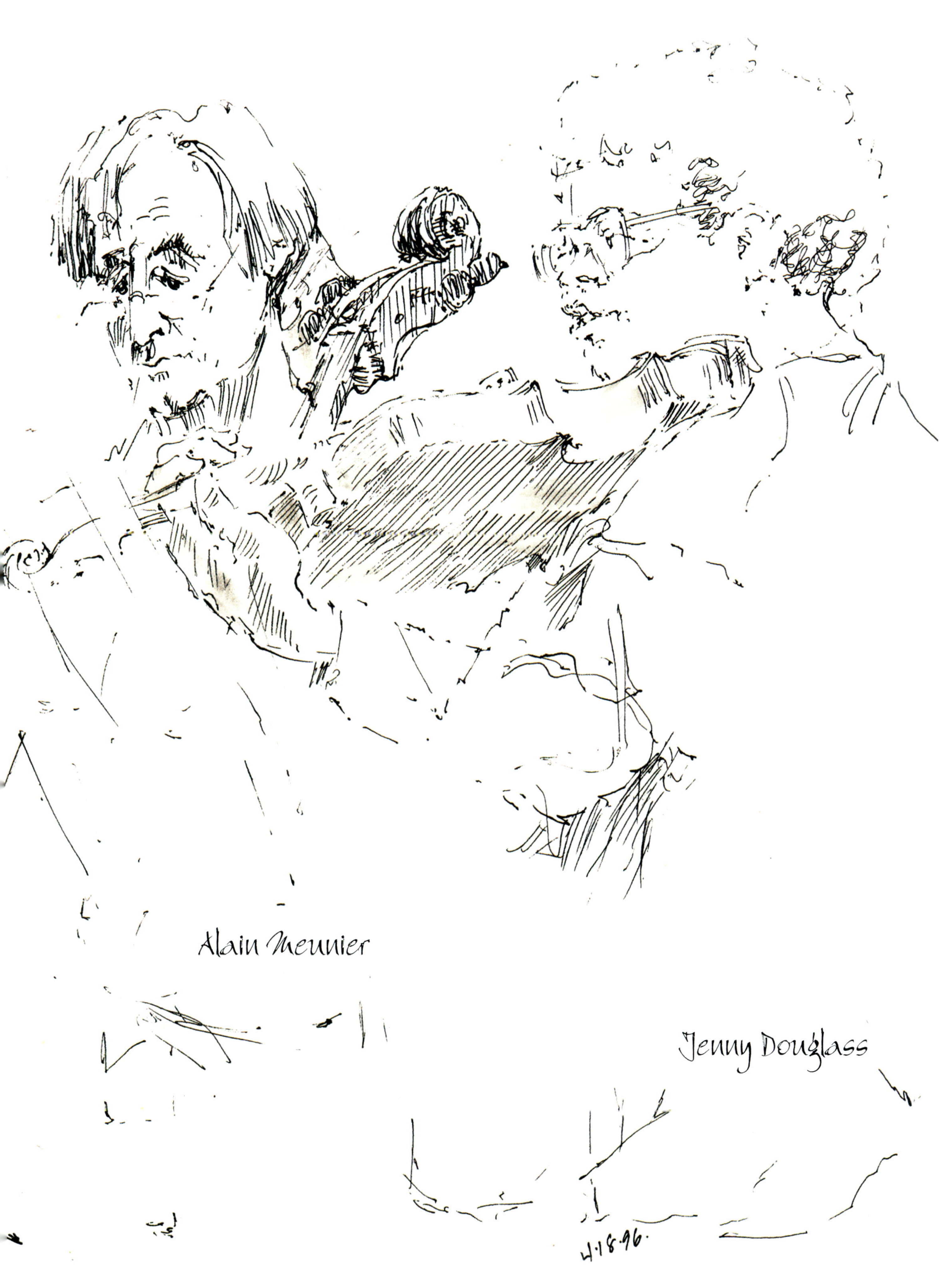

Alain Meunier
Jenny Douglass
4·18·96

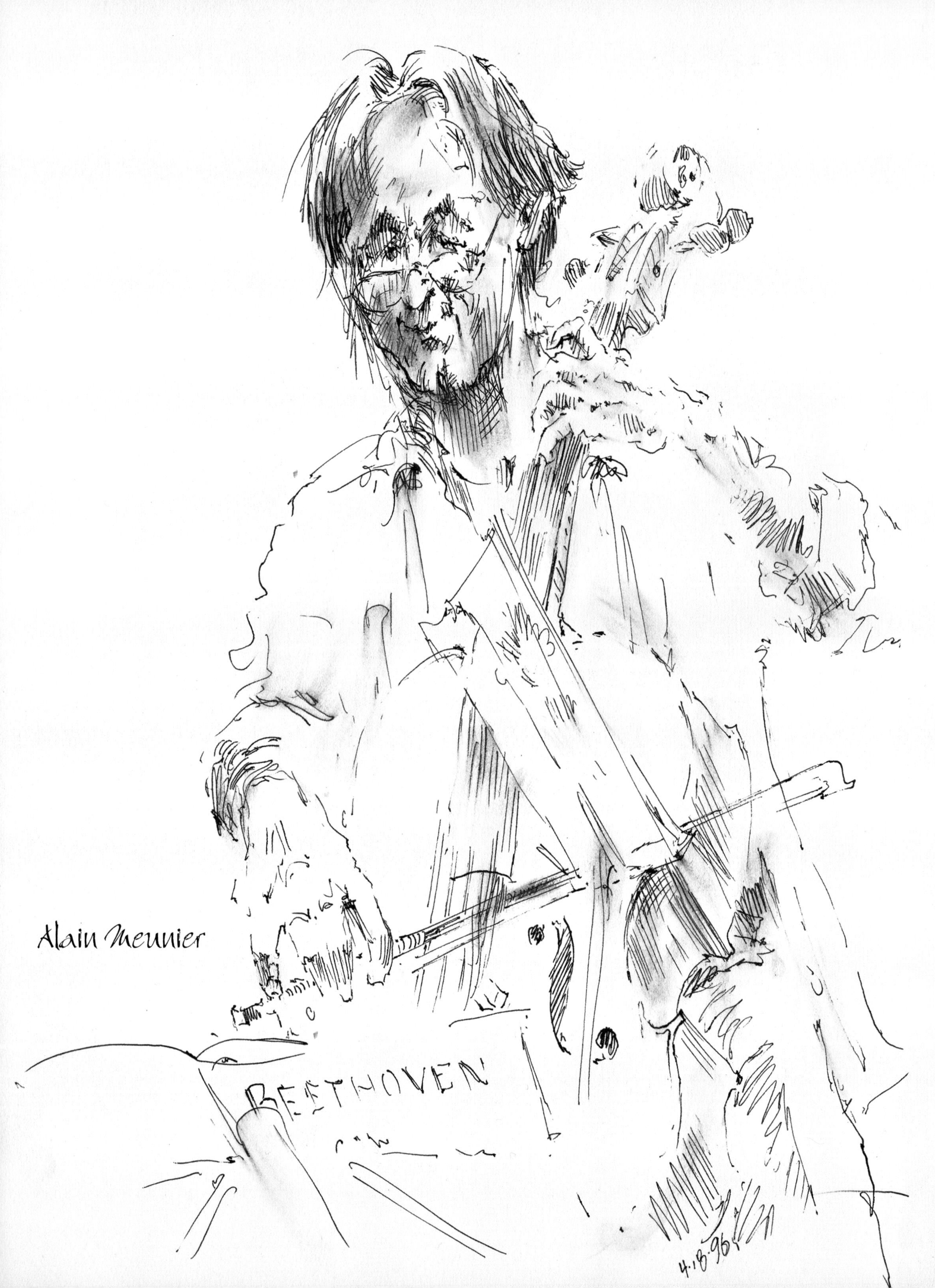
Alain Meunier
BEETHOVEN
4.18.96

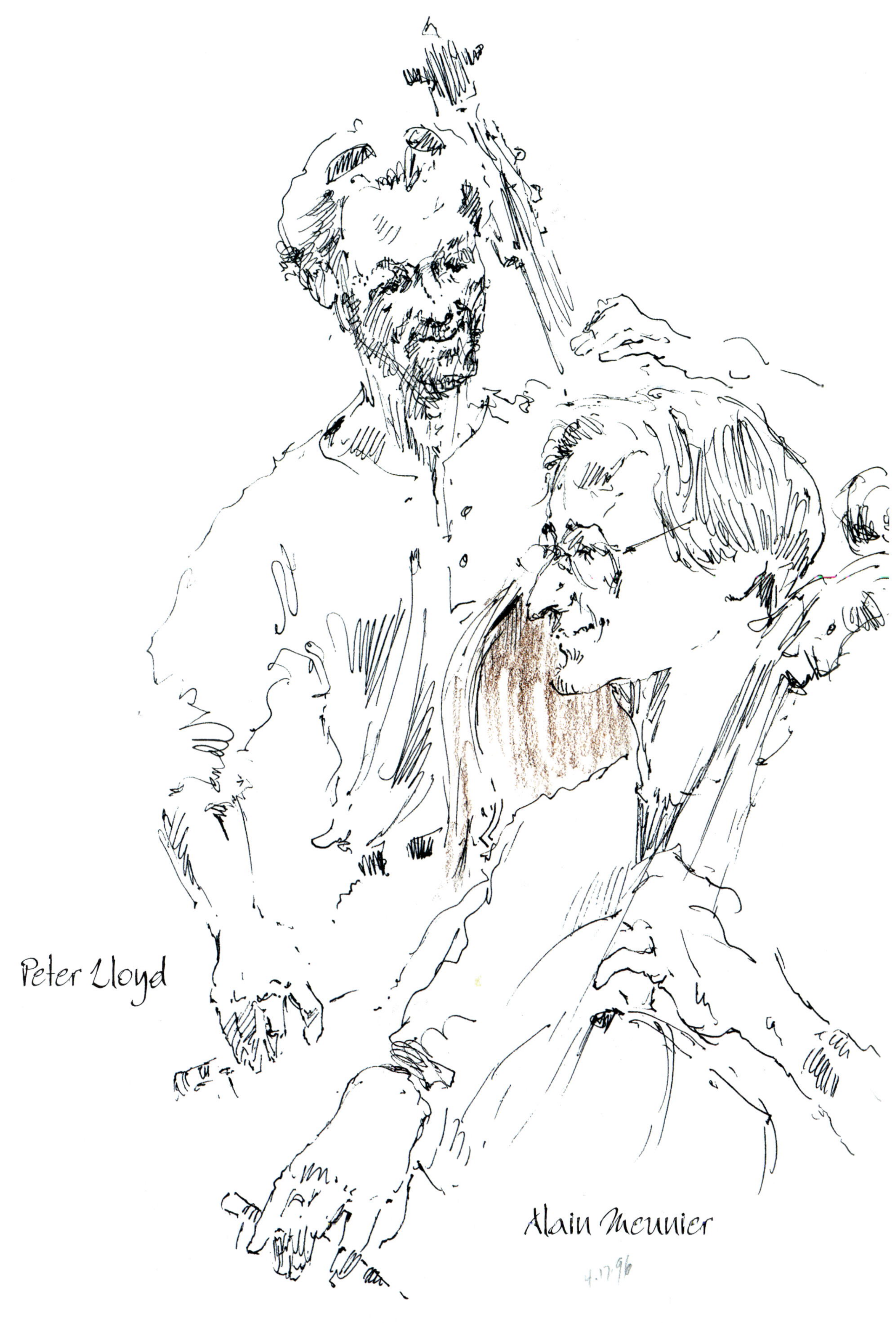
Peter Lloyd
Alain Meunier
4.17.96

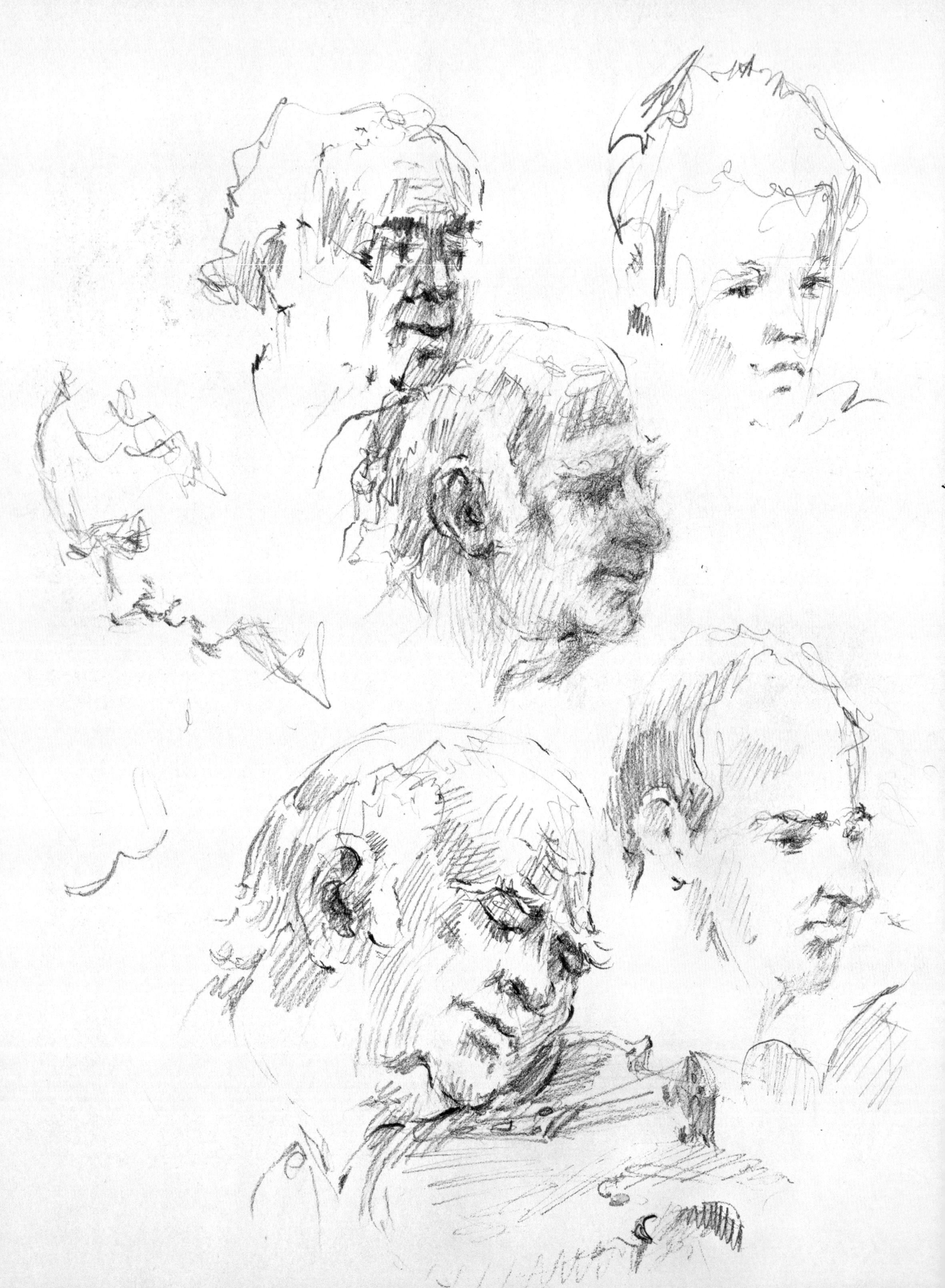

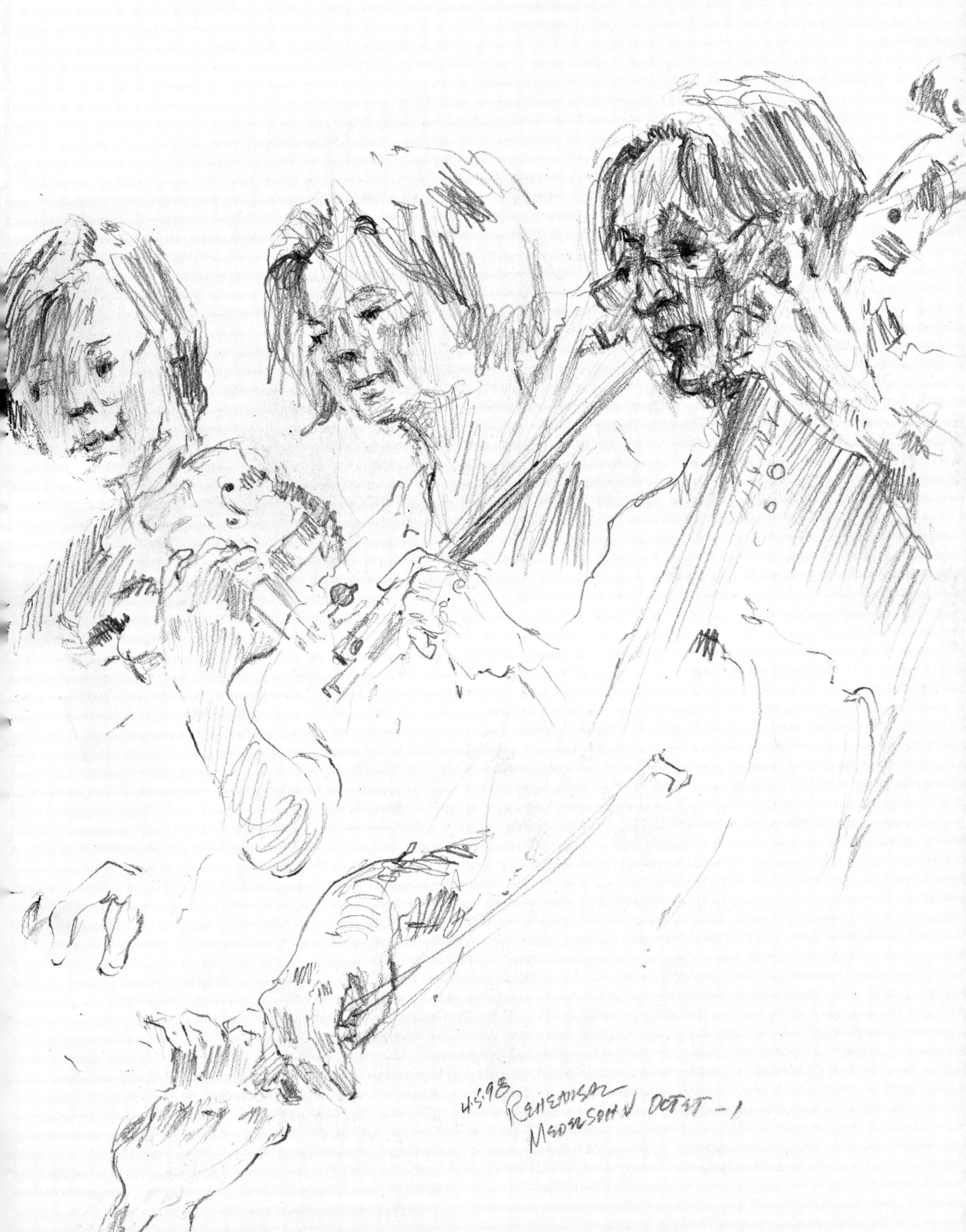
4.5.98 Rehearsal
Mendelssohn Octet – 1

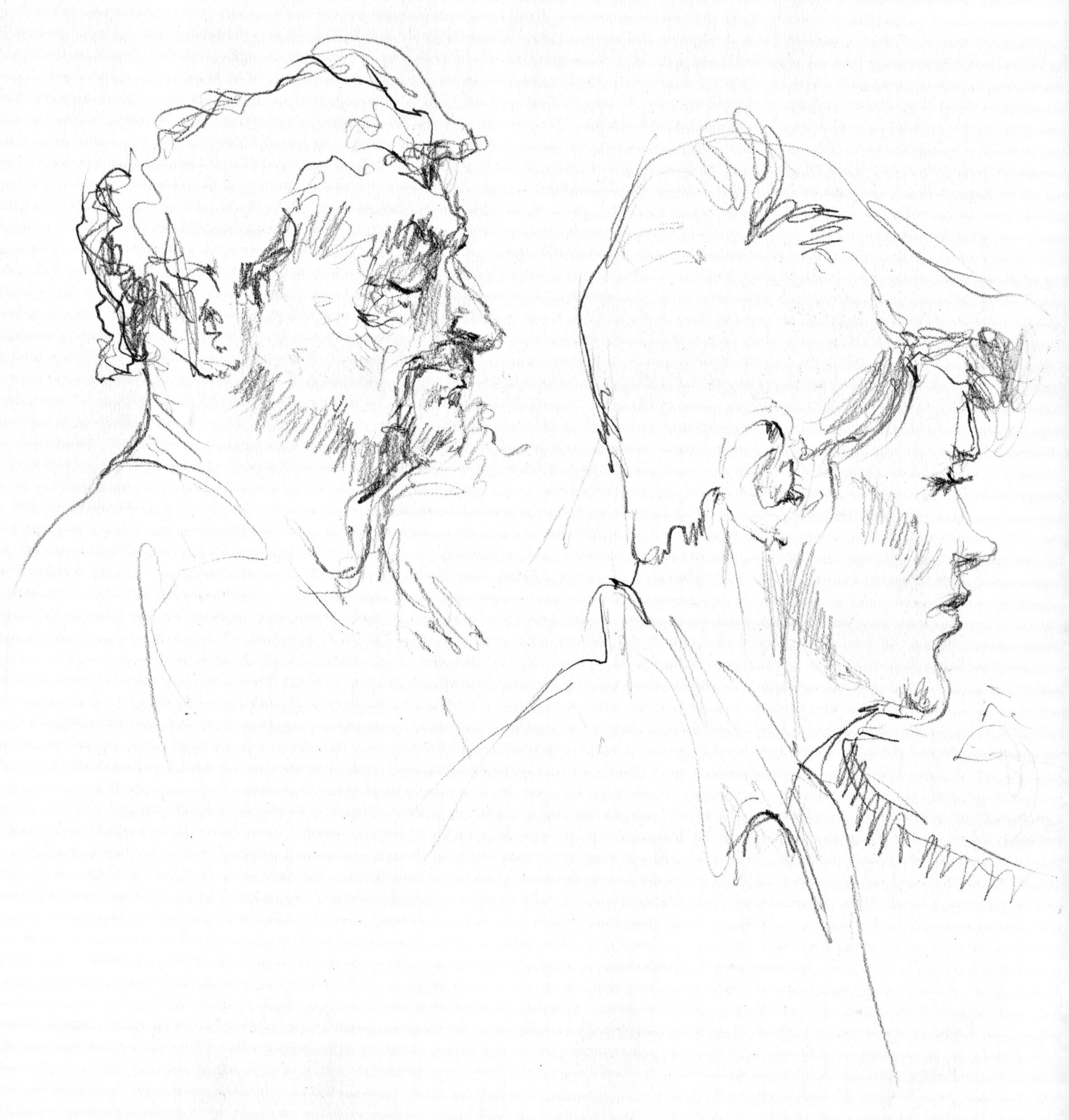

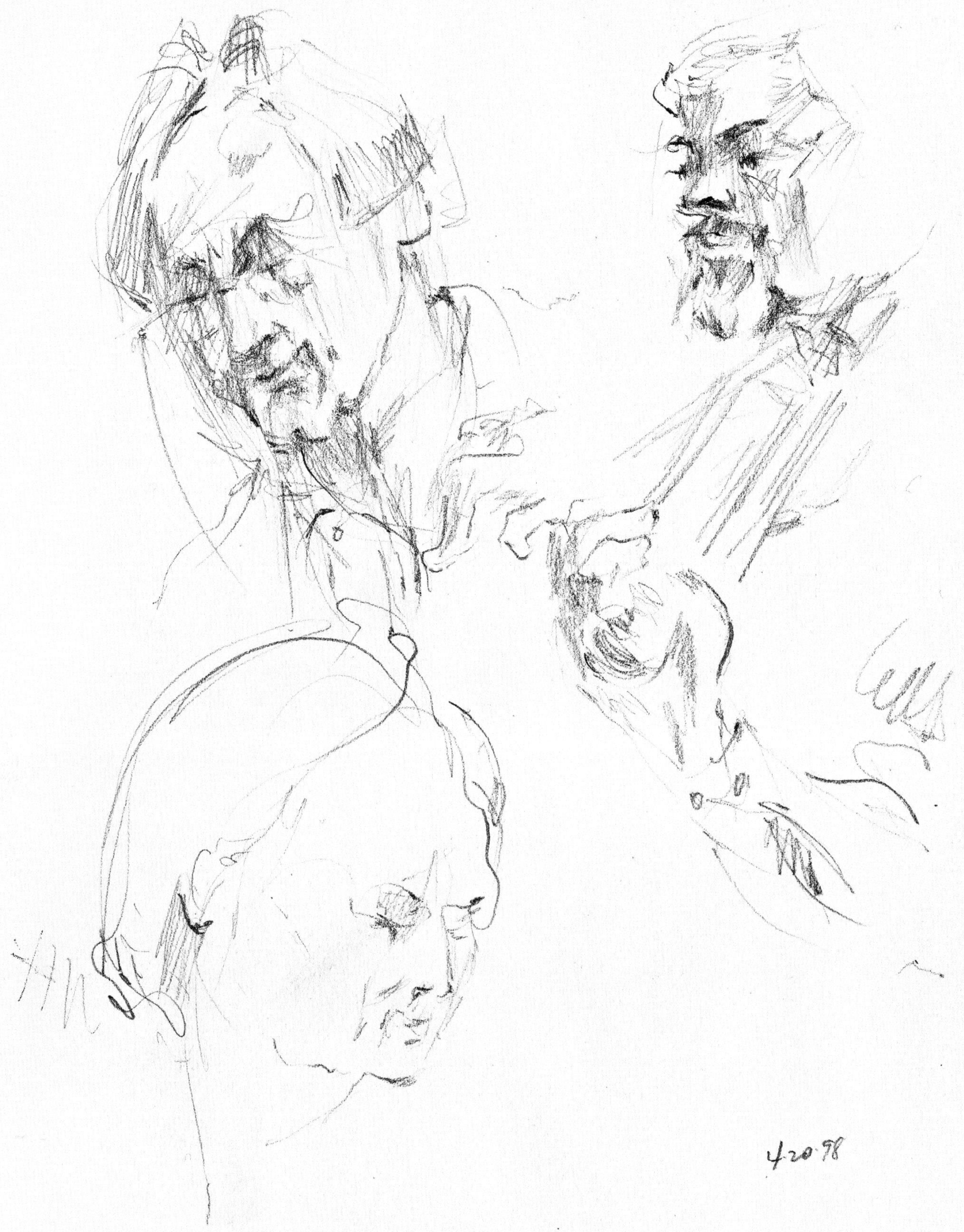
4.20.98

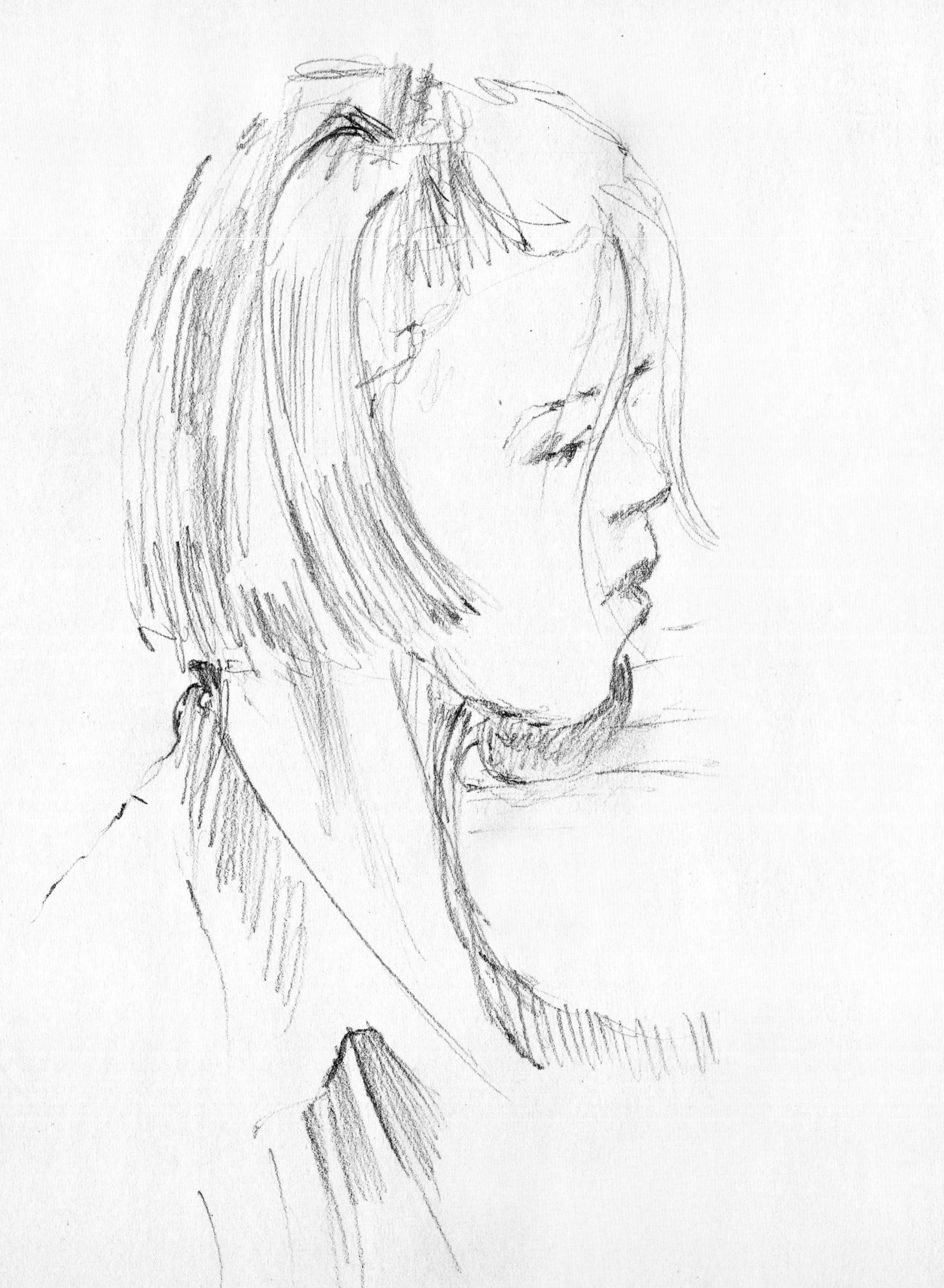

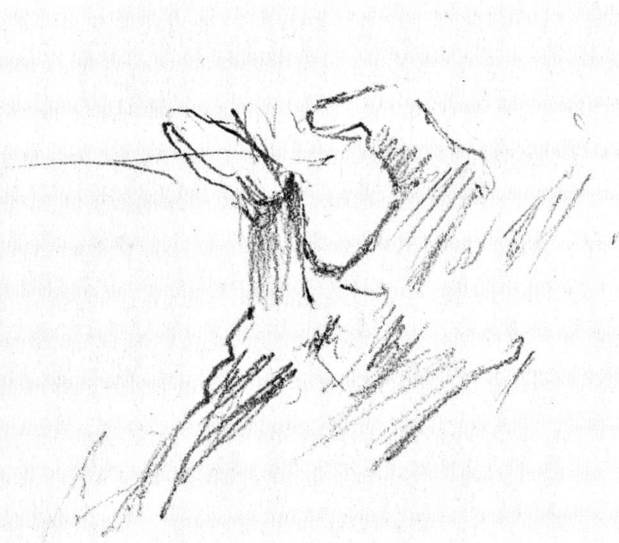

Isabelle Faust

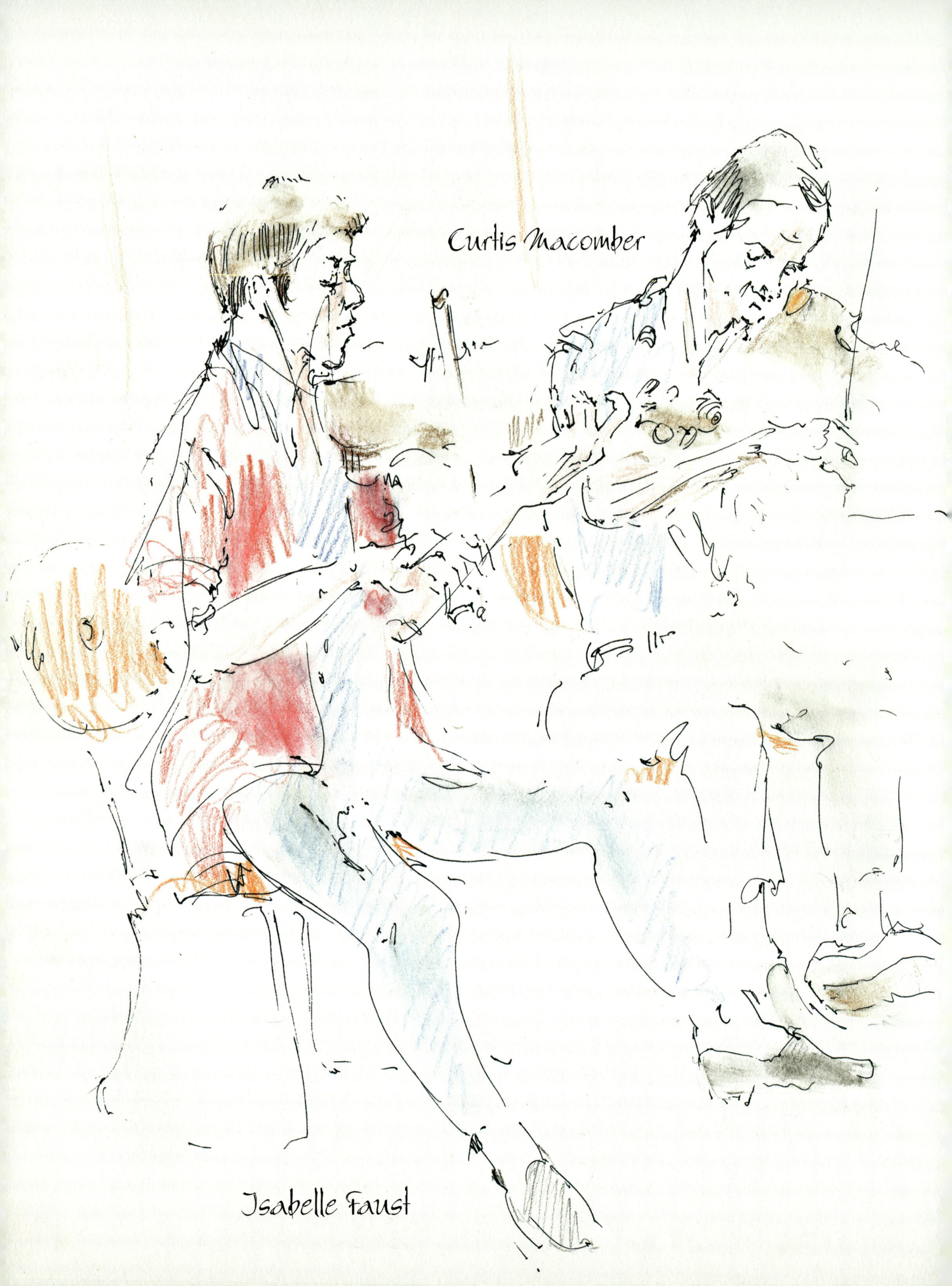
Curtis Macomber
Isabelle Faust

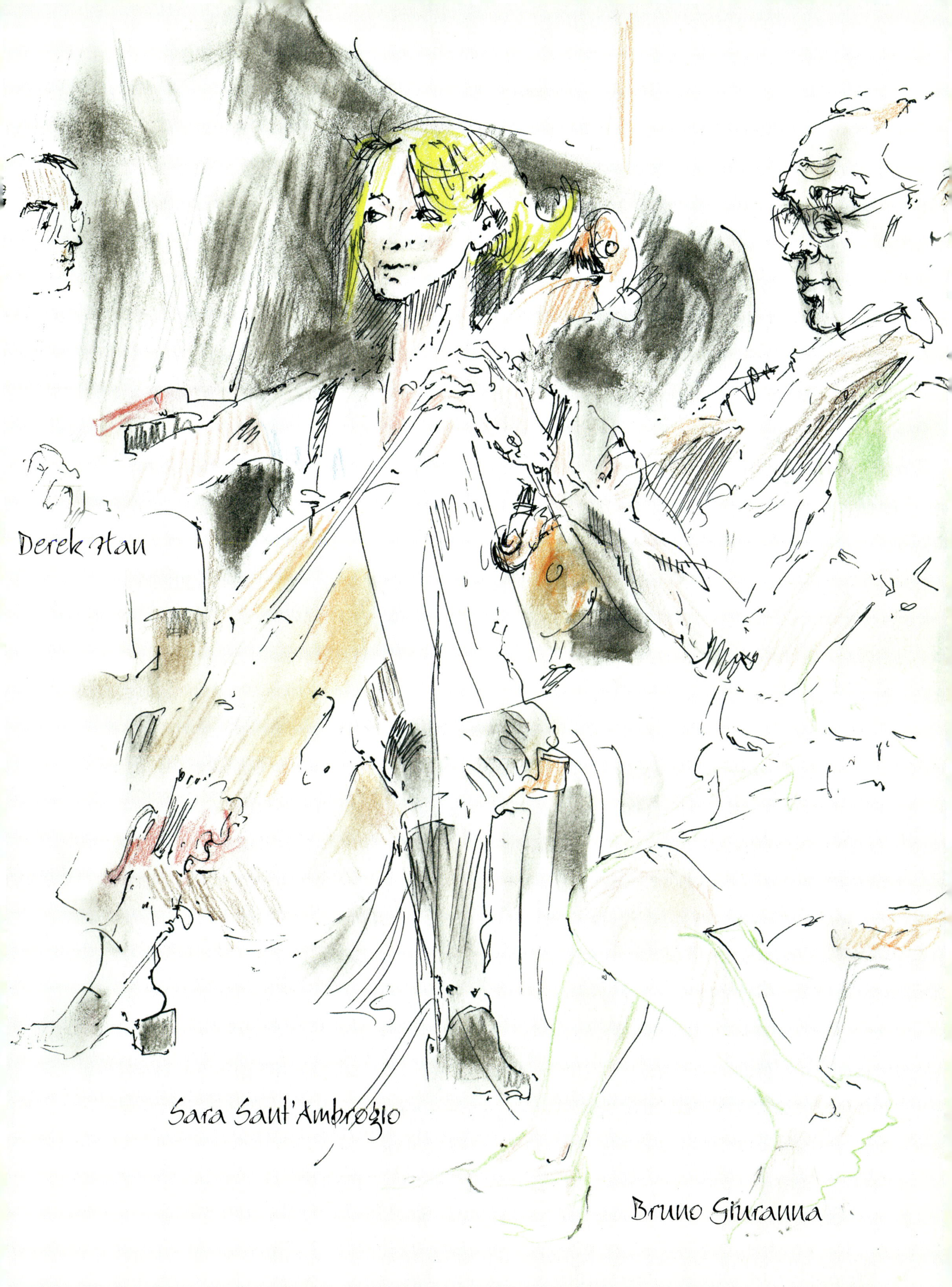
Derek Han
Sara Sant'Ambrogio
Bruno Giuranna

Dick Hyman is one of the most highly regarded jazz and classical musicians internationally. His skill as a pianist is legendary in that he can play in every jazz style.

For many years, he has been the Musical Director and Arranger for Woody Allen's films.

He resides in the Sarasota area and has performed with La Musica and been commissioned by them to compose an original work. These drawings illustrate him lecturing and performing his new work in rehearsal.

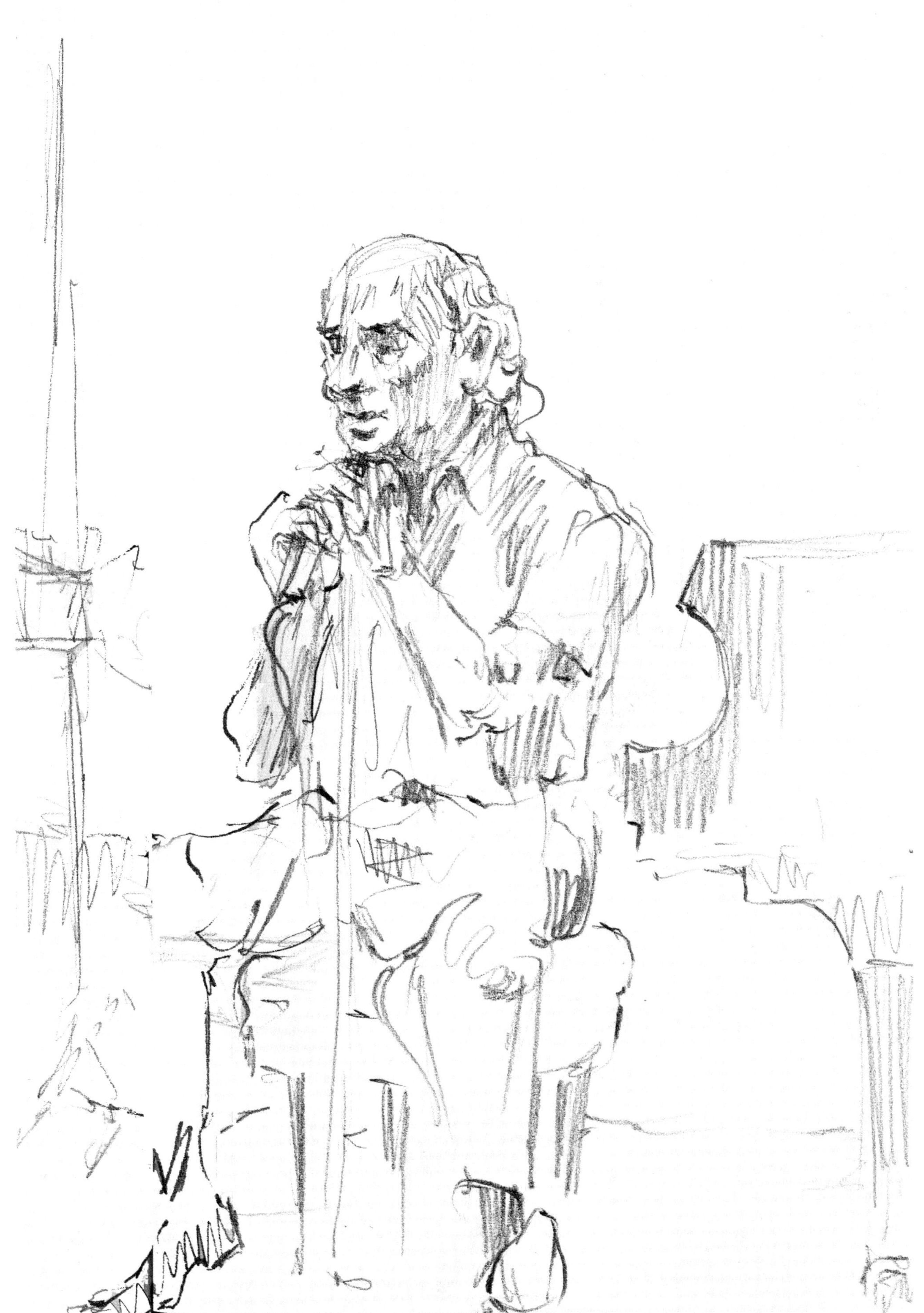

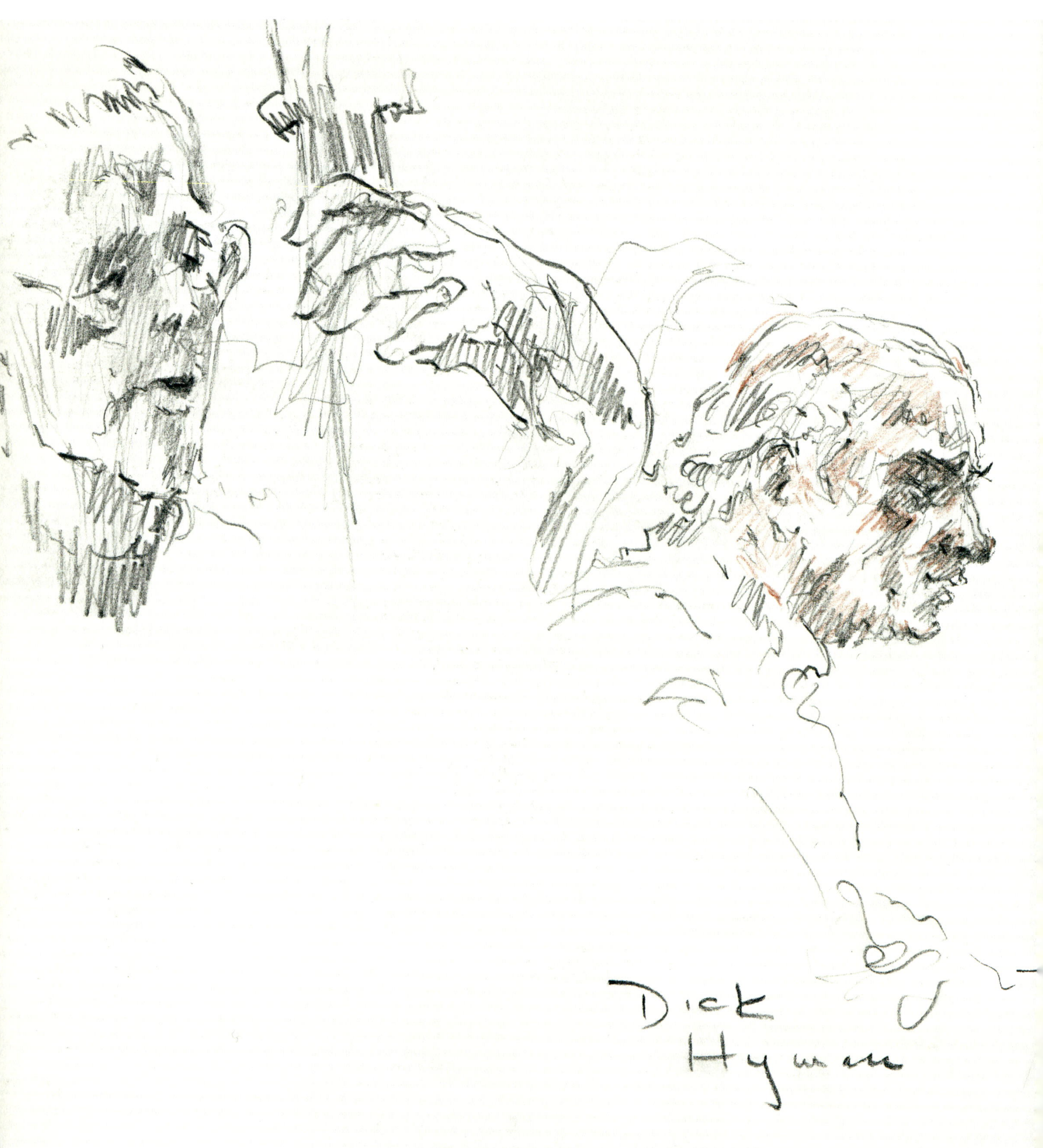
Dick
Hyman

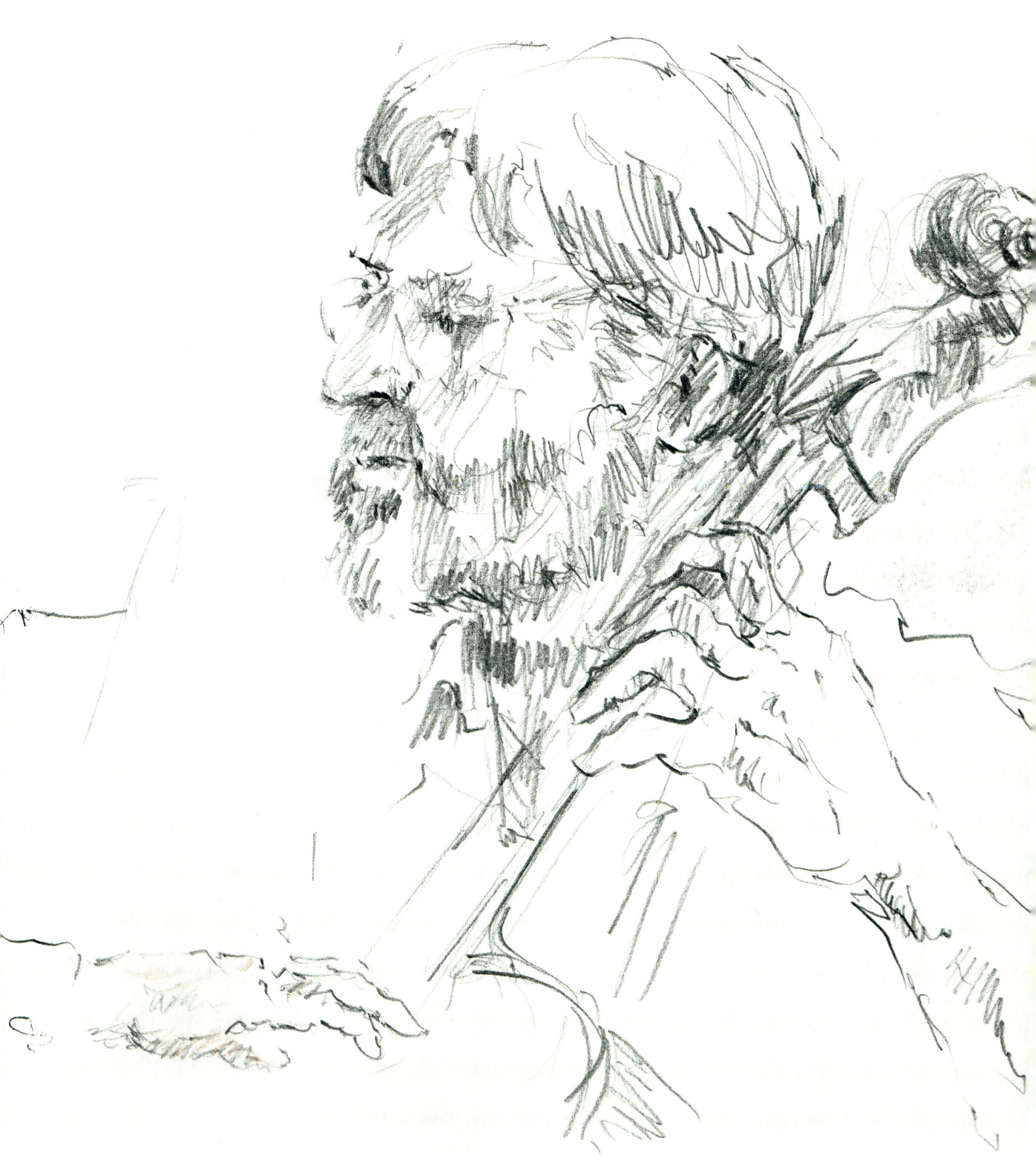

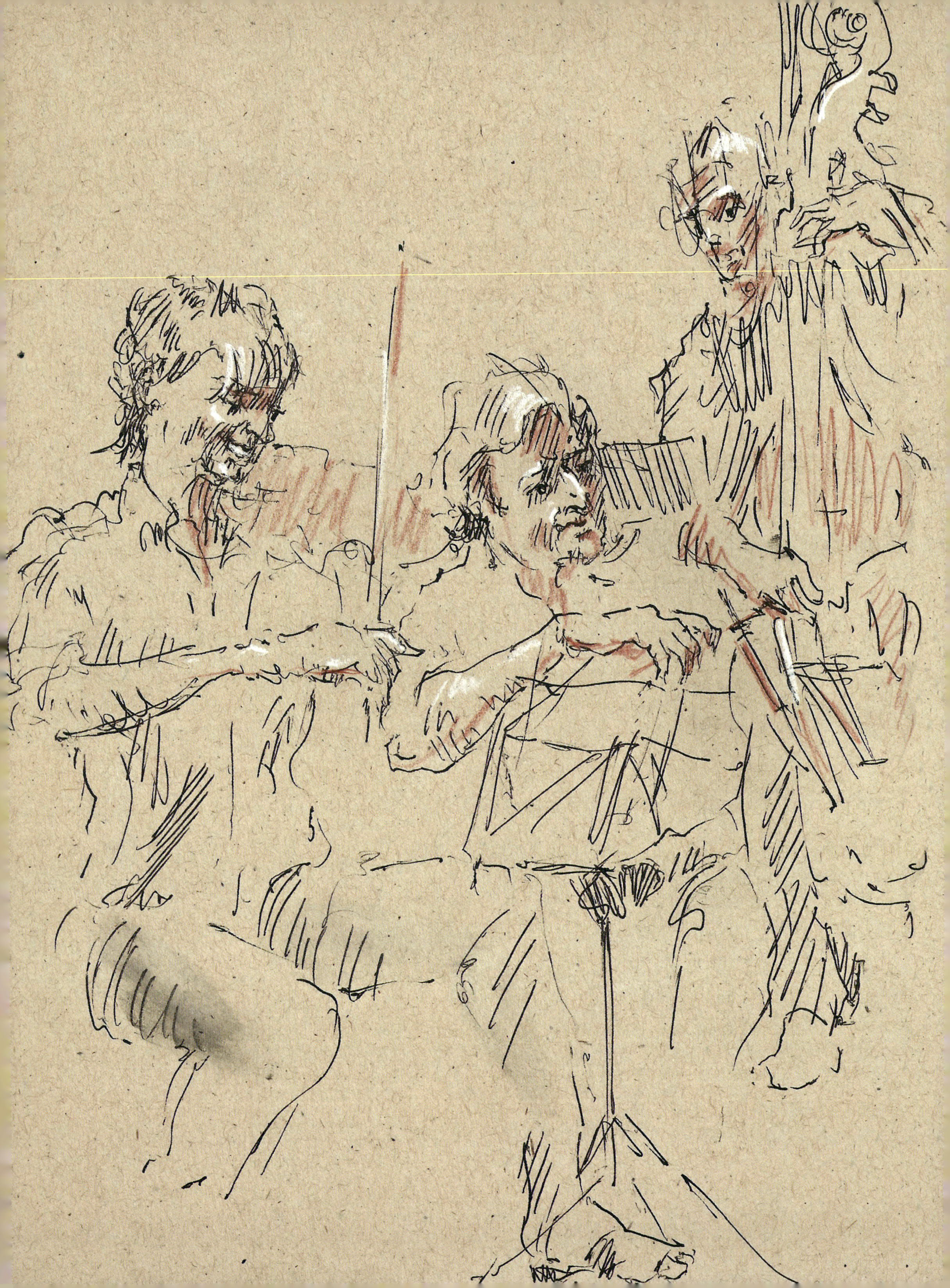

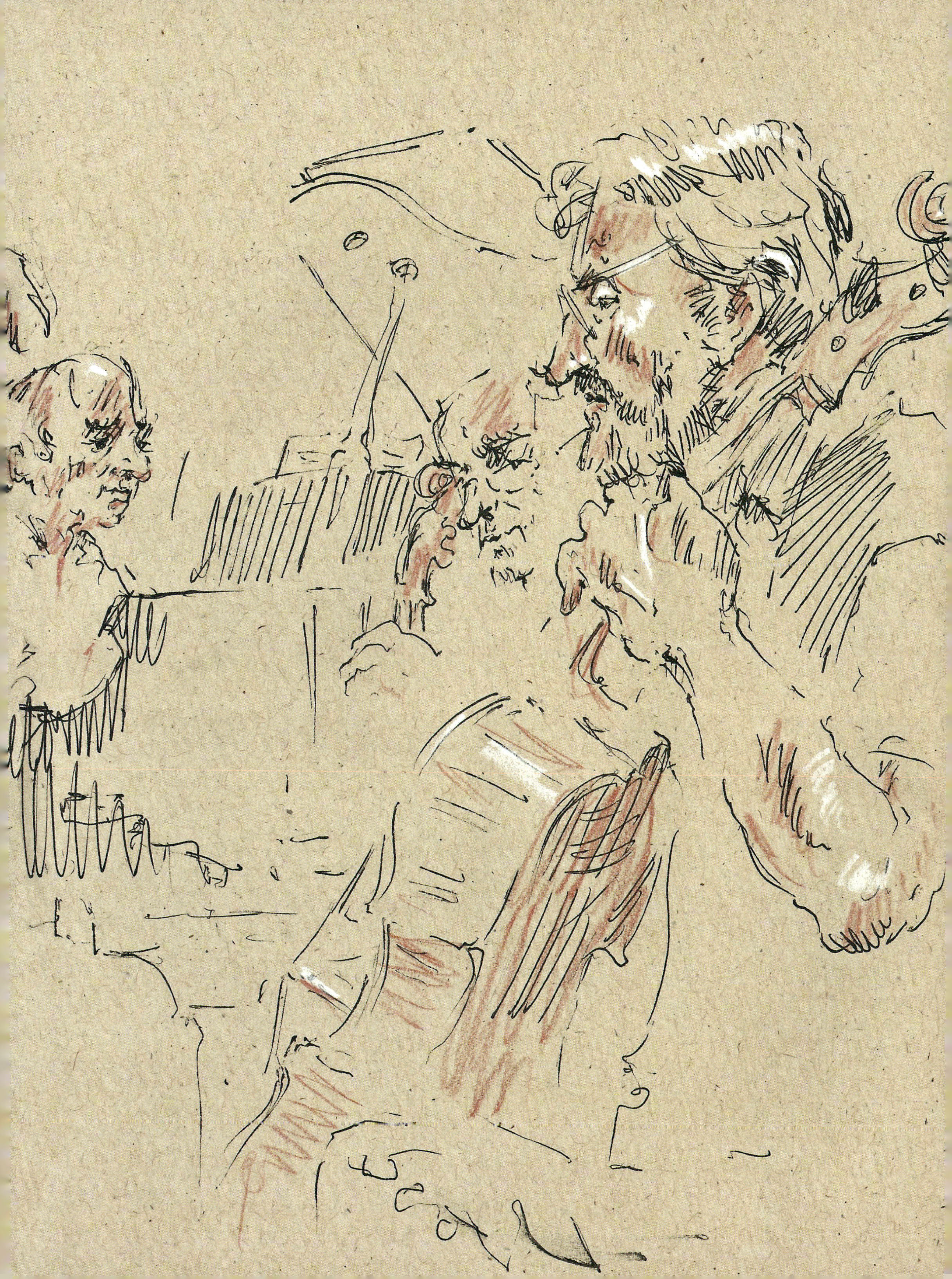

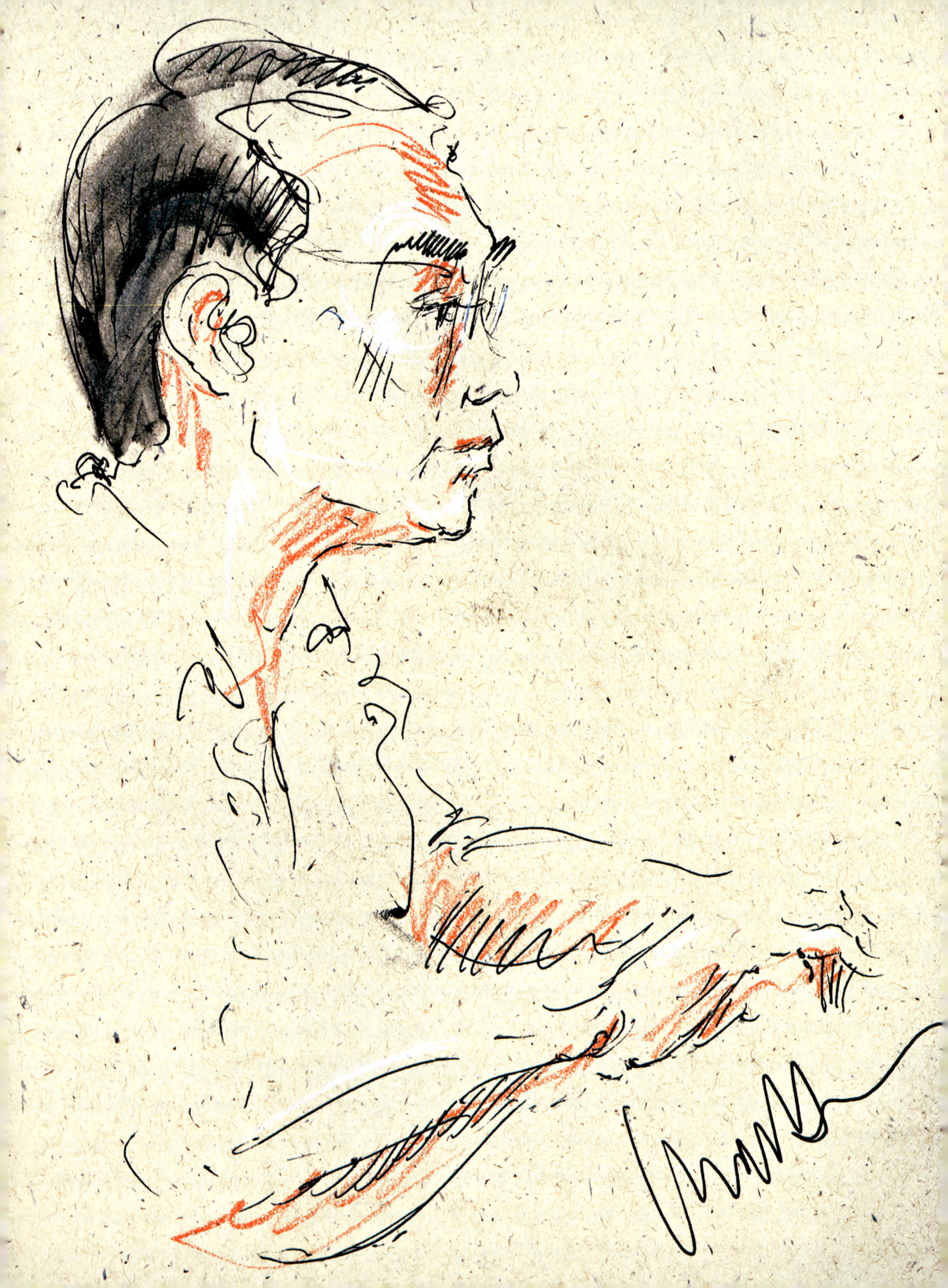

Derek Han, pianist and Associate Artistic Director of La Musica, was a graduate of the Juilliard School of Music at age 18. He studied with the famed Gina Bachauer and Lily Kraus. He won first prize at the Athens International Piano Competition.

Mr. Han has accompanied almost every visiting artist over the last 27 years at La Musica. On the next page is a watercolor of Han performing the Bruch Trio with Cynthia Phelps and David Schifrin.

"This book shares a journey over the years, as La Musica with its masterworks of chamber music is joined together with the beautifully artistic work of Sol Schwartz in the love of art."

– Derek Han

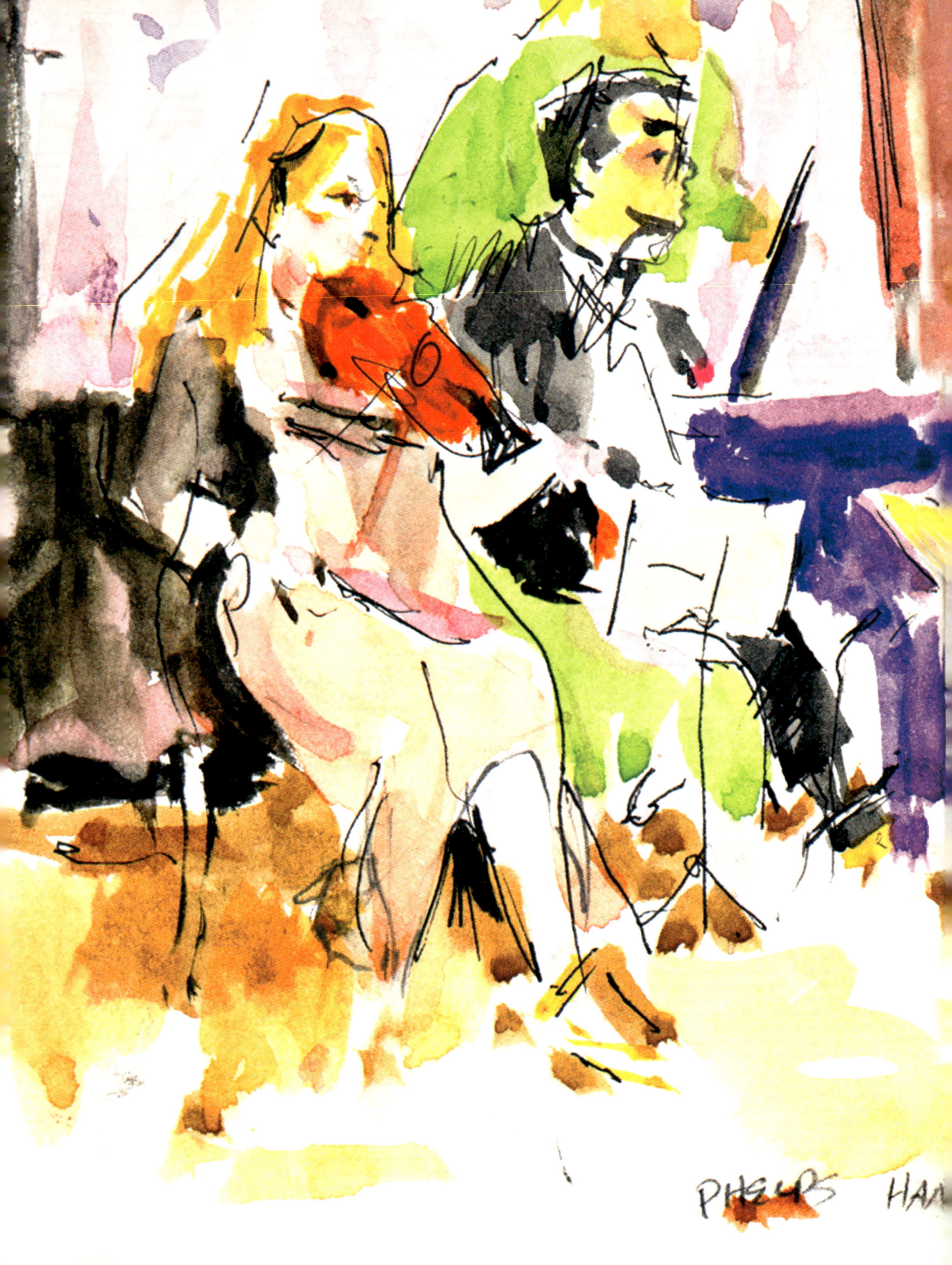
PHELPS

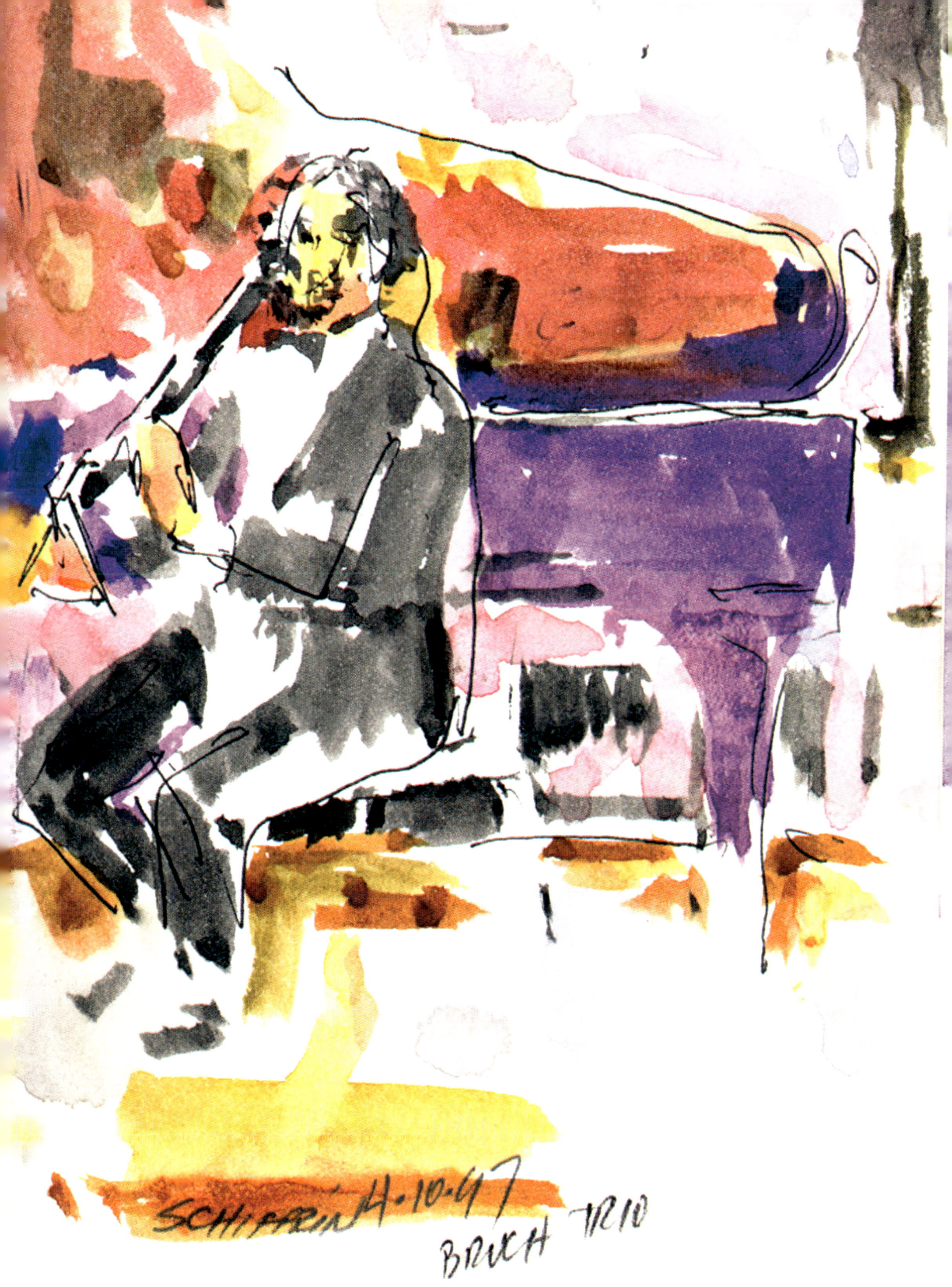
4·10·97
BRUCH TRIO

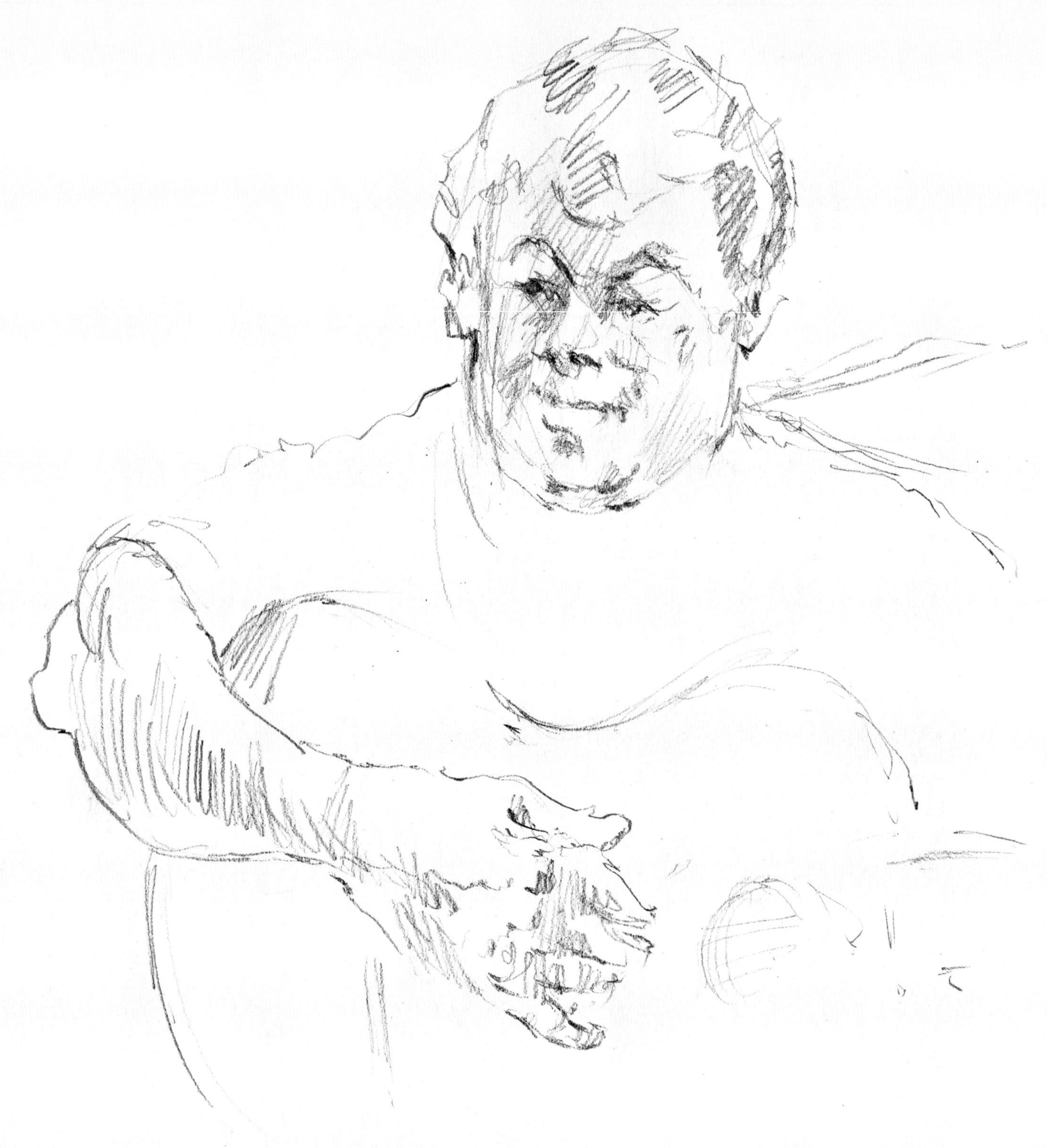

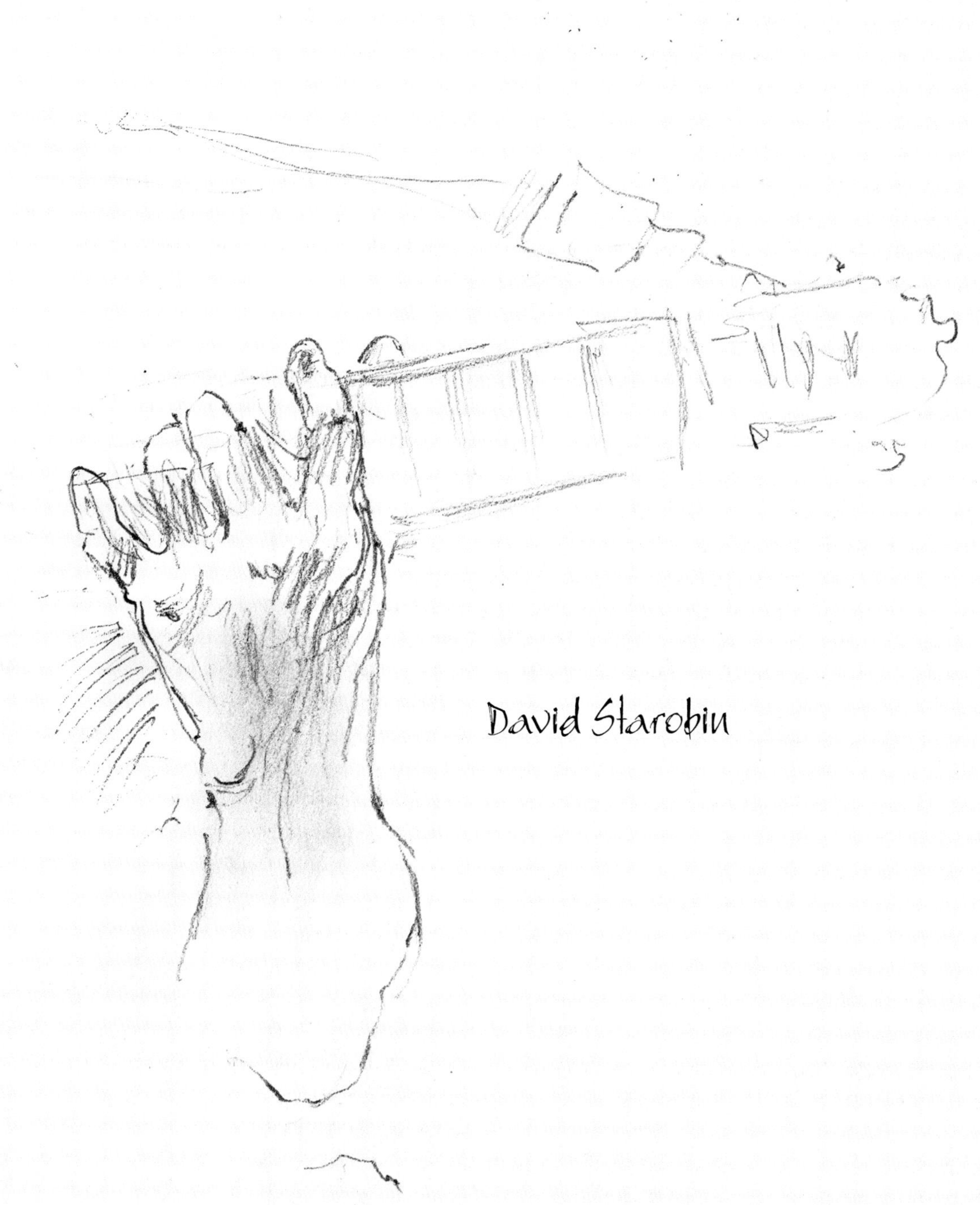

David Starobin

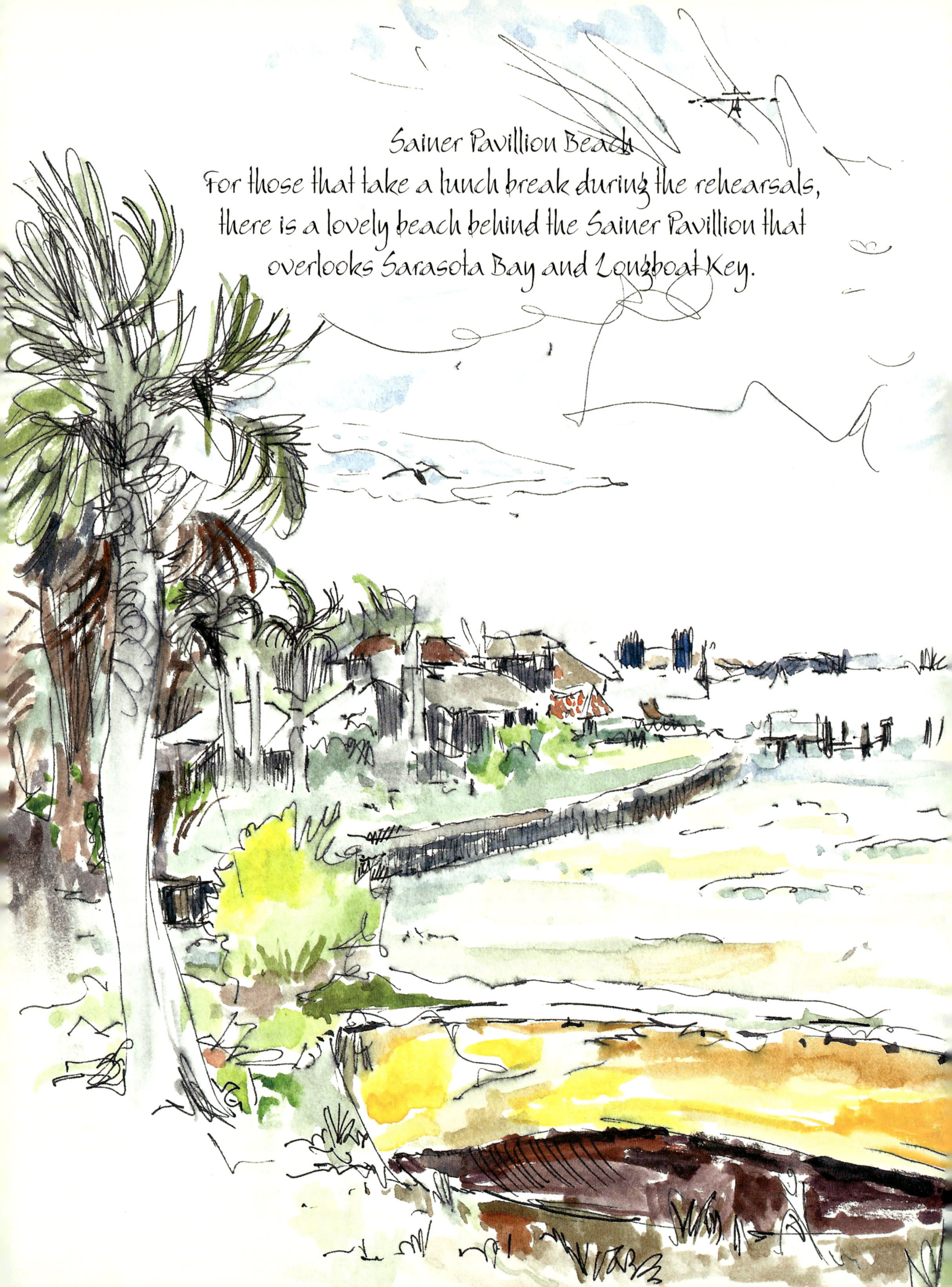
Sainer Pavillion Beach
For those that take a lunch break during the rehearsals,
there is a lovely beach behind the Sainer Pavillion that
overlooks Sarasota Bay and Longboat Key.

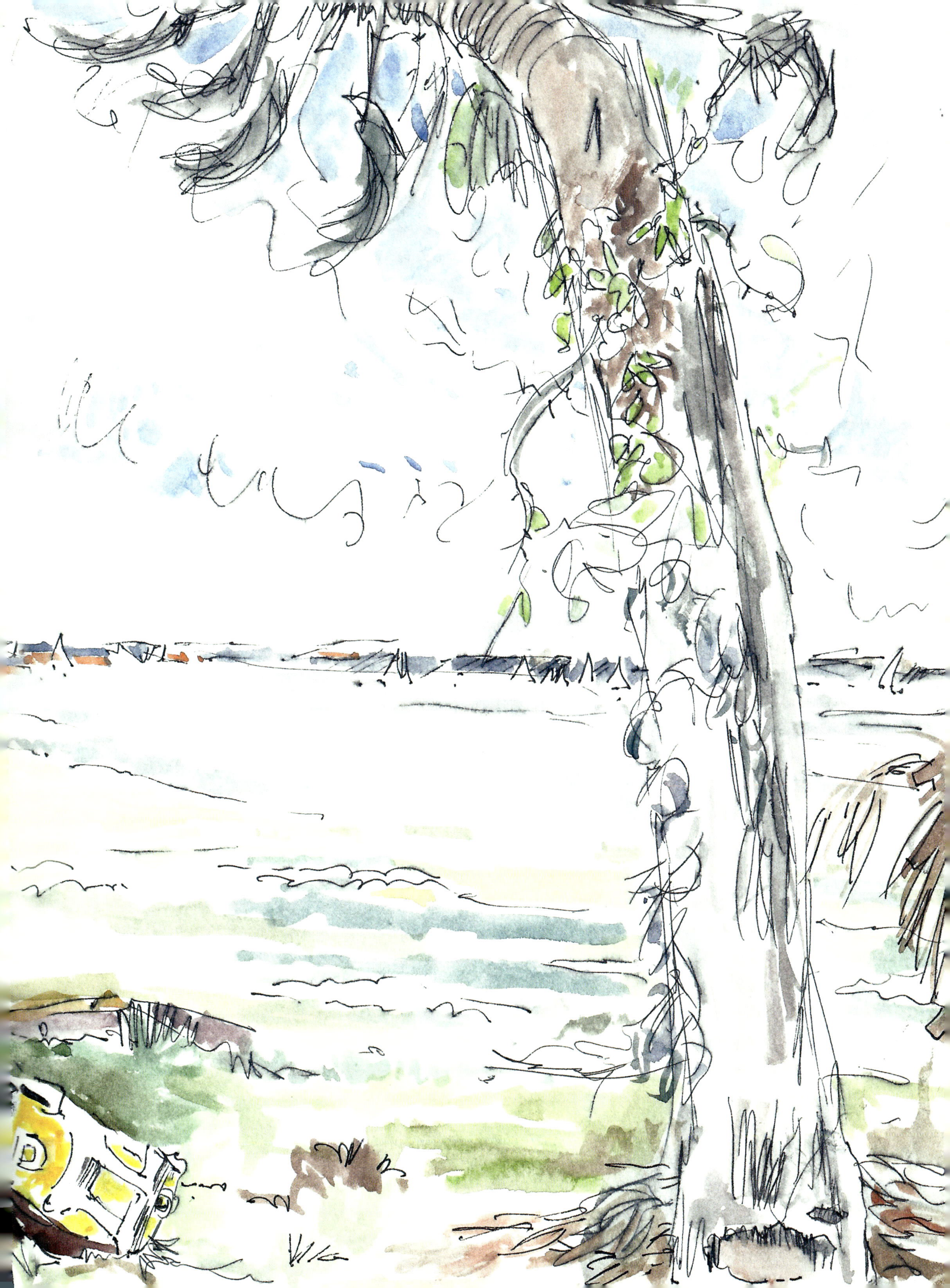

Francesco Petracchi, bassist

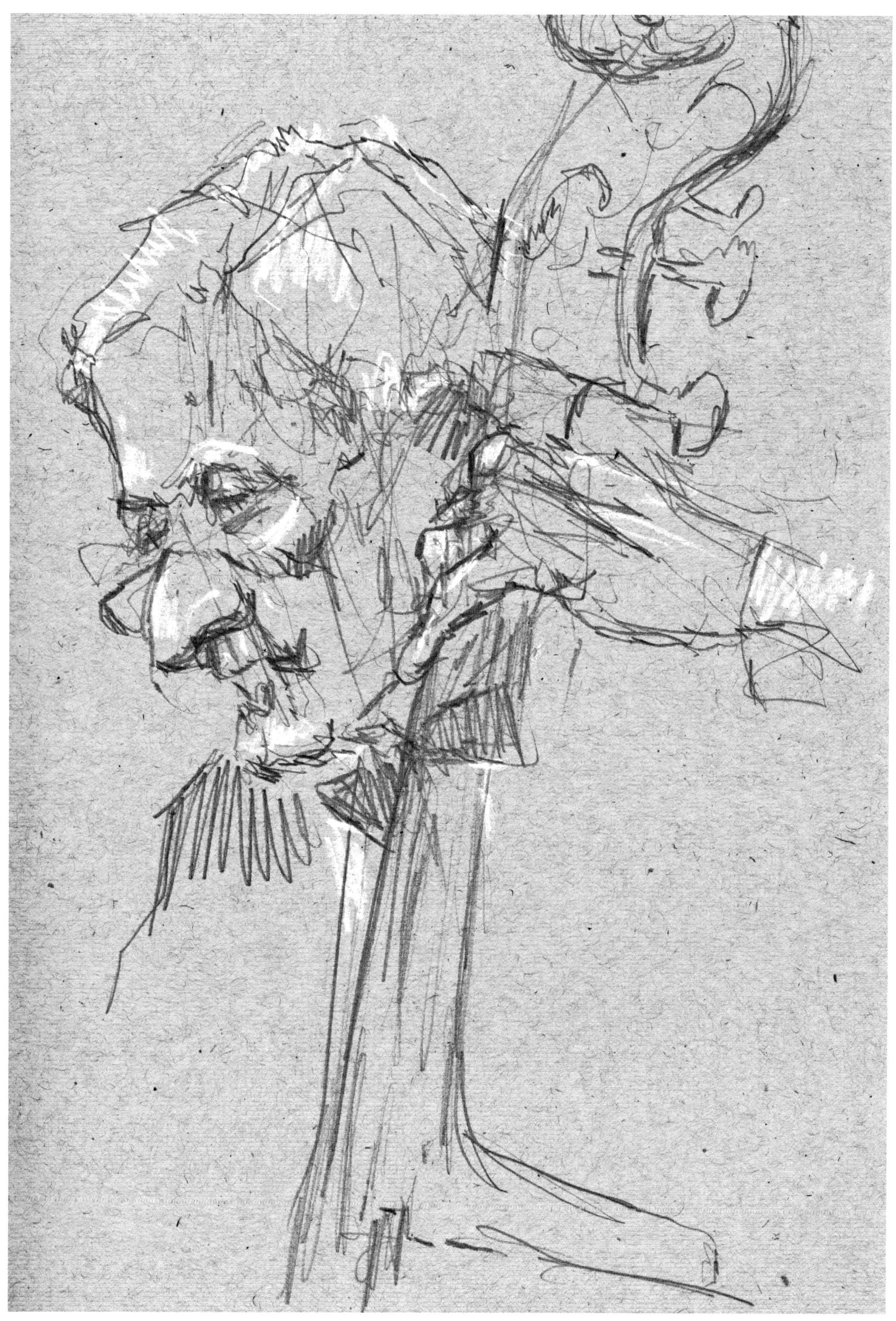

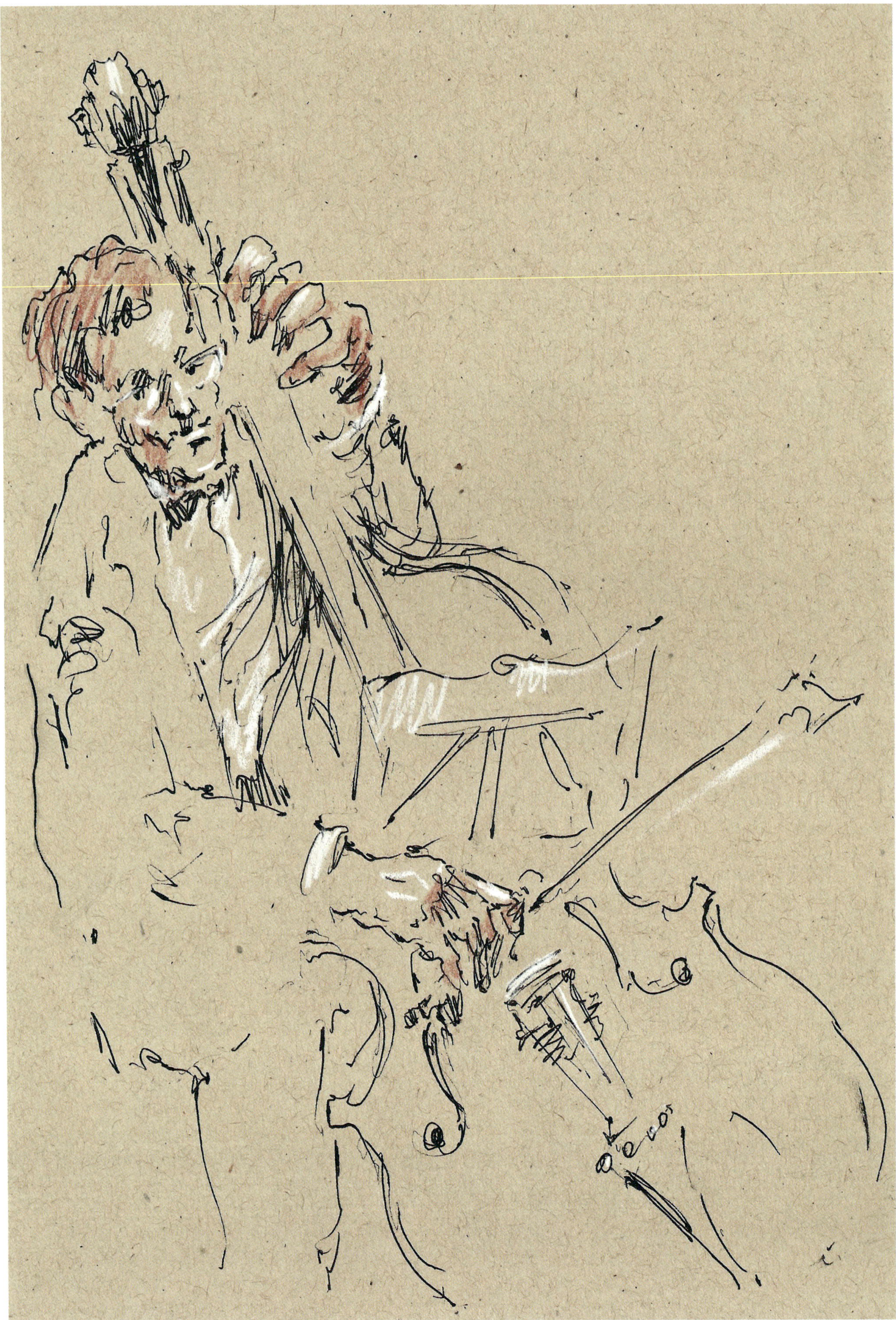

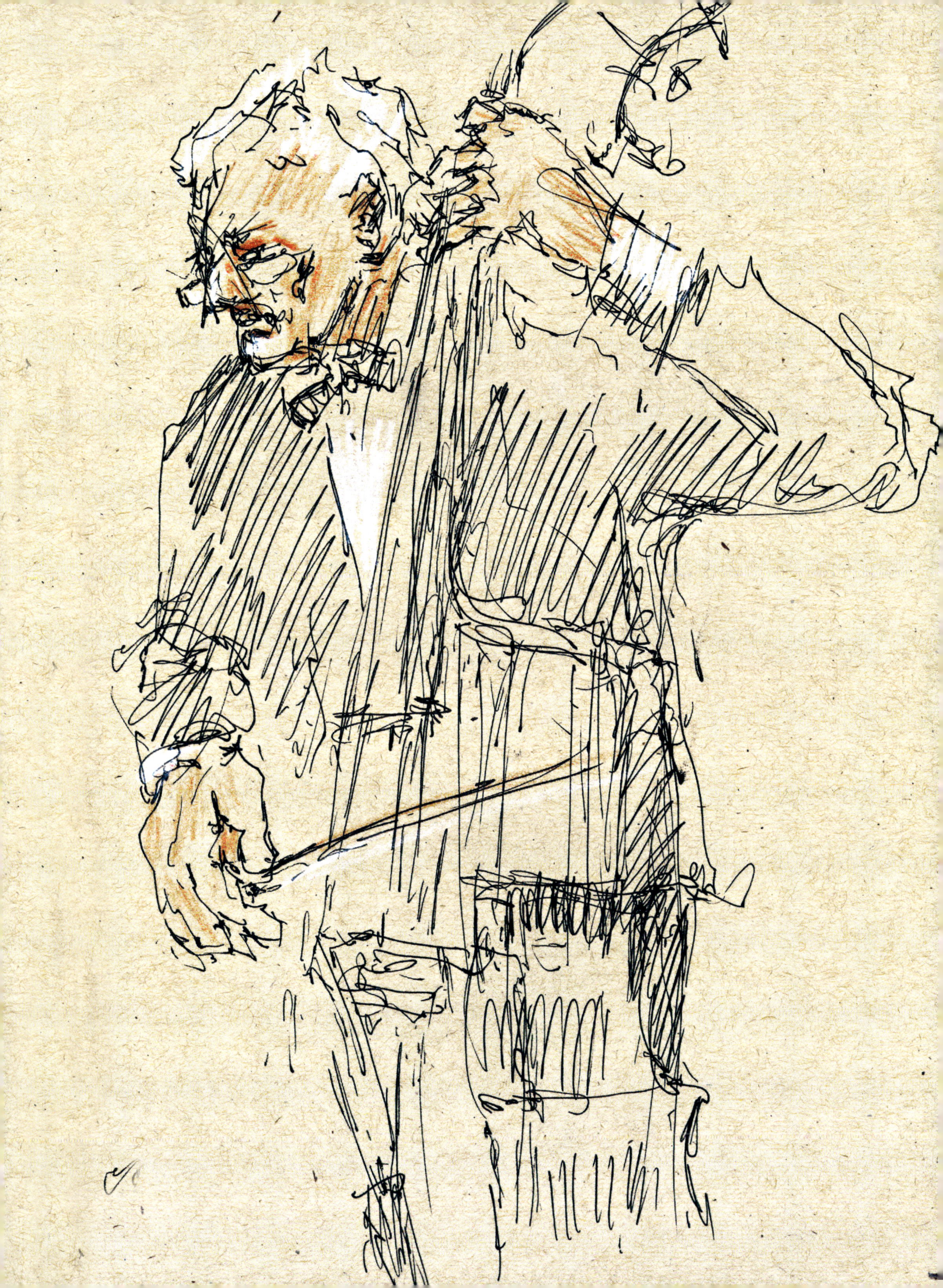

Eric Kim is an American cellist who is a graduate of the Juilliard School of Music, where he studied with Leonard Rose and Lynn Harrell. Mr. Kim received the first William Schuman Prize at Juilliard. He has become a regular at the La Musica Festival. Mr. Kim is on the faculty of the Indiana University Jacobs School of Music. In addition to his skills as a cellist, Mr. Kim is noted for his abilities as a chef. This year (2013) Mr. Kim and Mr. Avshalomov will have a cooking contest in front of a fortunate audience at Michael's On East in Sarasota.

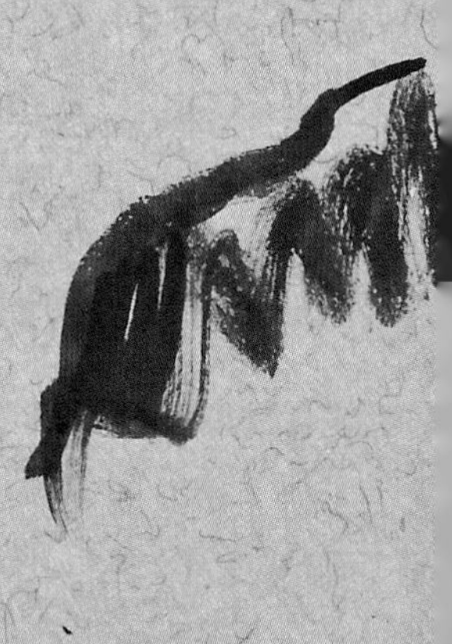

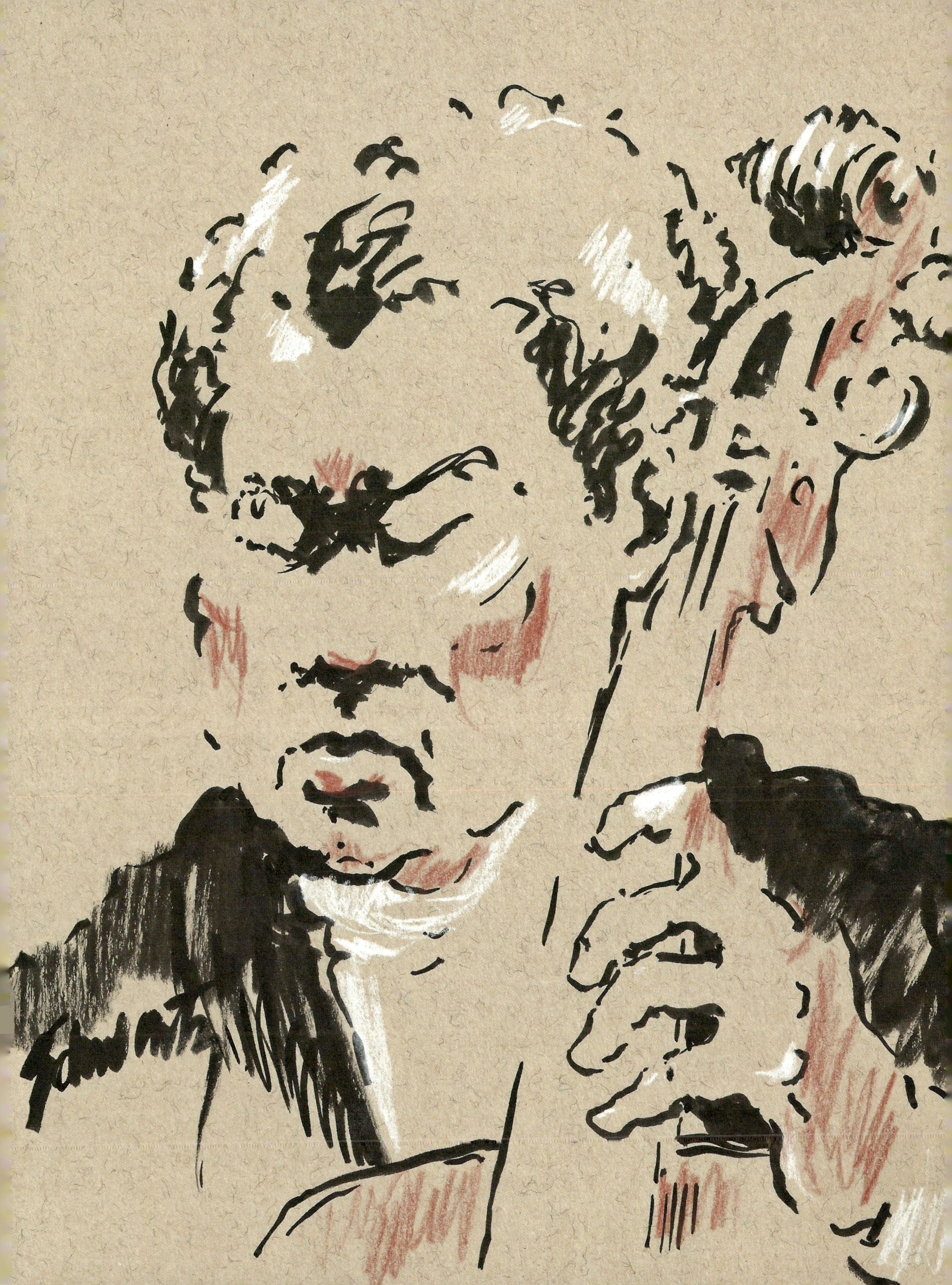

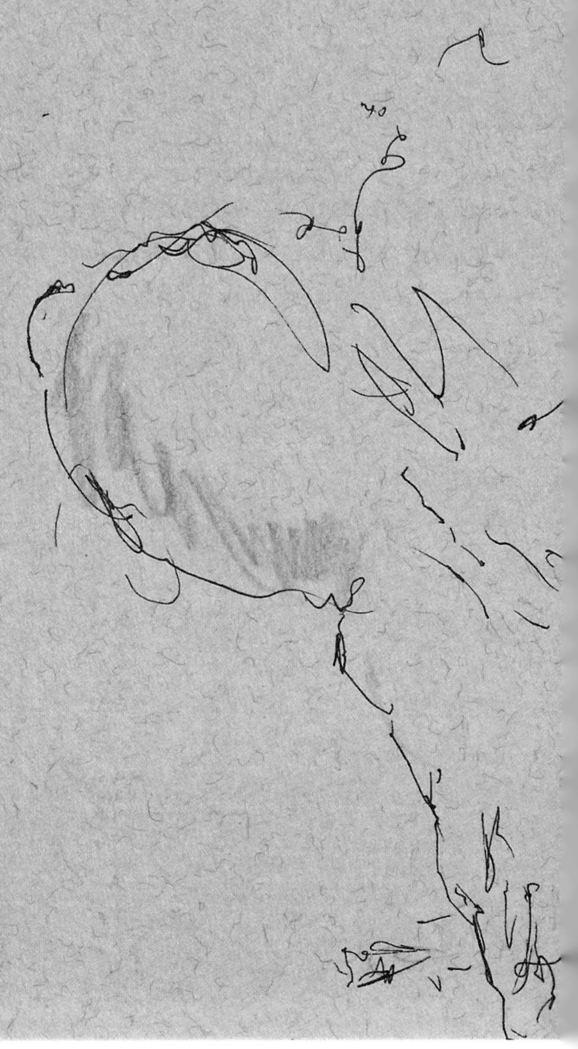

2.10.10

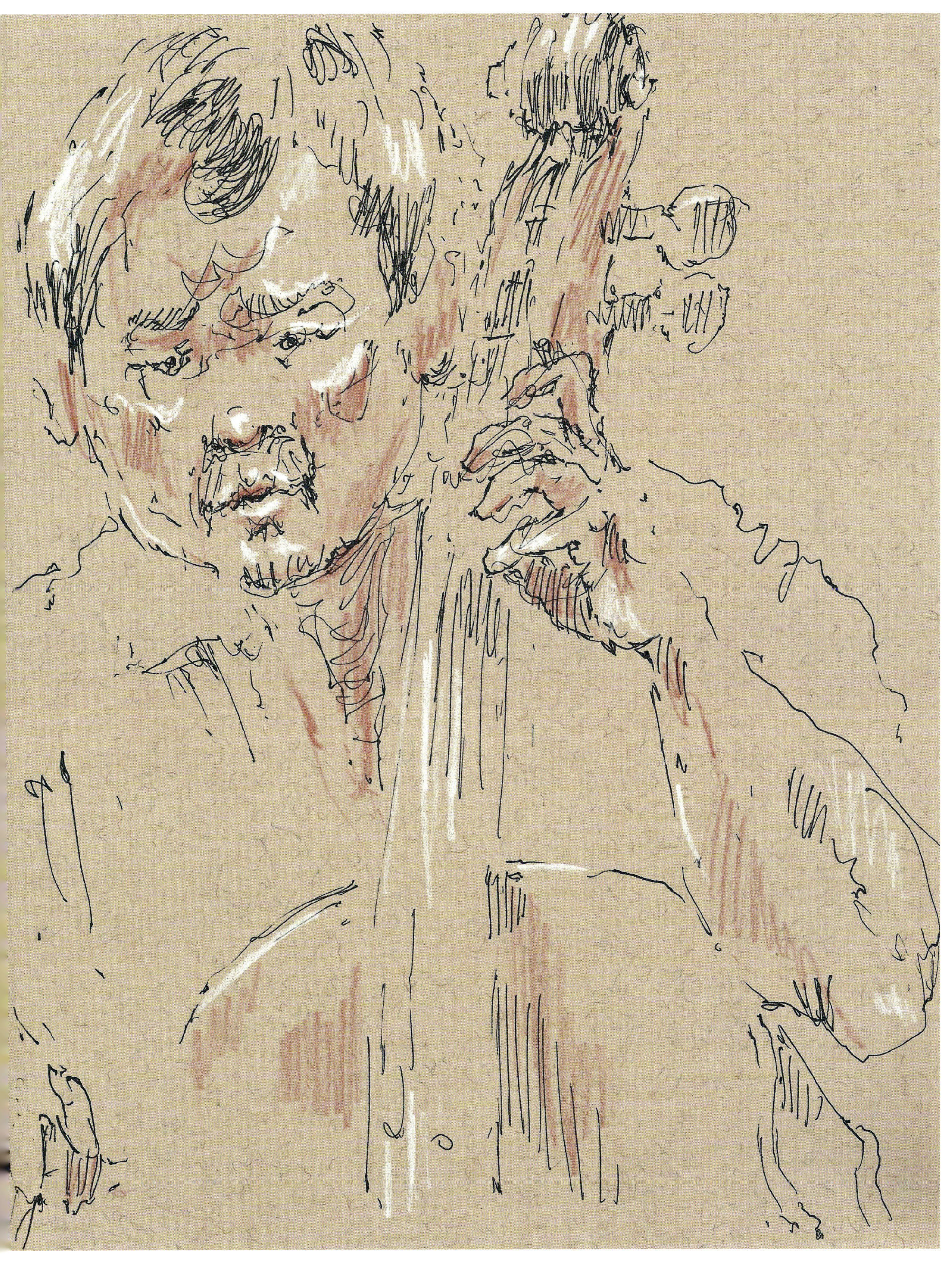

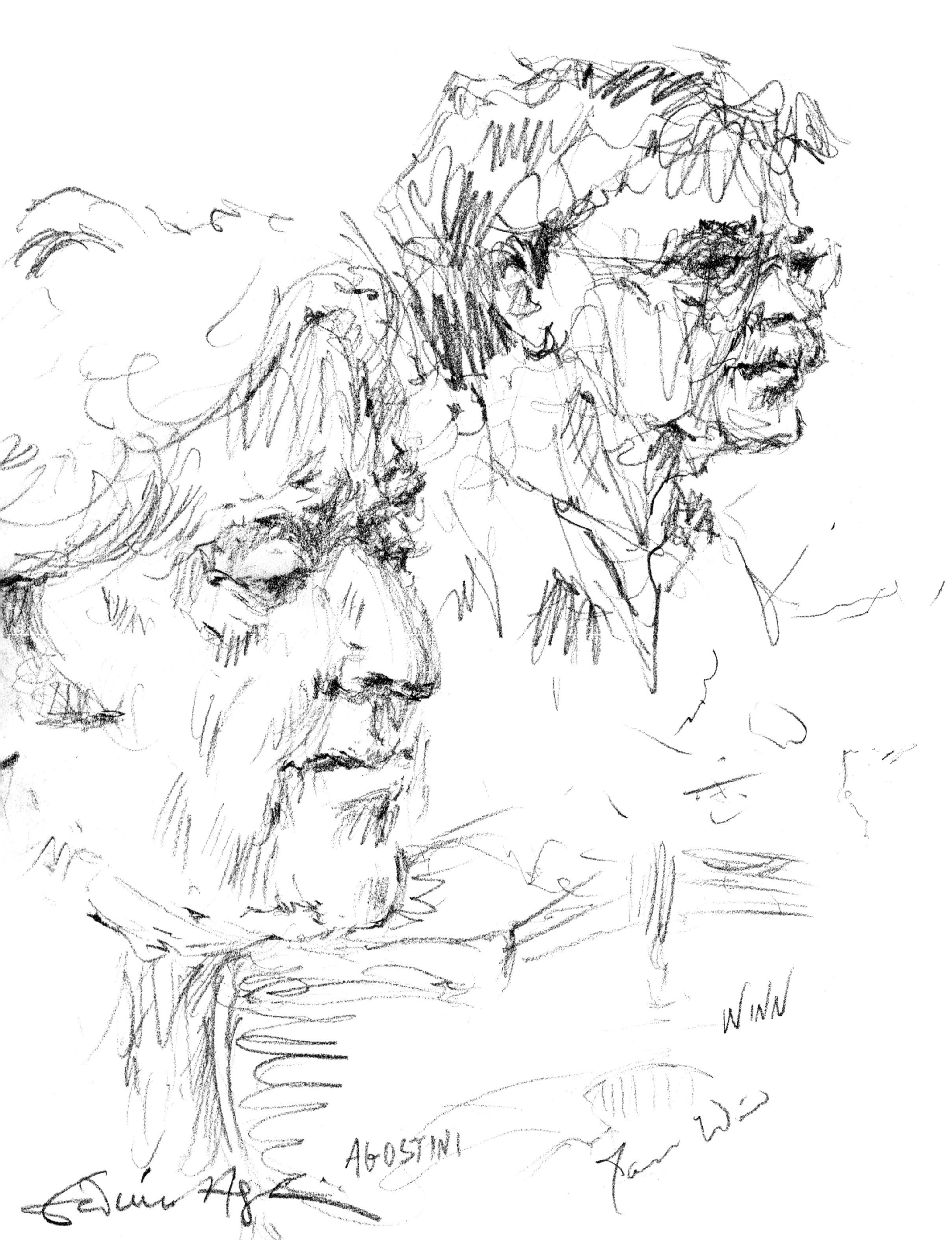
WINN
AGOSTINI

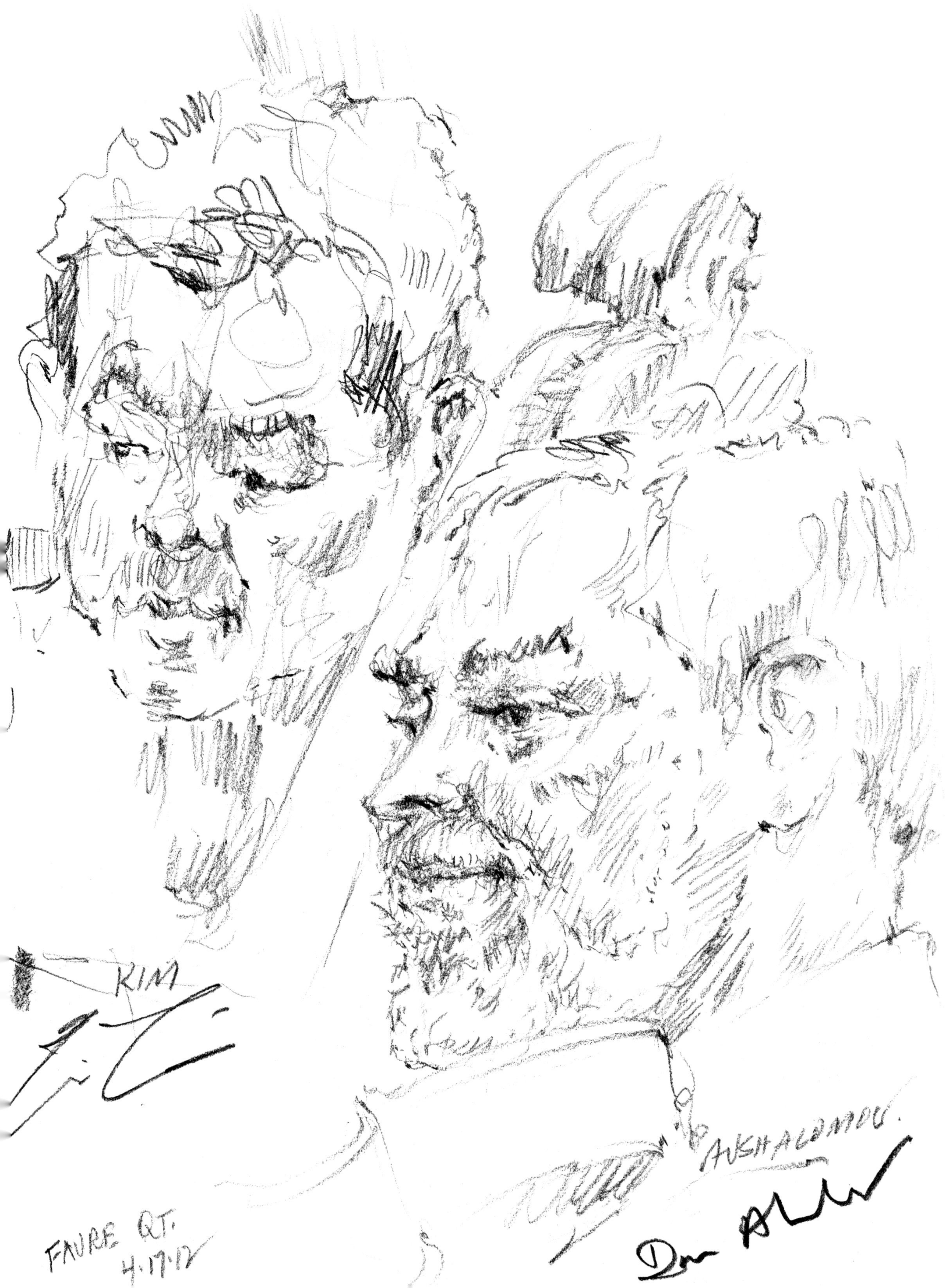
KIM
AUSHALOMOV.
FAURE QT.
4.17.12

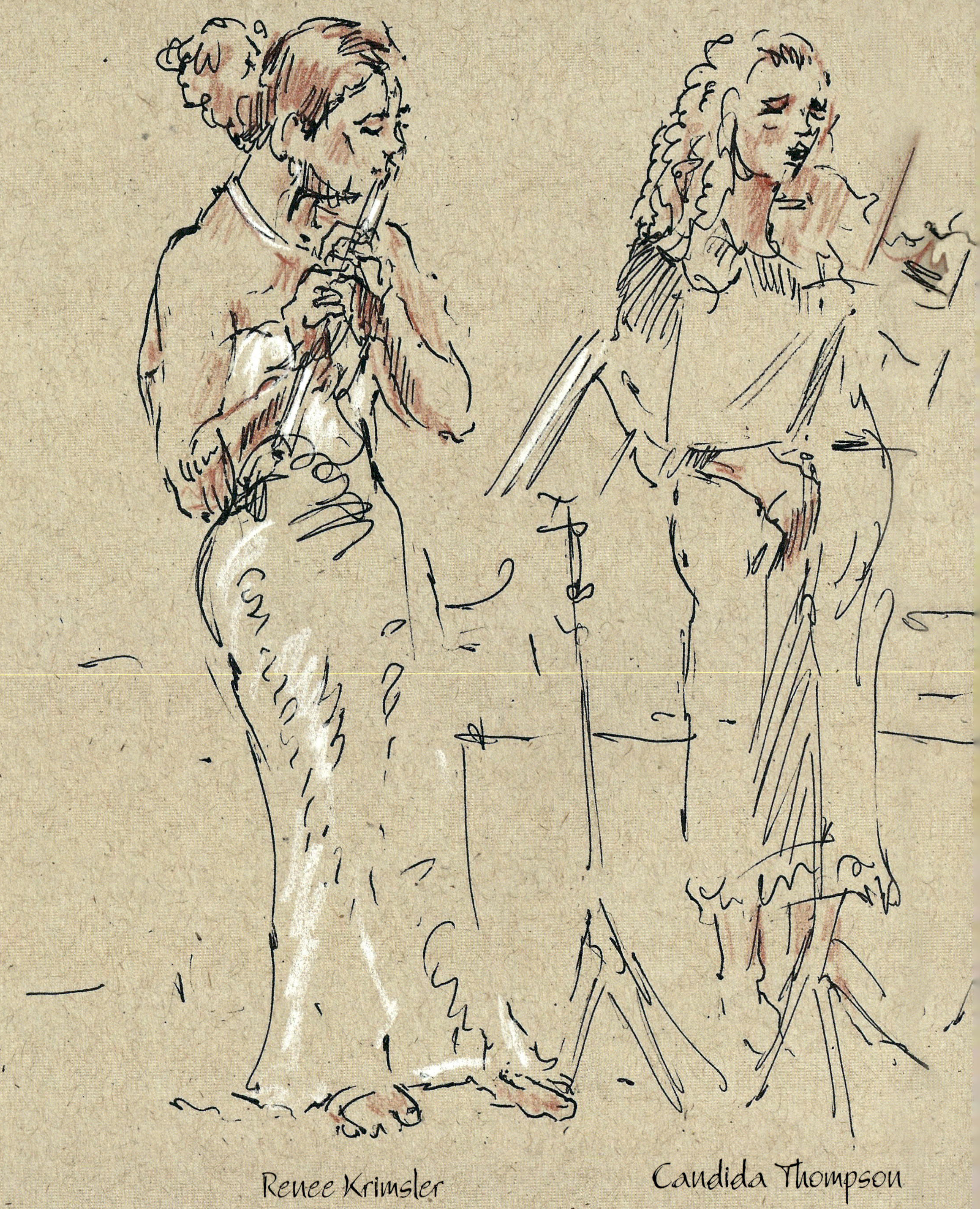
Renee Krimsler
Candida Thompson

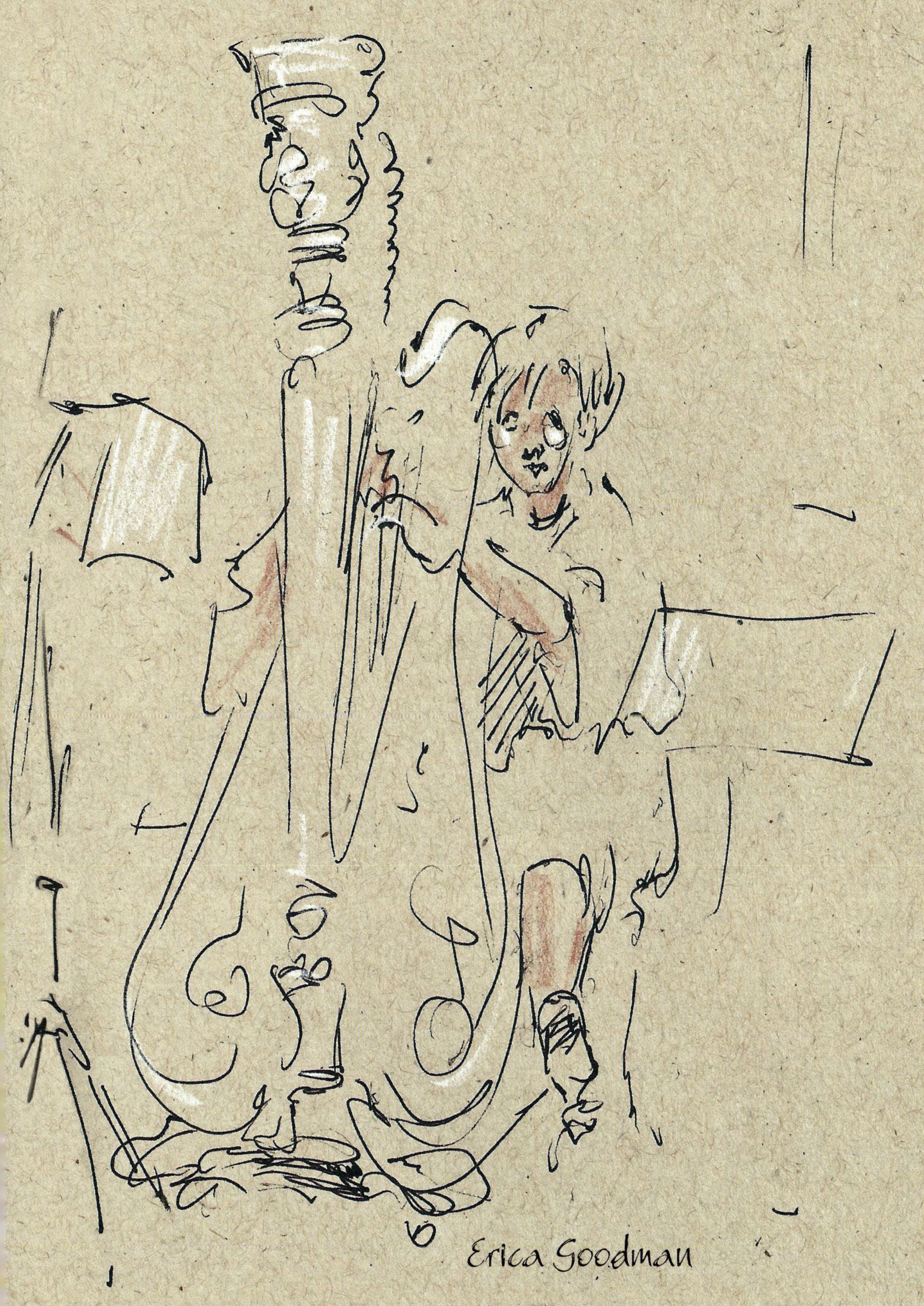
Erica Goodman
GOODMAN
GIBAIDULINA
4.12.01

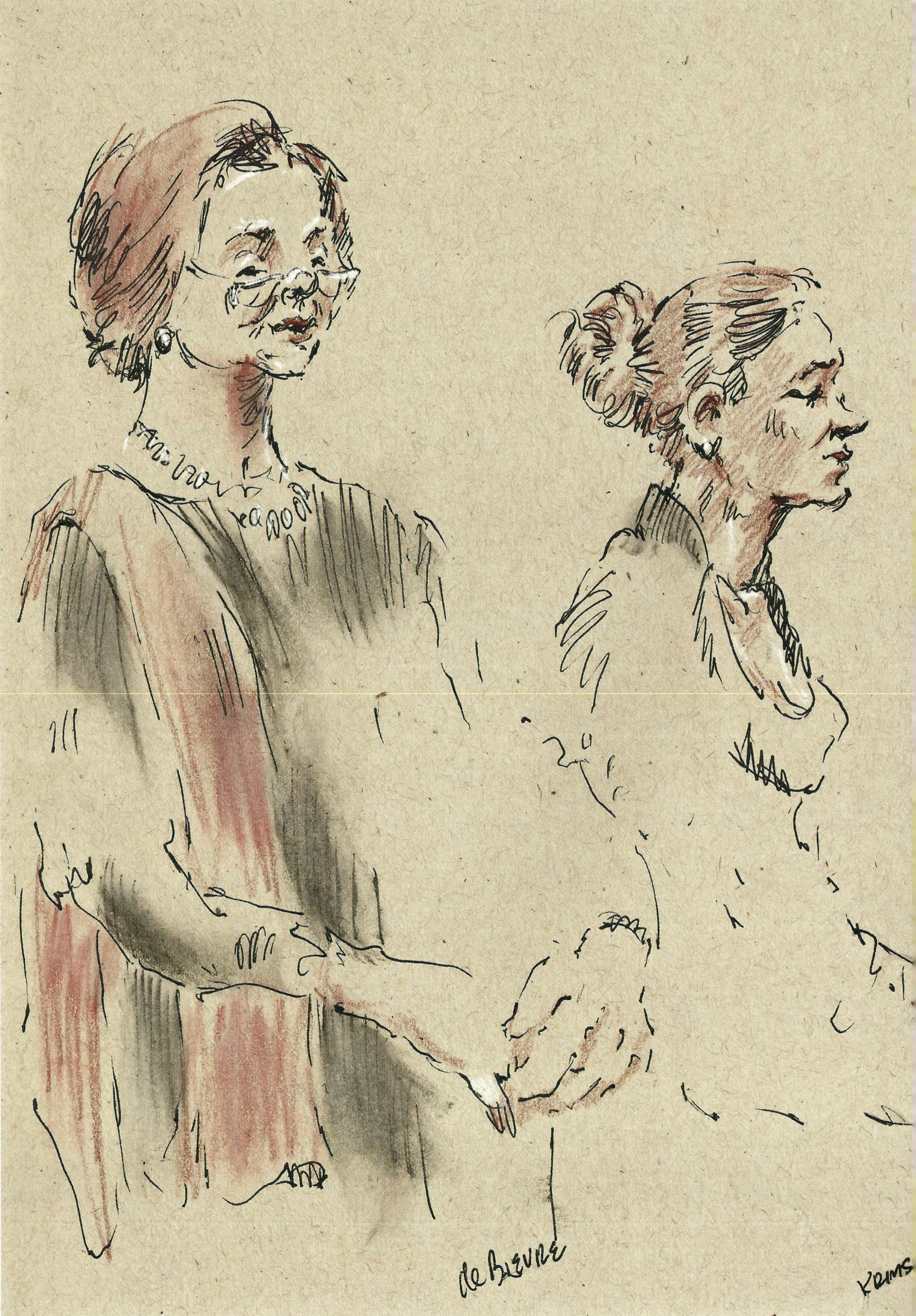
de BIEVRE
KRIMS

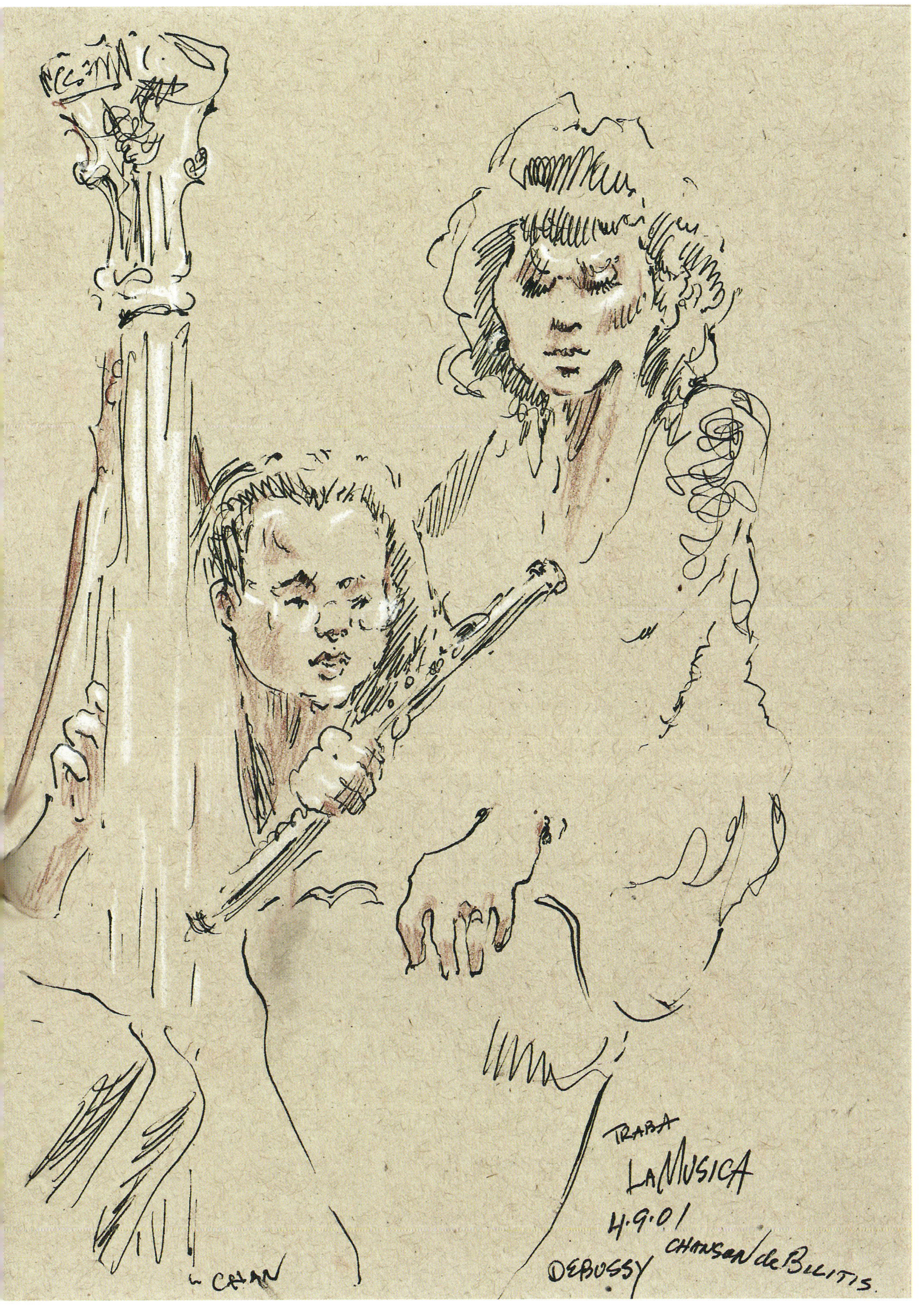
TRABA
LA MUSICA
4.9.01
DEBUSSY
CHANSON de BILITIS.
CHAN

John Zirbel, French horn

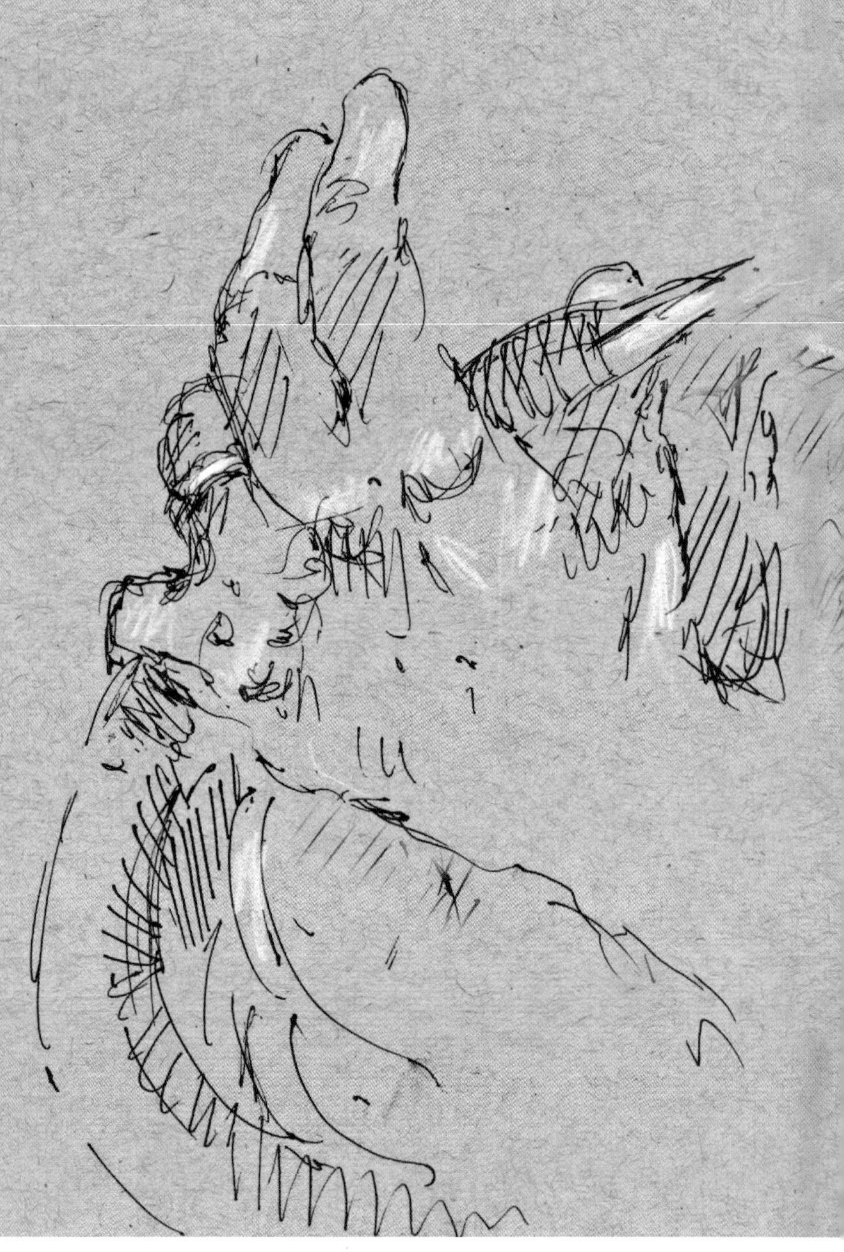

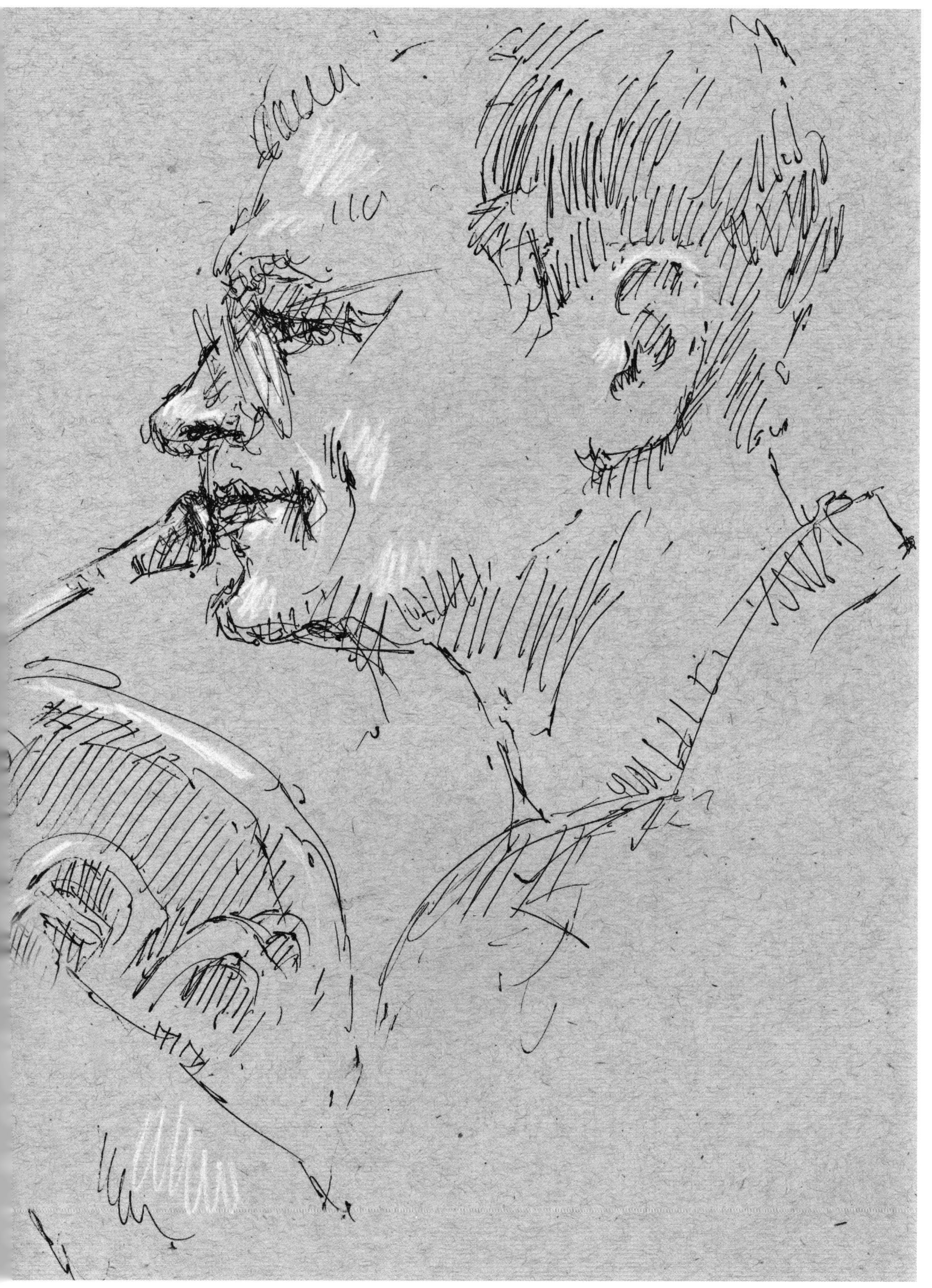

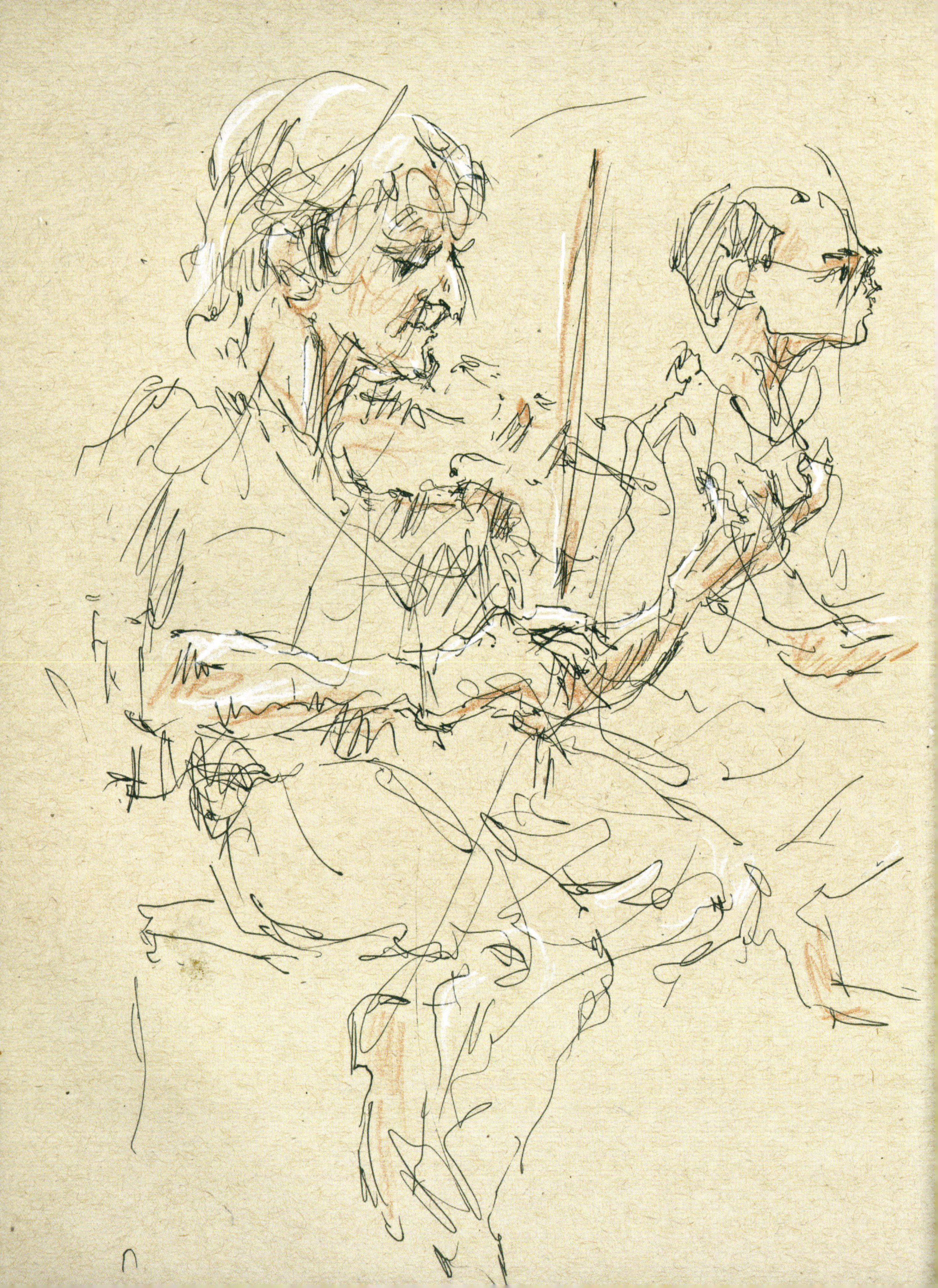

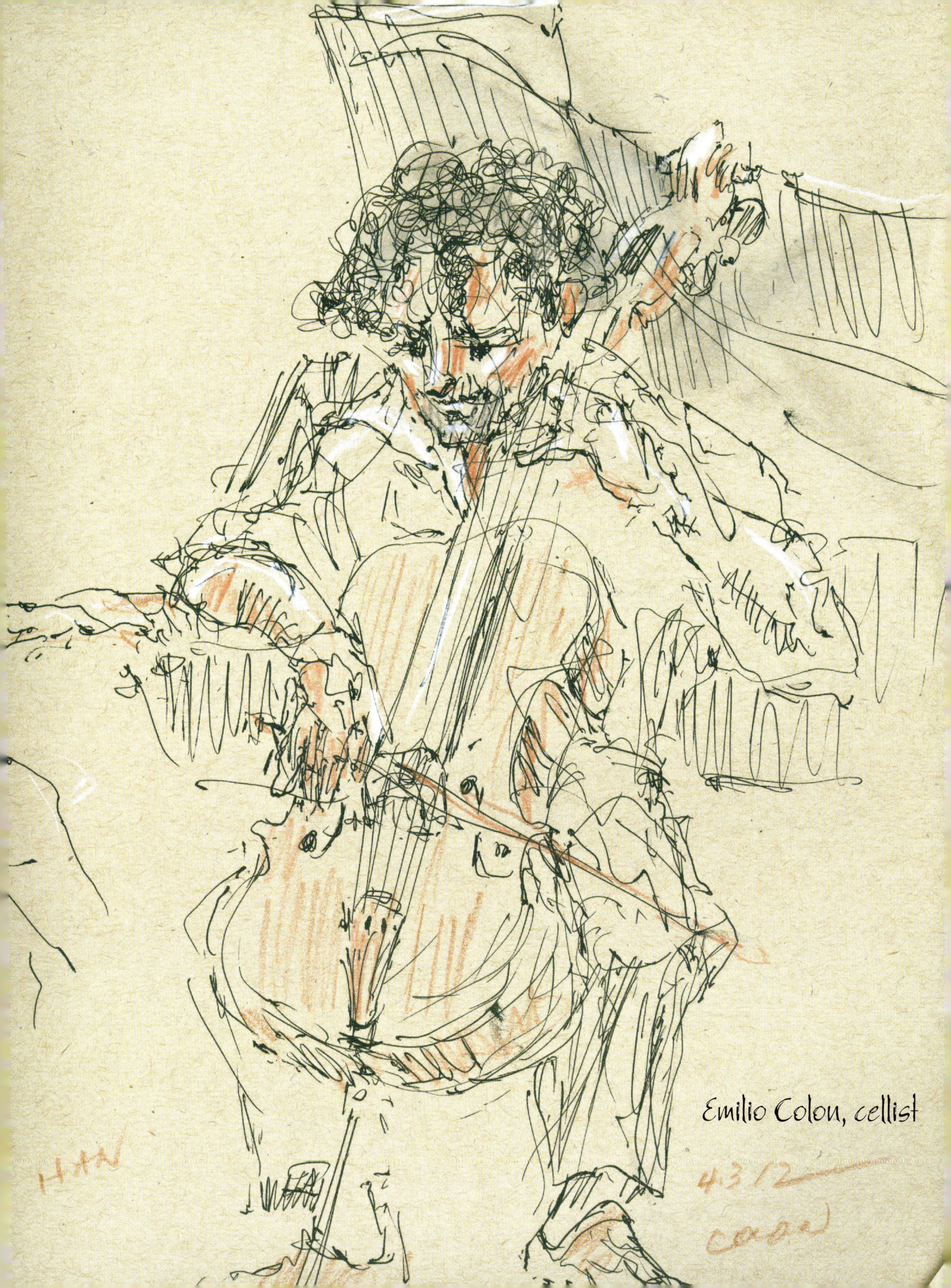

Emilio Colon, cellist

Xenia Jankovic

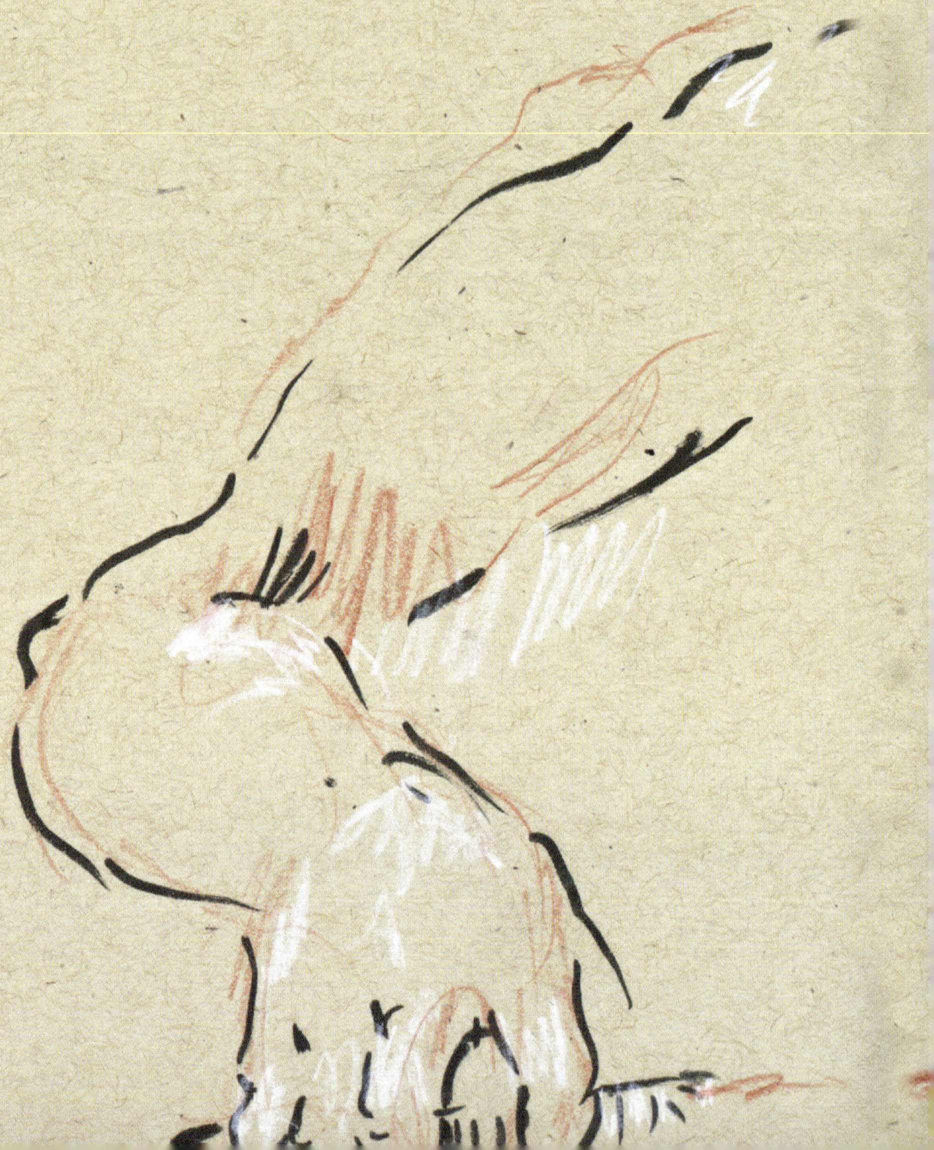

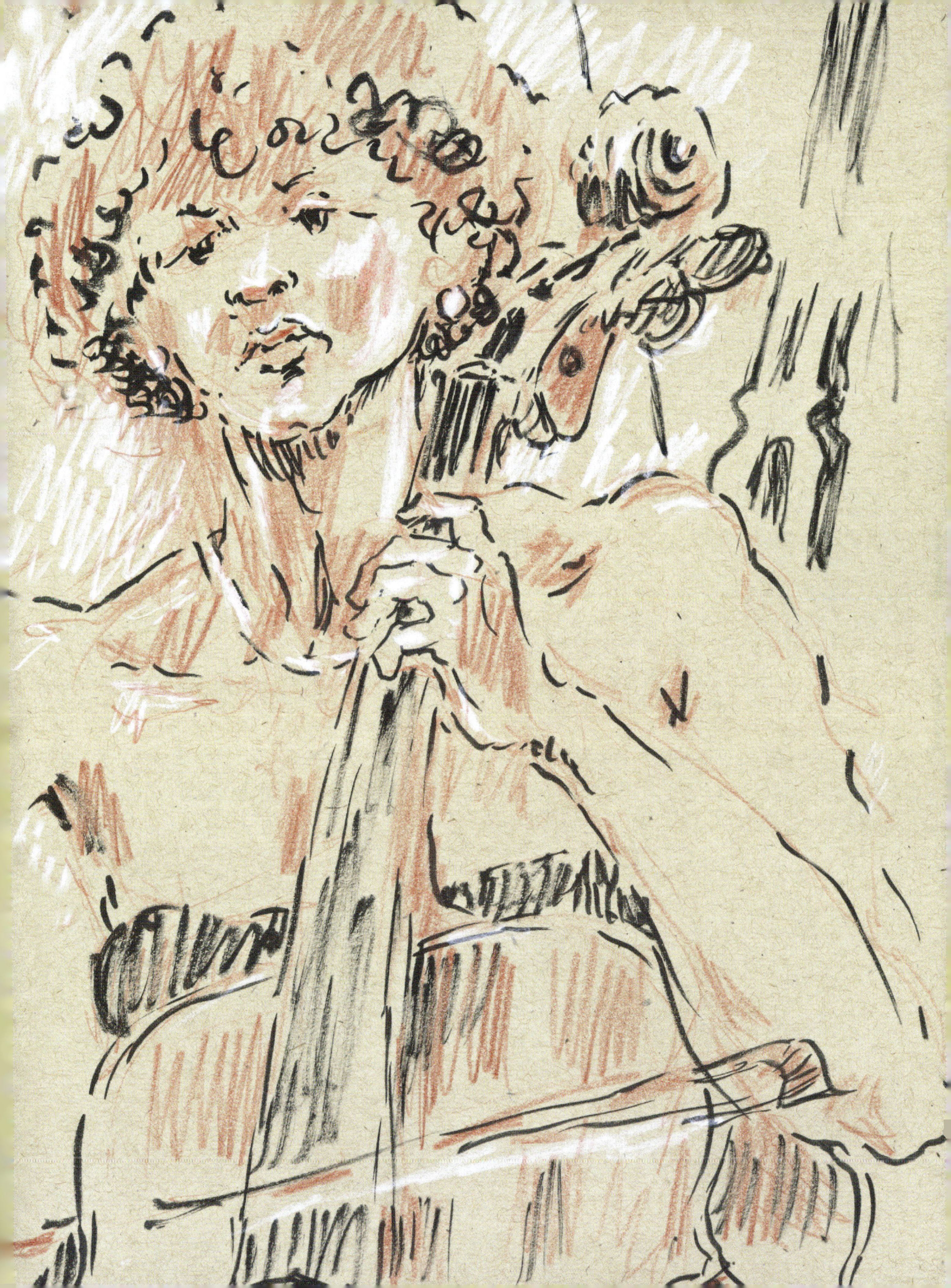

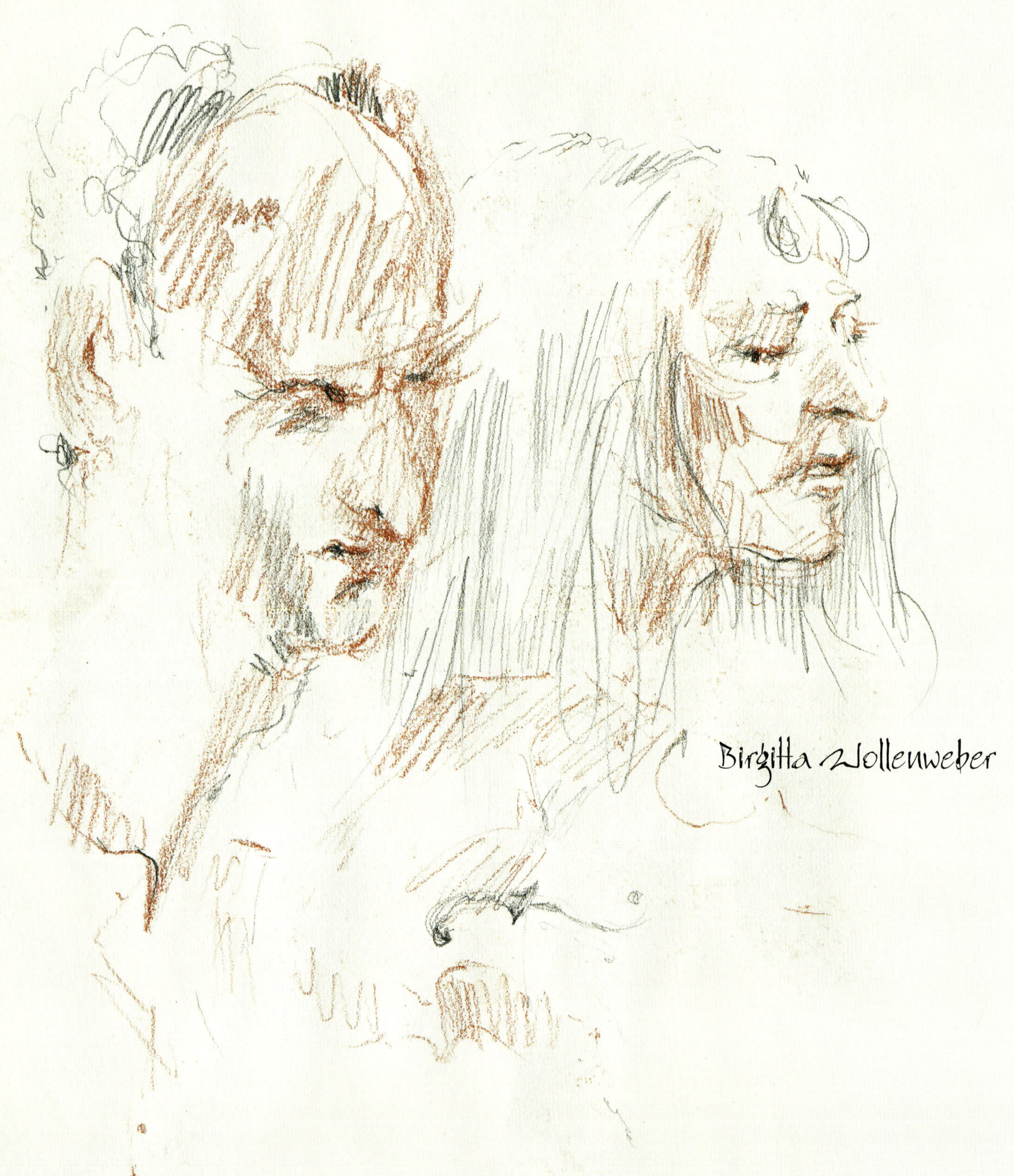
Birgitta Wollenweber
Massimo Quarta

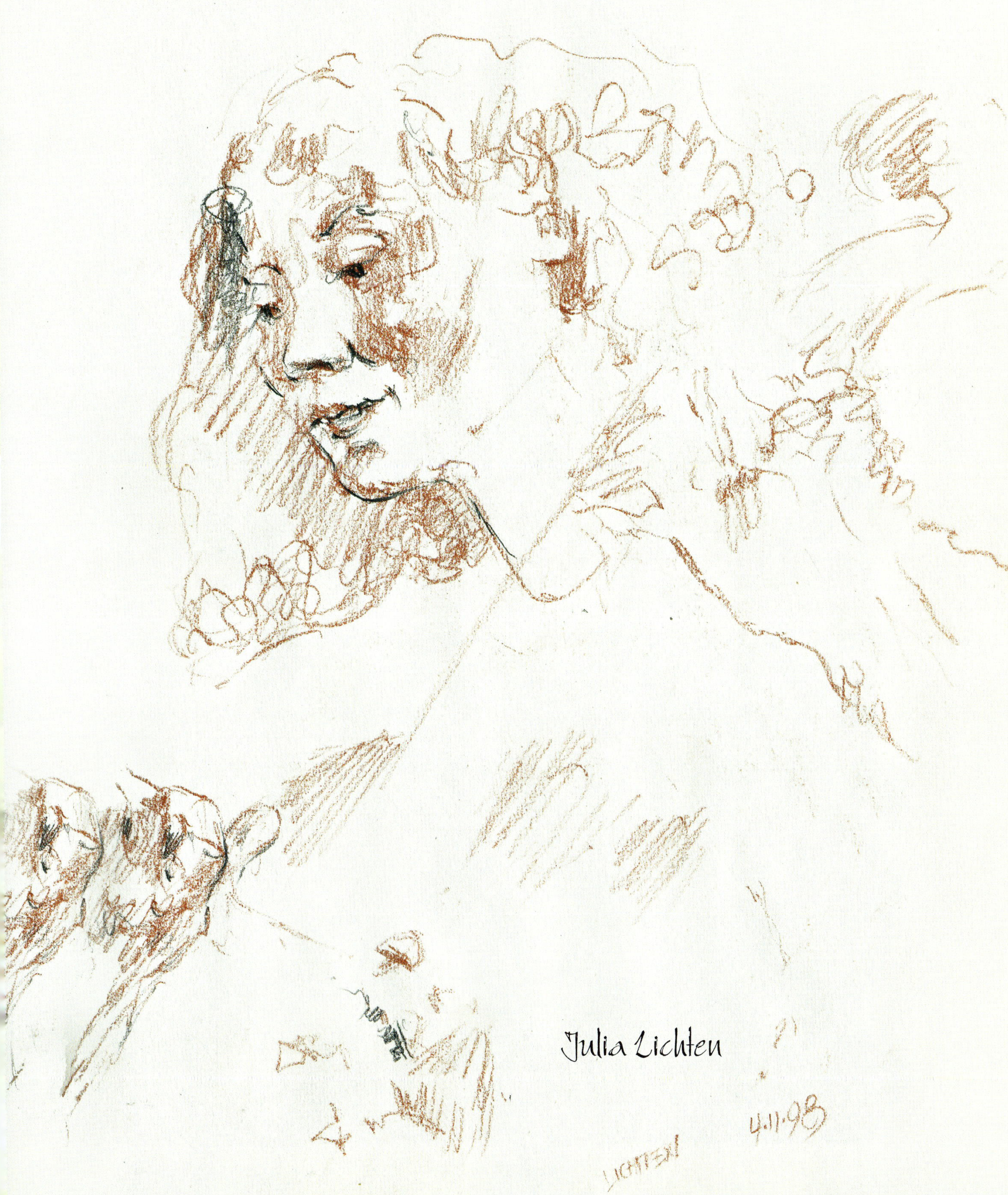

Julia Lichten

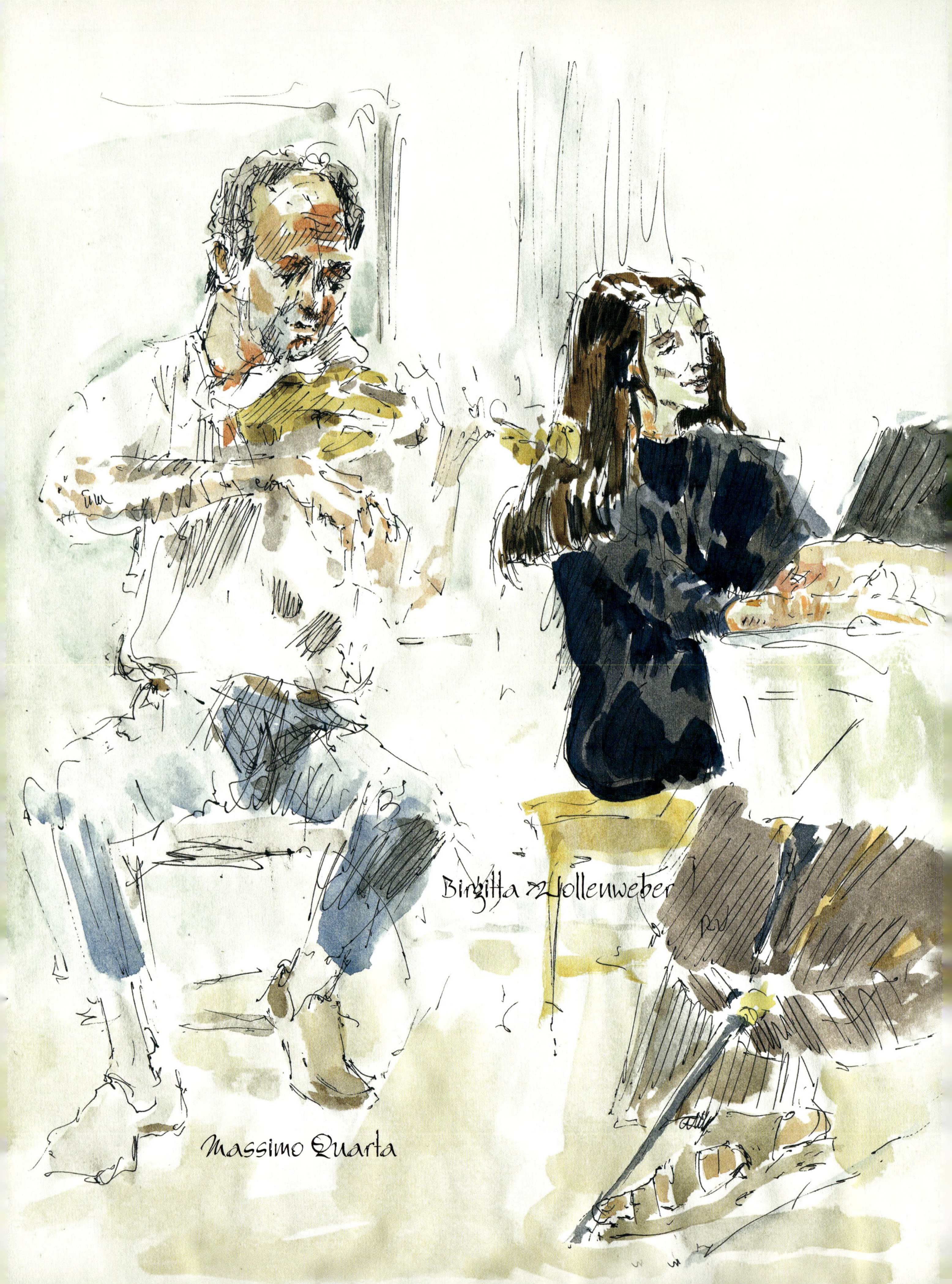
Birgitta Wollenweber
Massimo Quarta

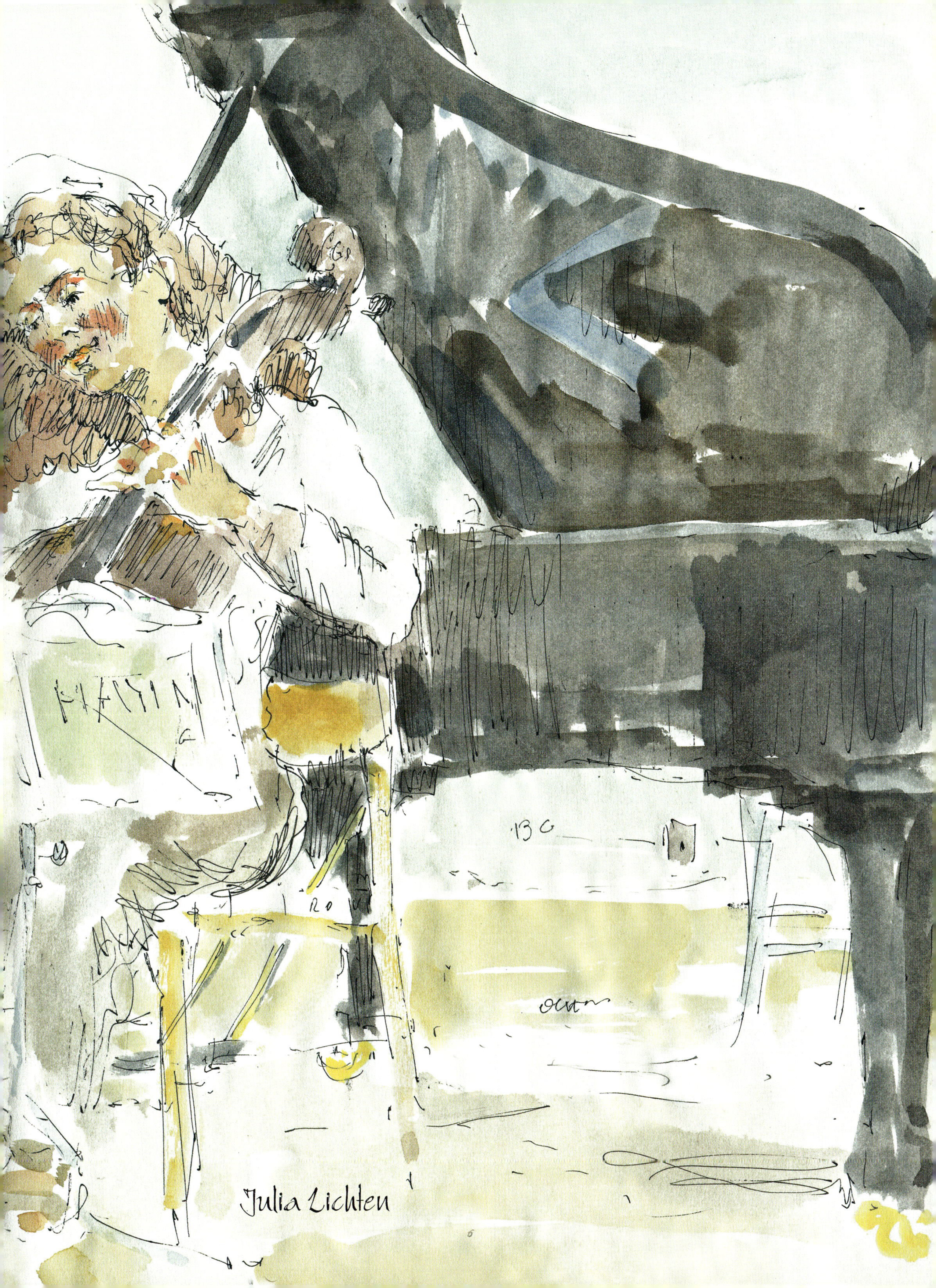
Julia Lichten

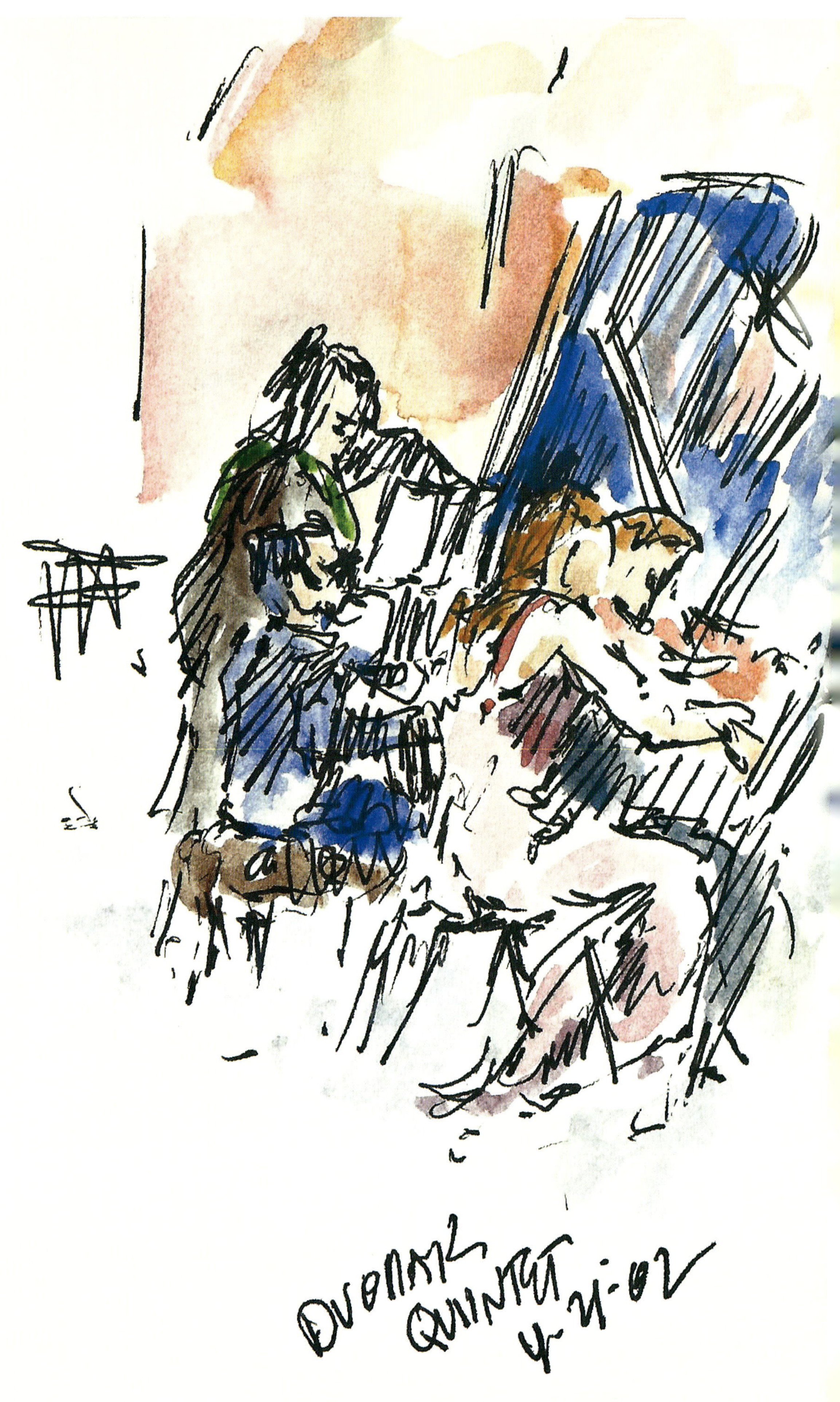
DVORAK
QUINTET
4-21-02

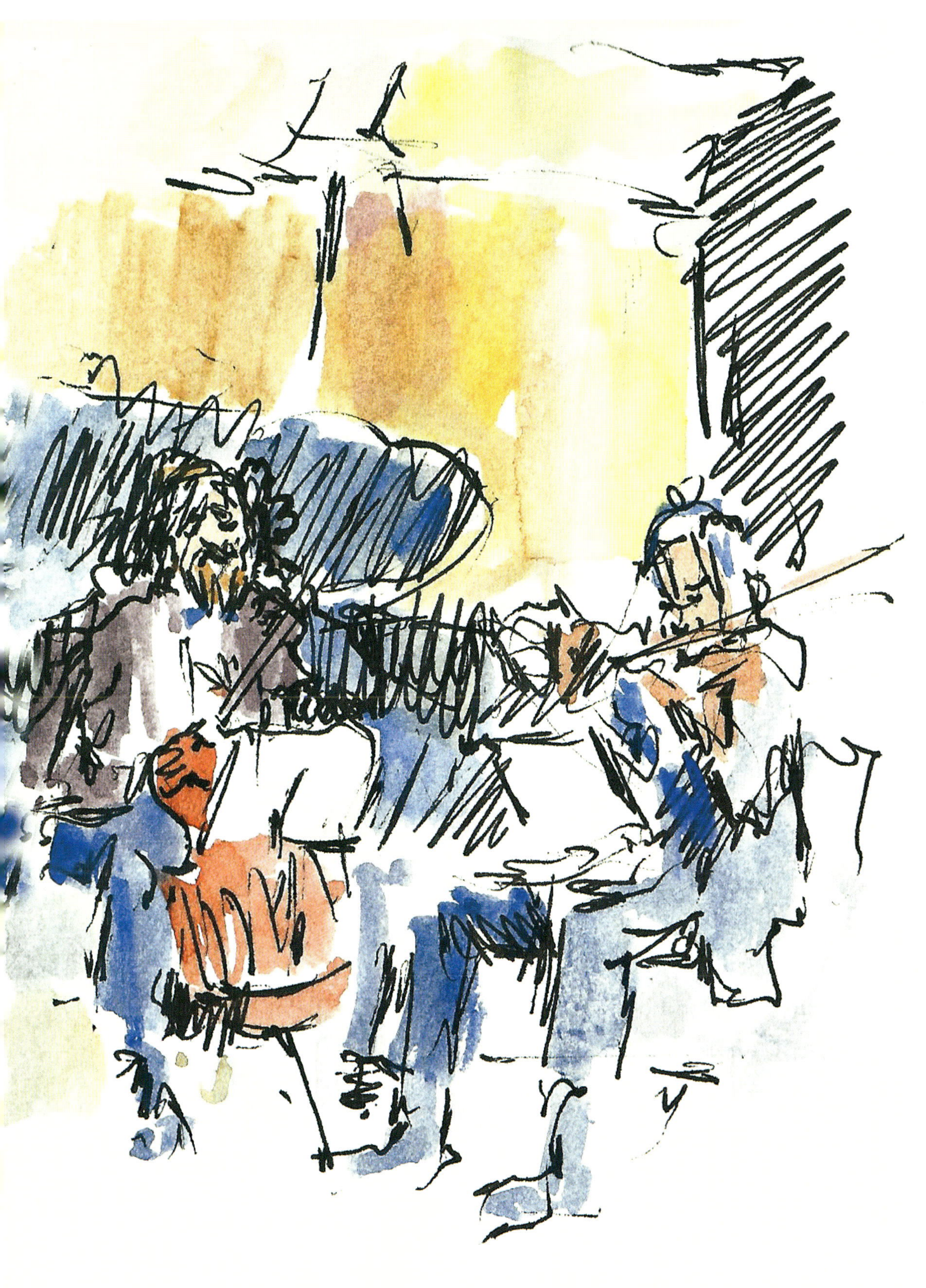

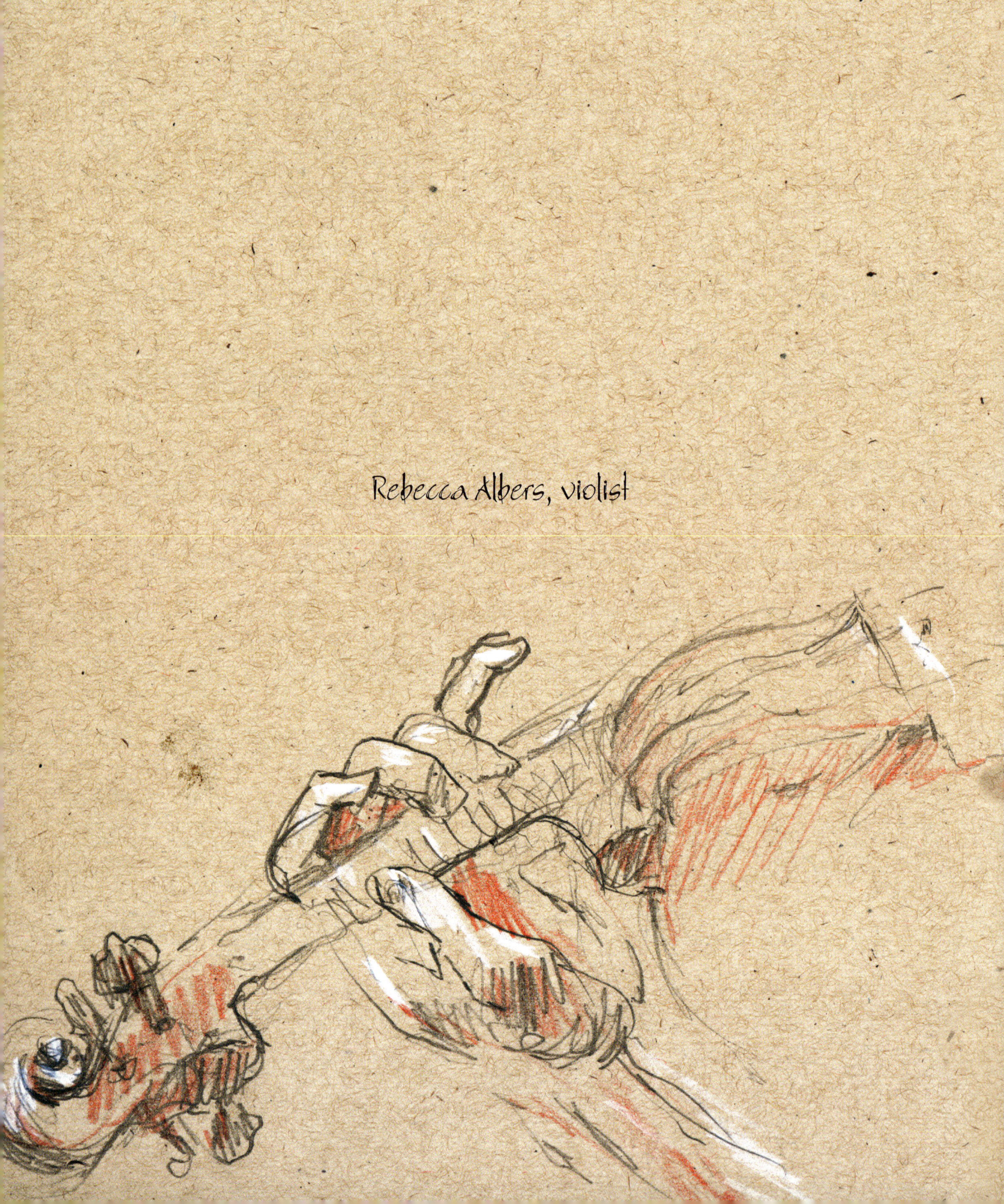

Rebecca Albers, violist

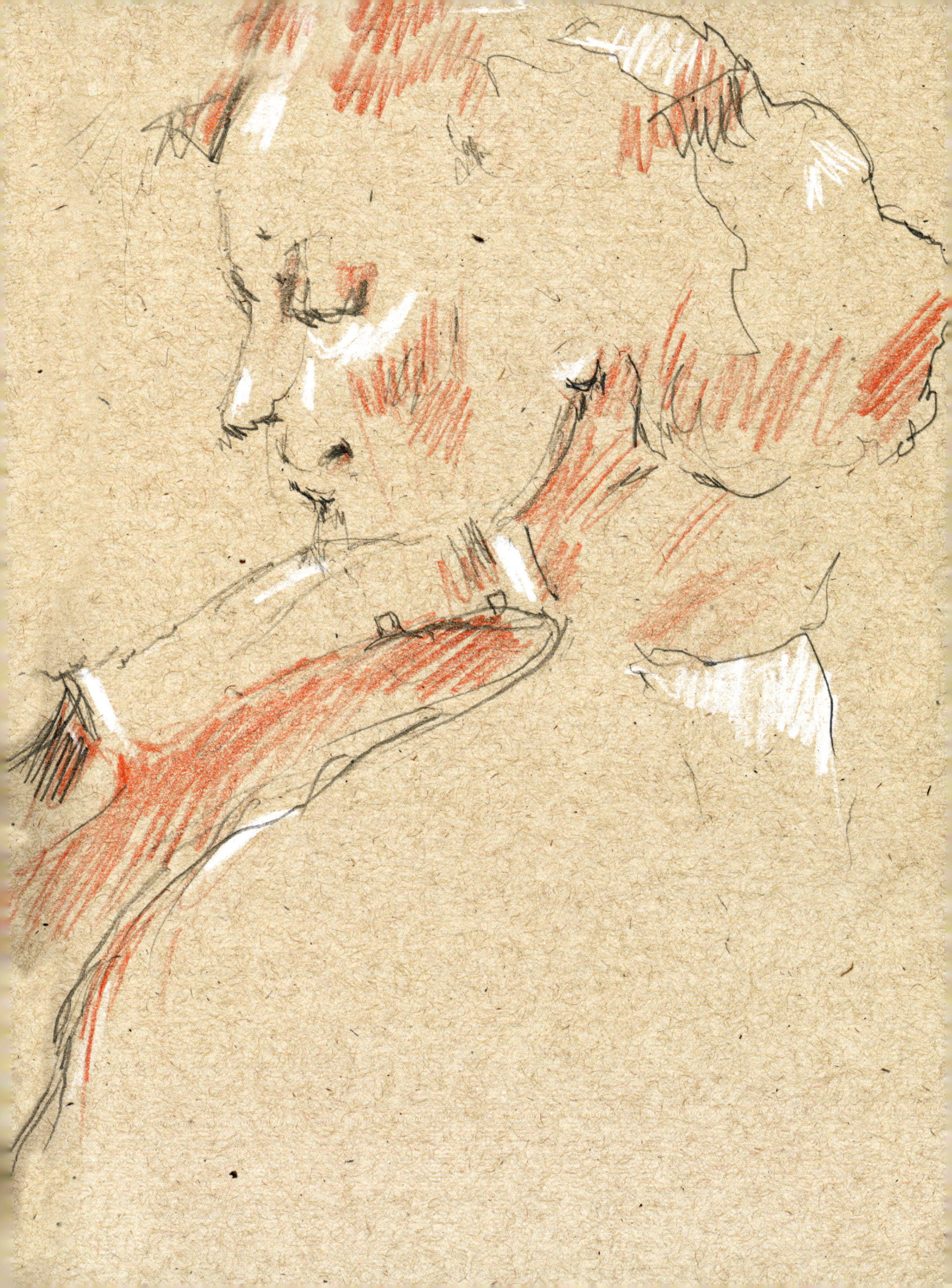

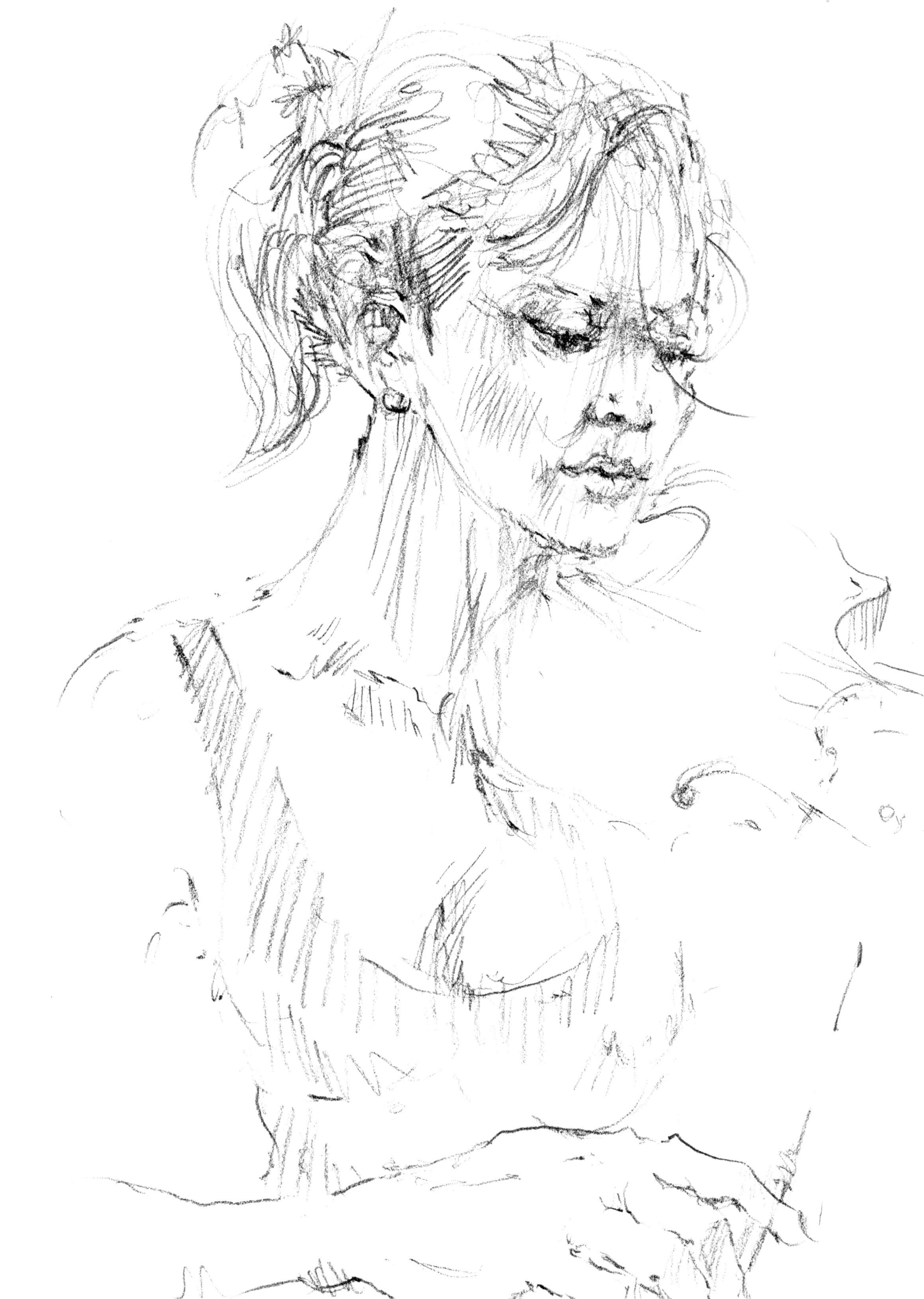

Anne Schoenhoelz, violinist

4/12 ANNE

Nokuthula Ngwenyama, violinist

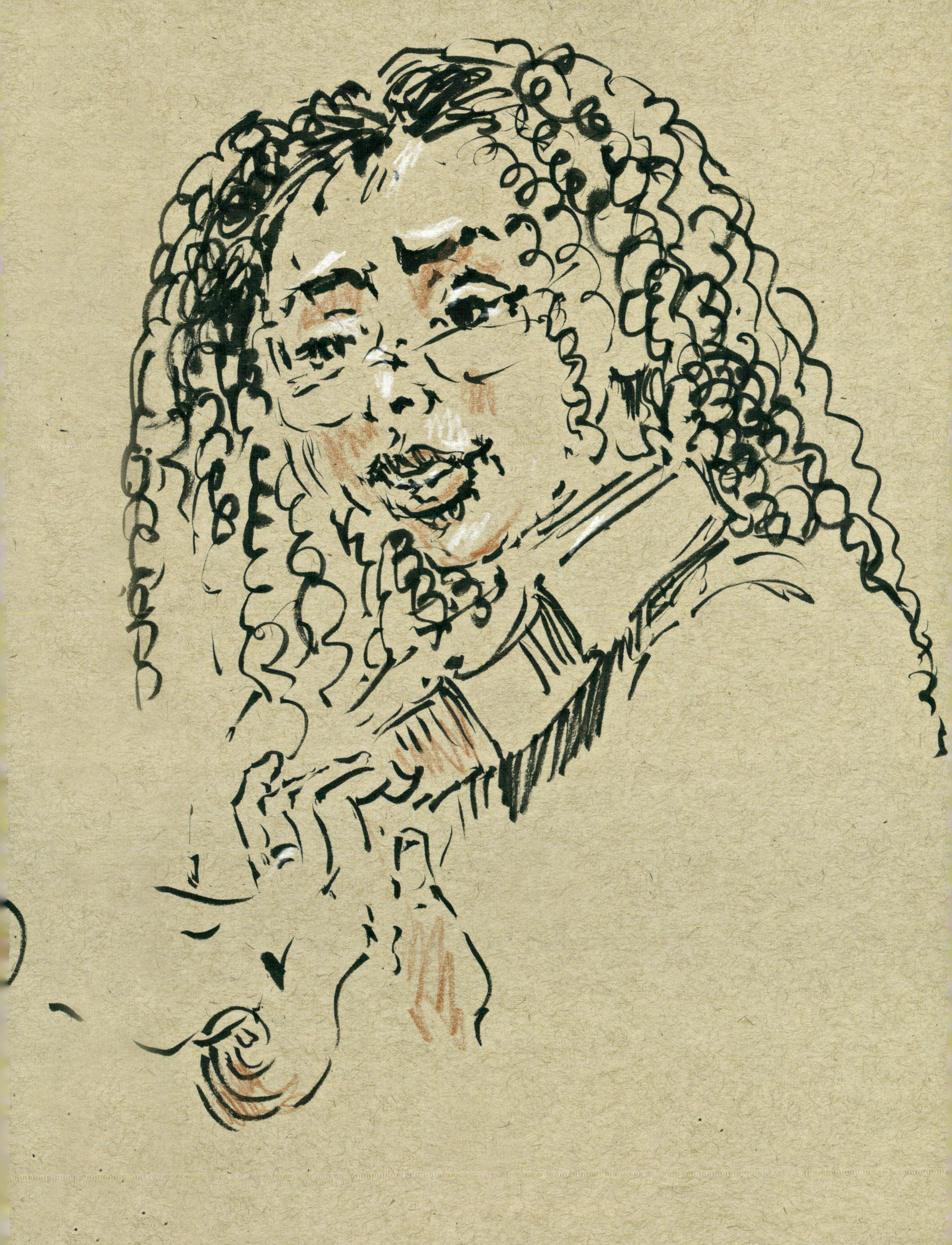

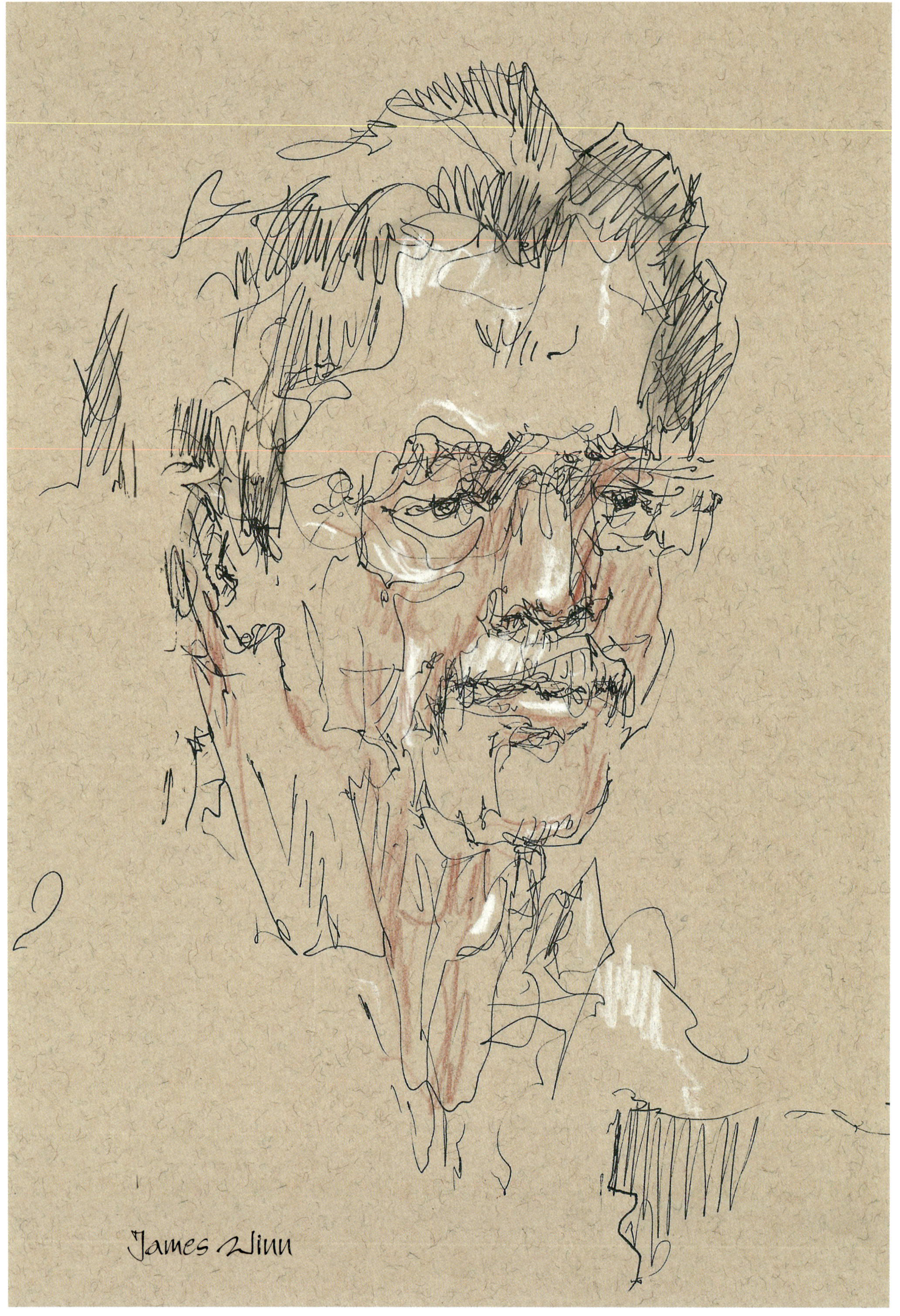
James Winn

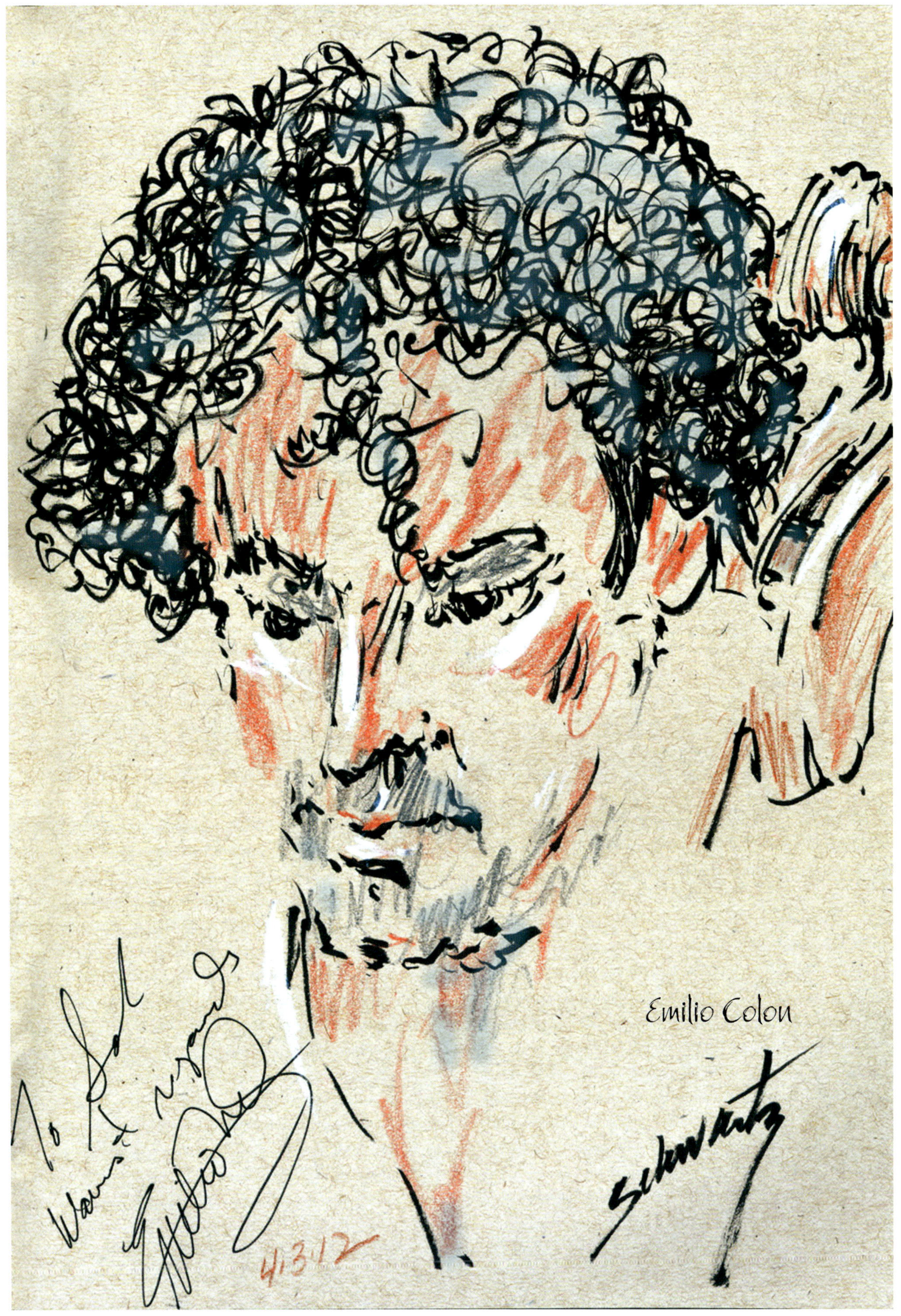
Emilio Colon
Schwartz
4/3/12

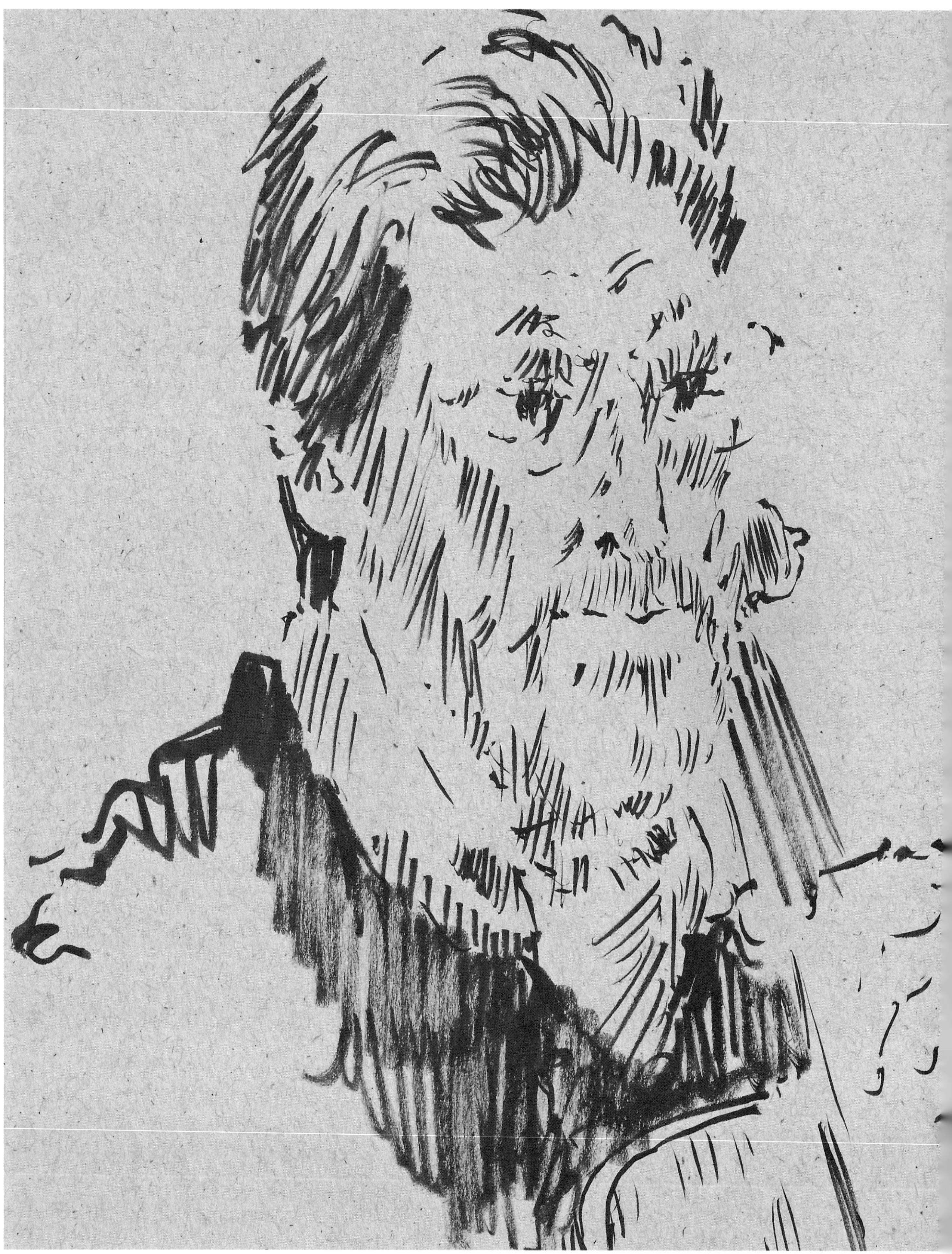

Rocco Filippini

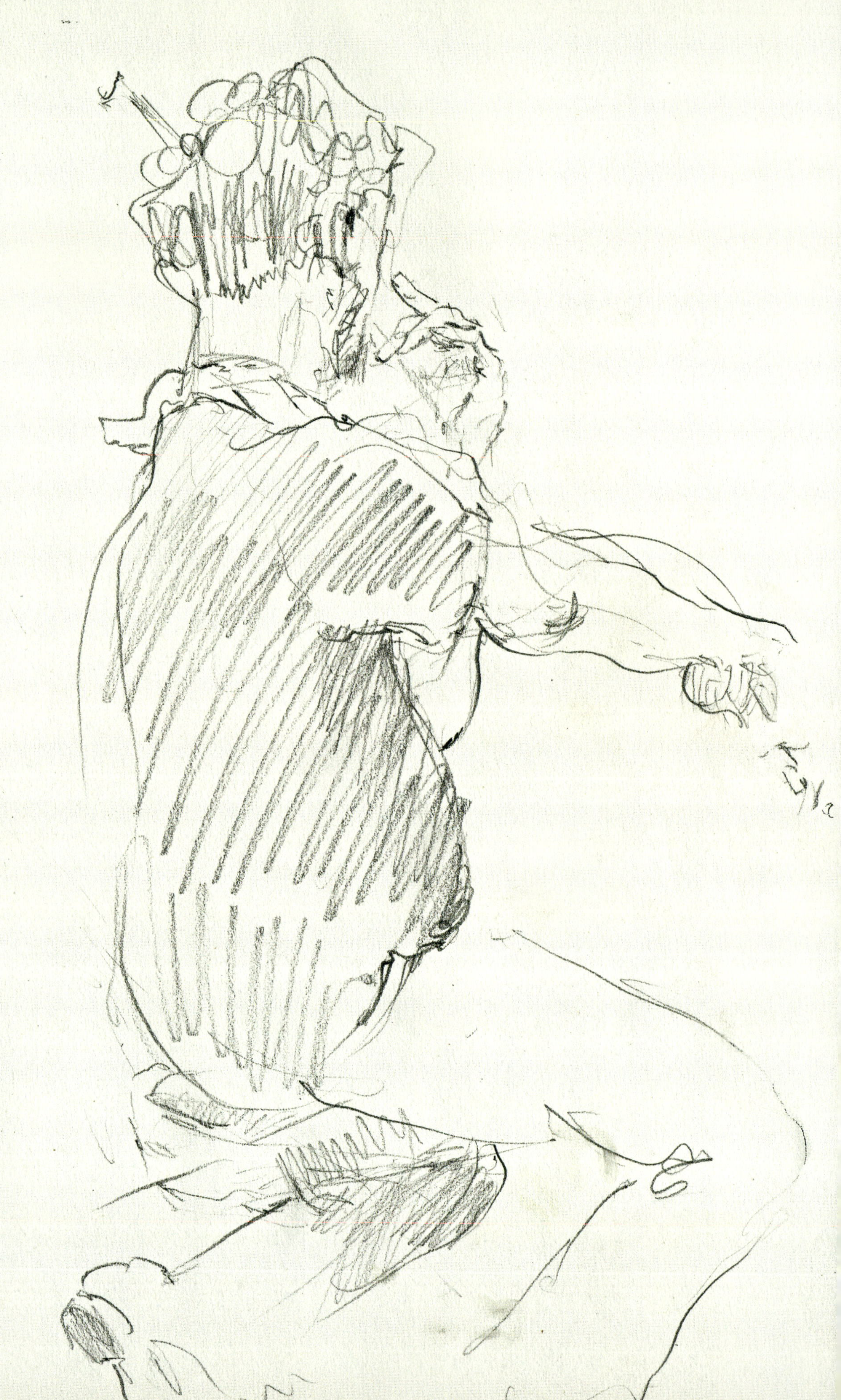

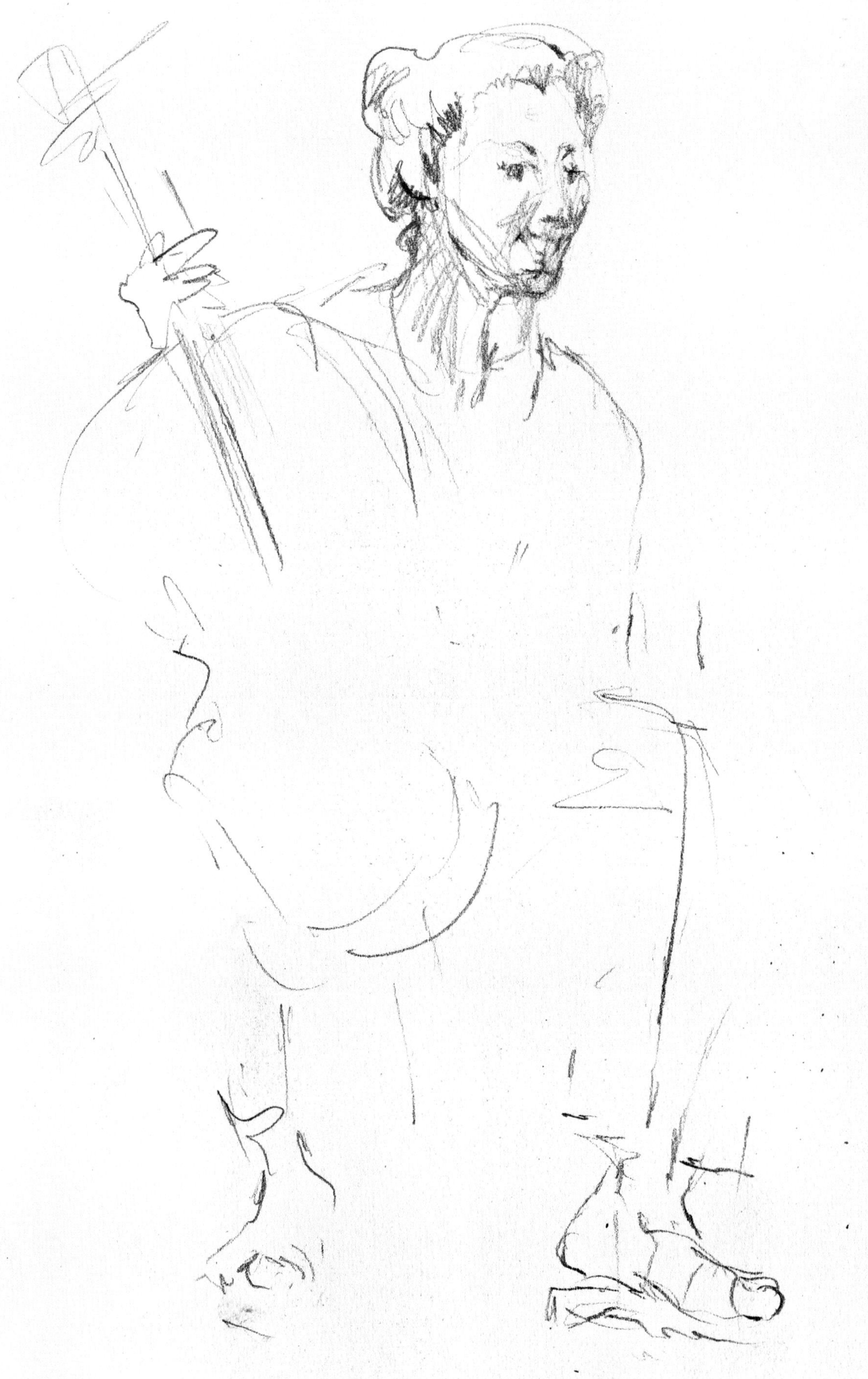

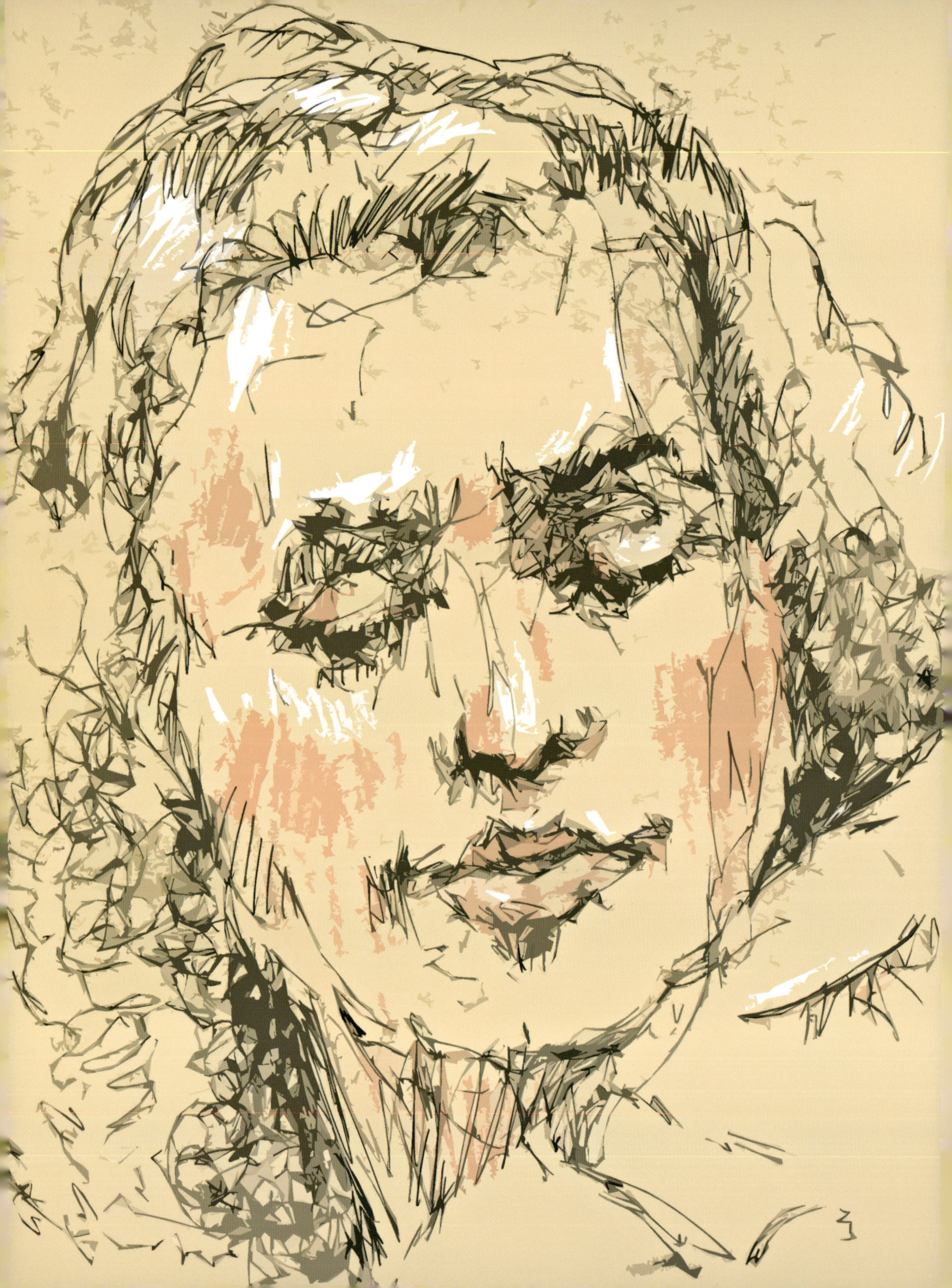

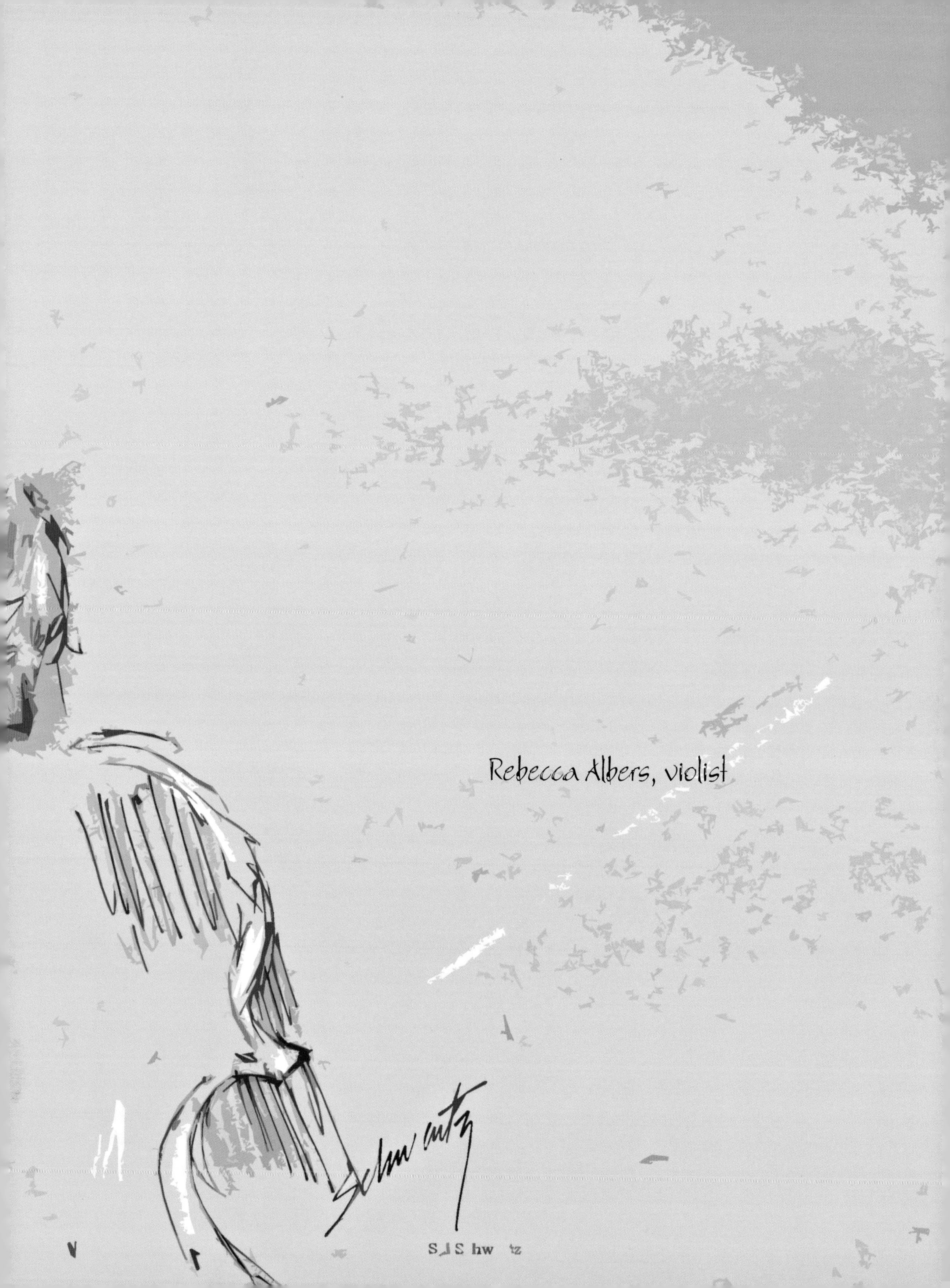

Rebecca Albers, violist

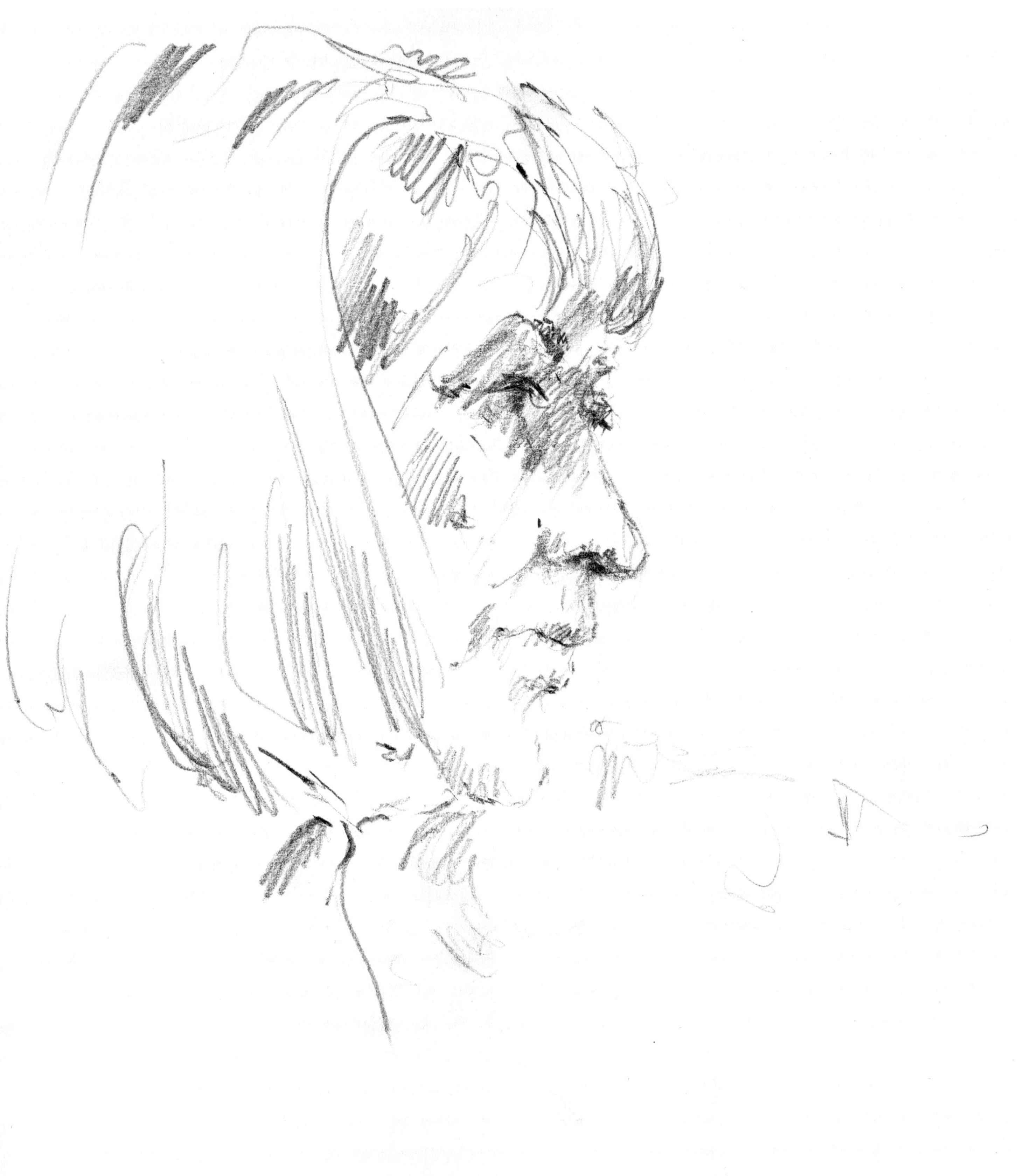

Ani Kavafian, violinist

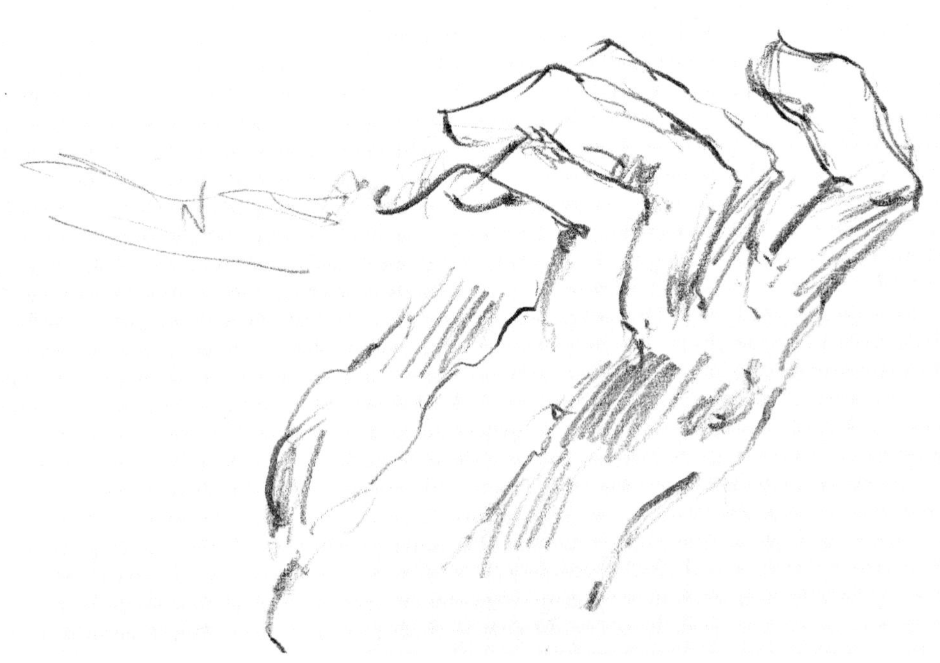

La Music

25th YEAR

Suggested poster for the 25th
anniversary of La Musica

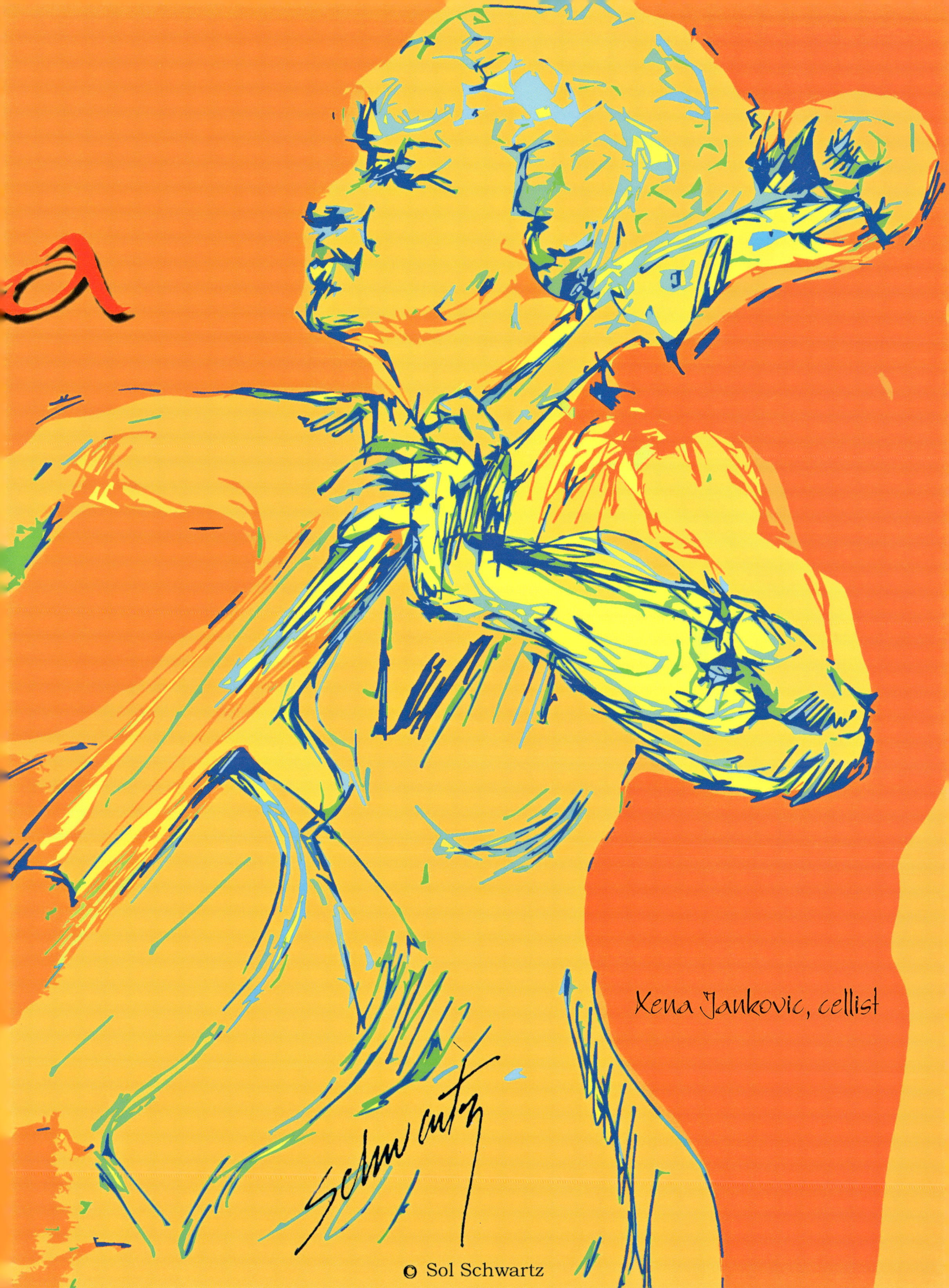

Xena Jankovic, cellist

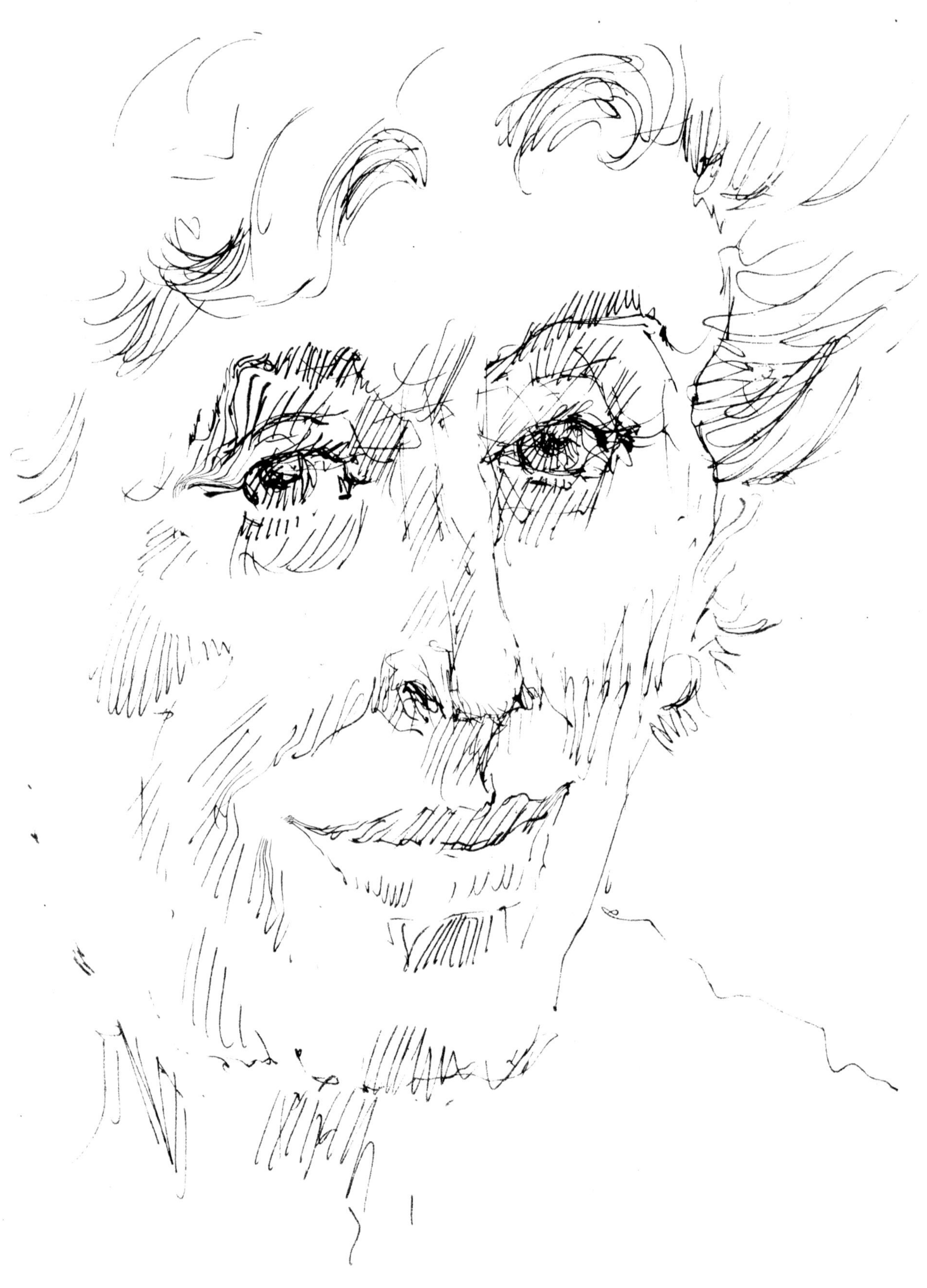

Elayne Bernstein

Audience

members

Elinor Choynik
46.09

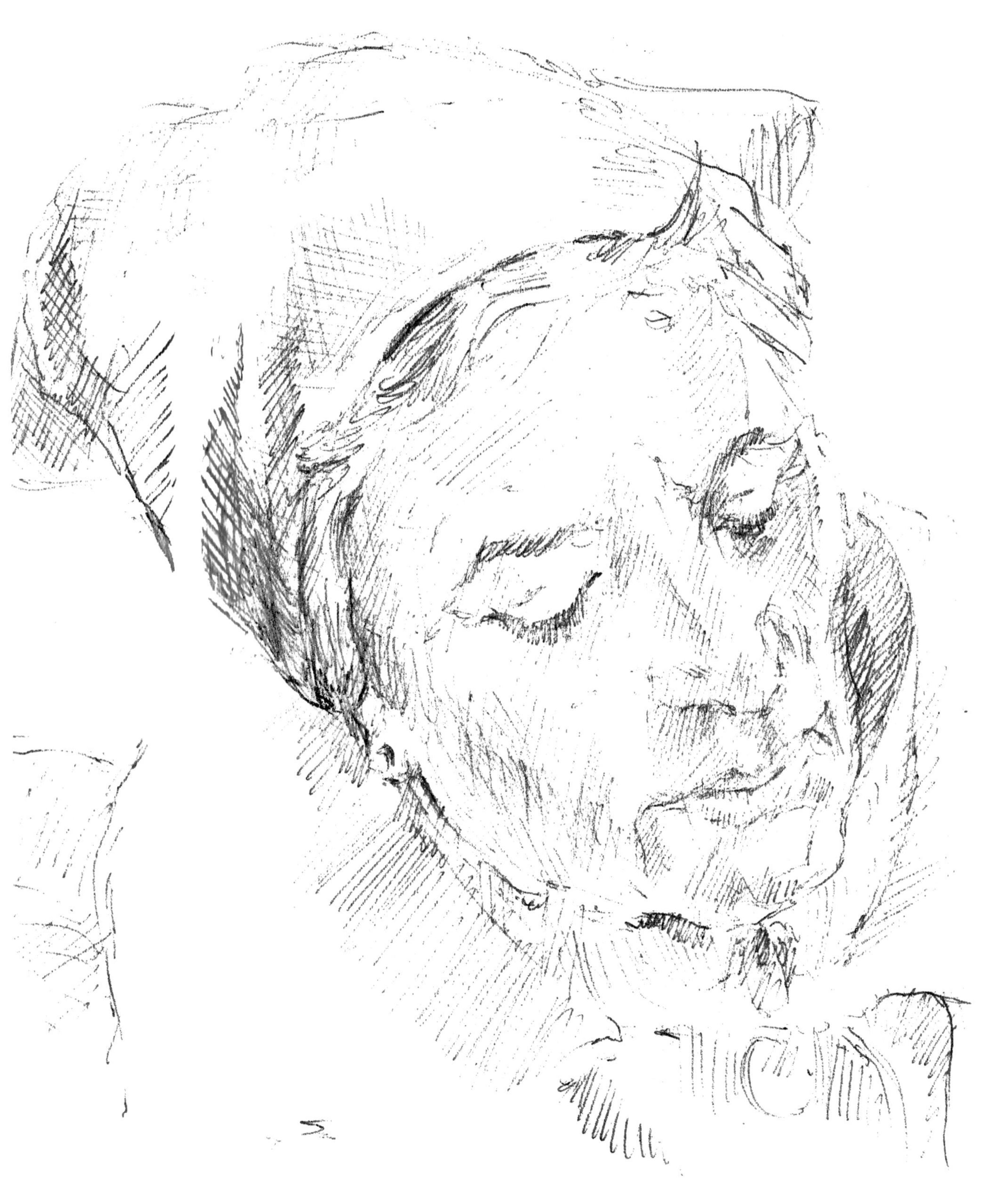

Lillian Schwartz

Audience

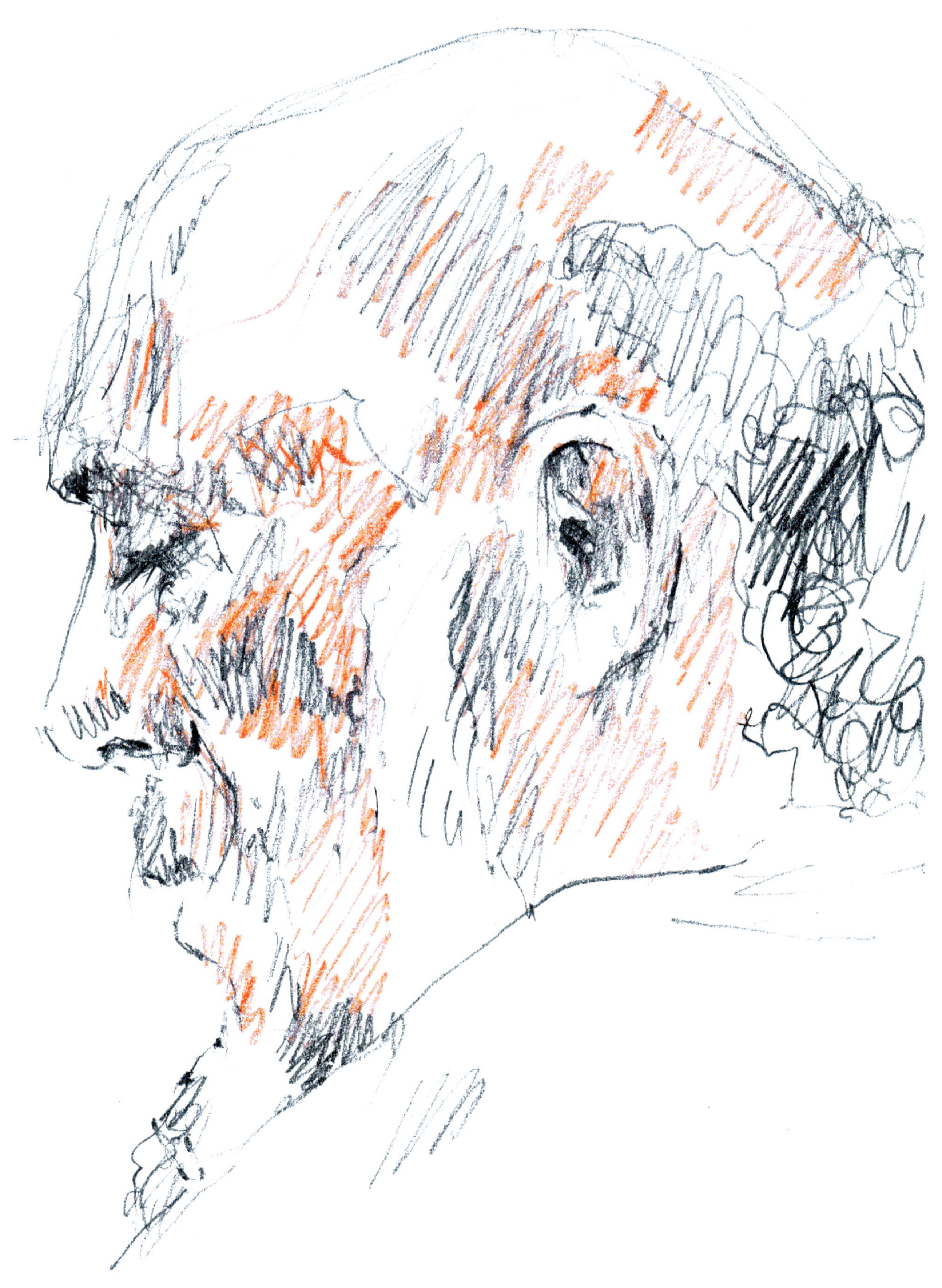

members

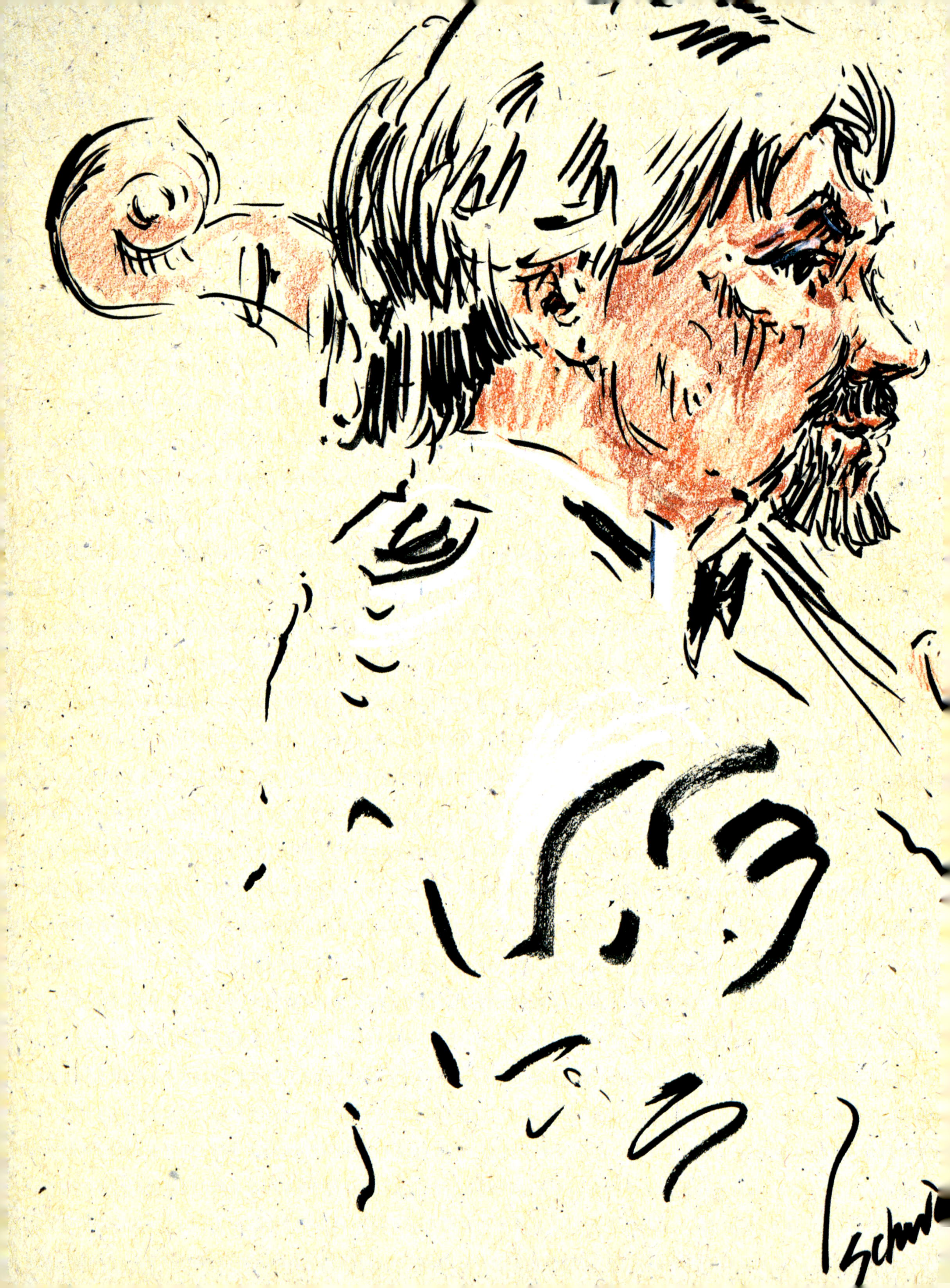

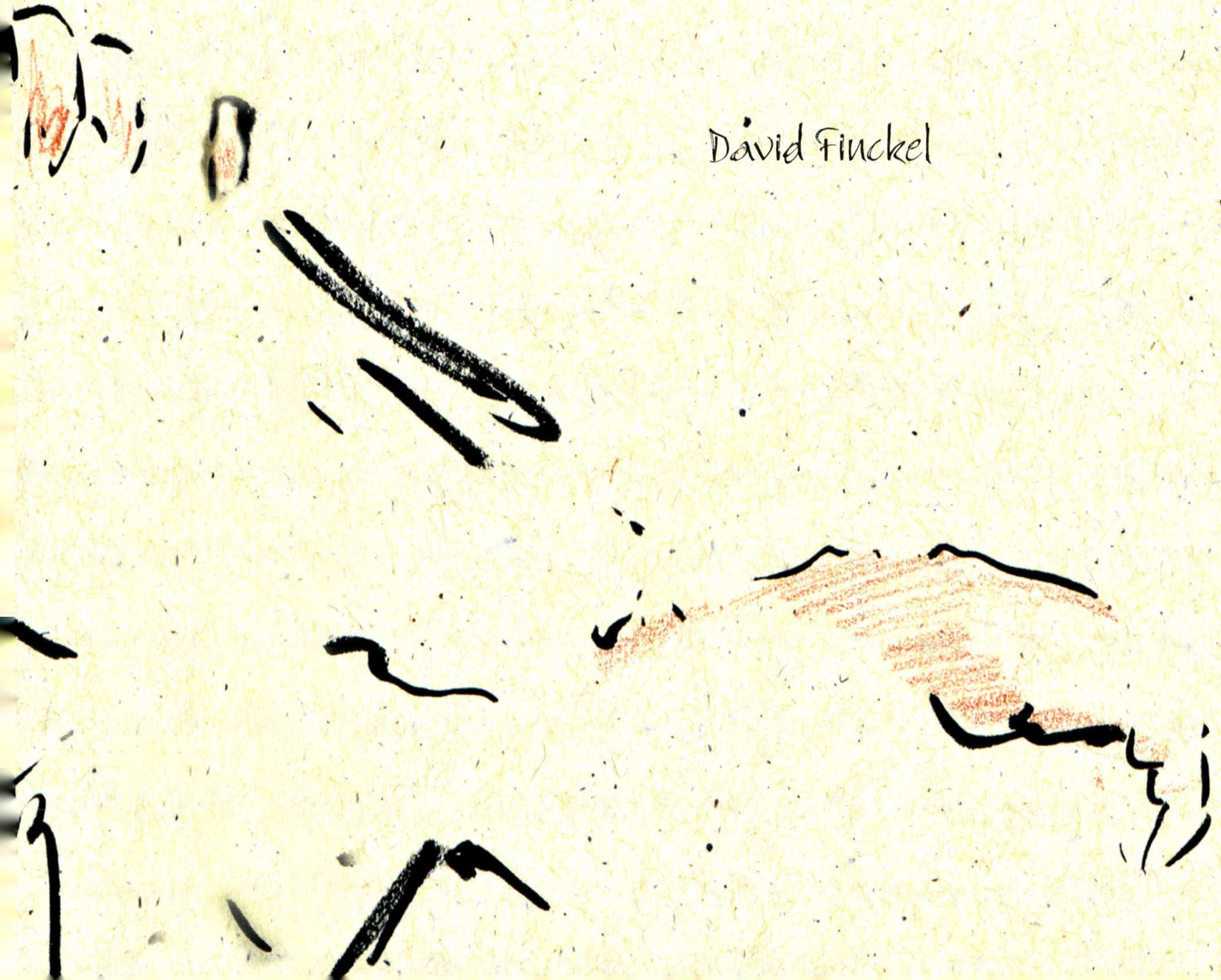

David Finckel

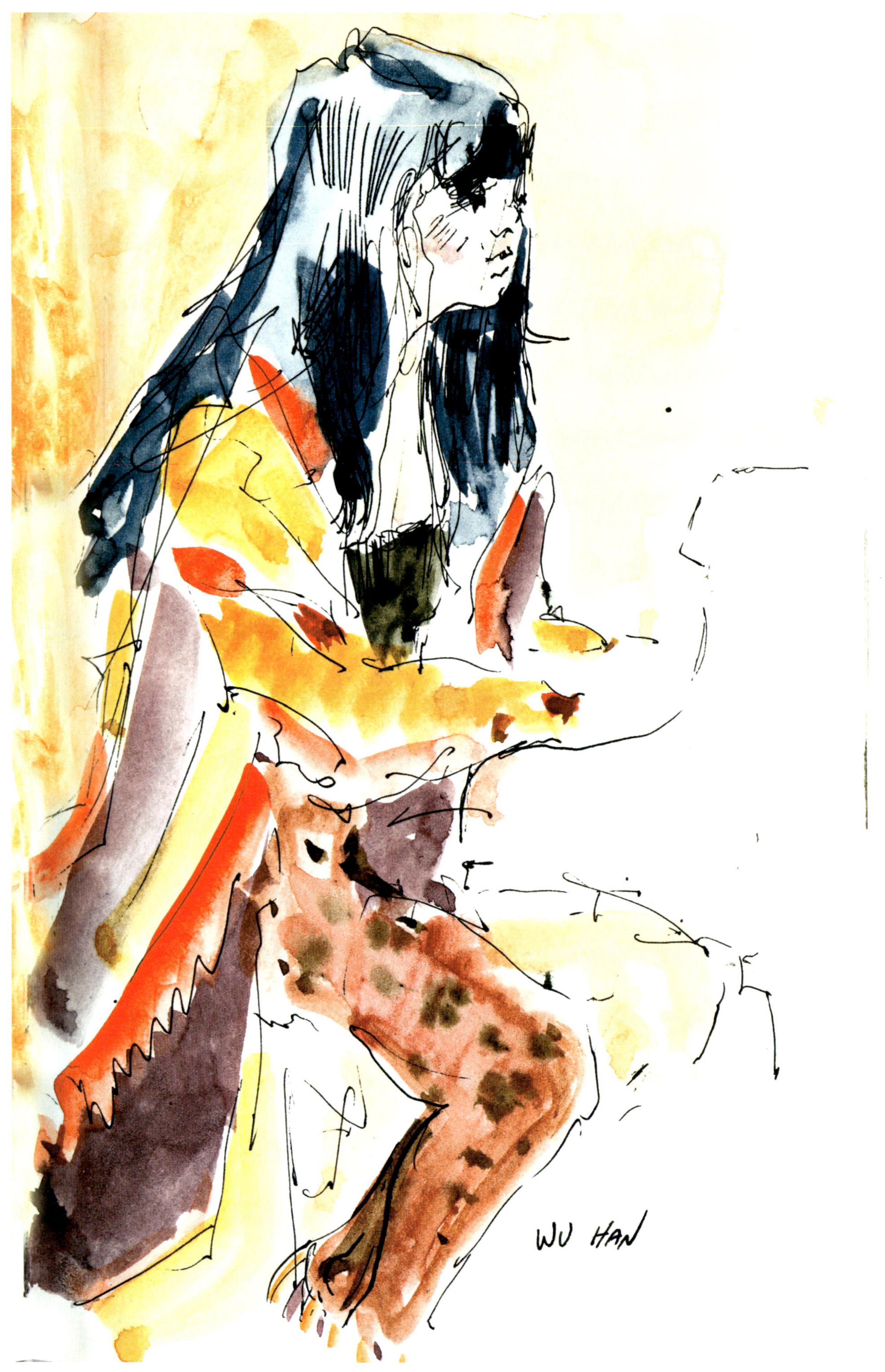
WU HAN

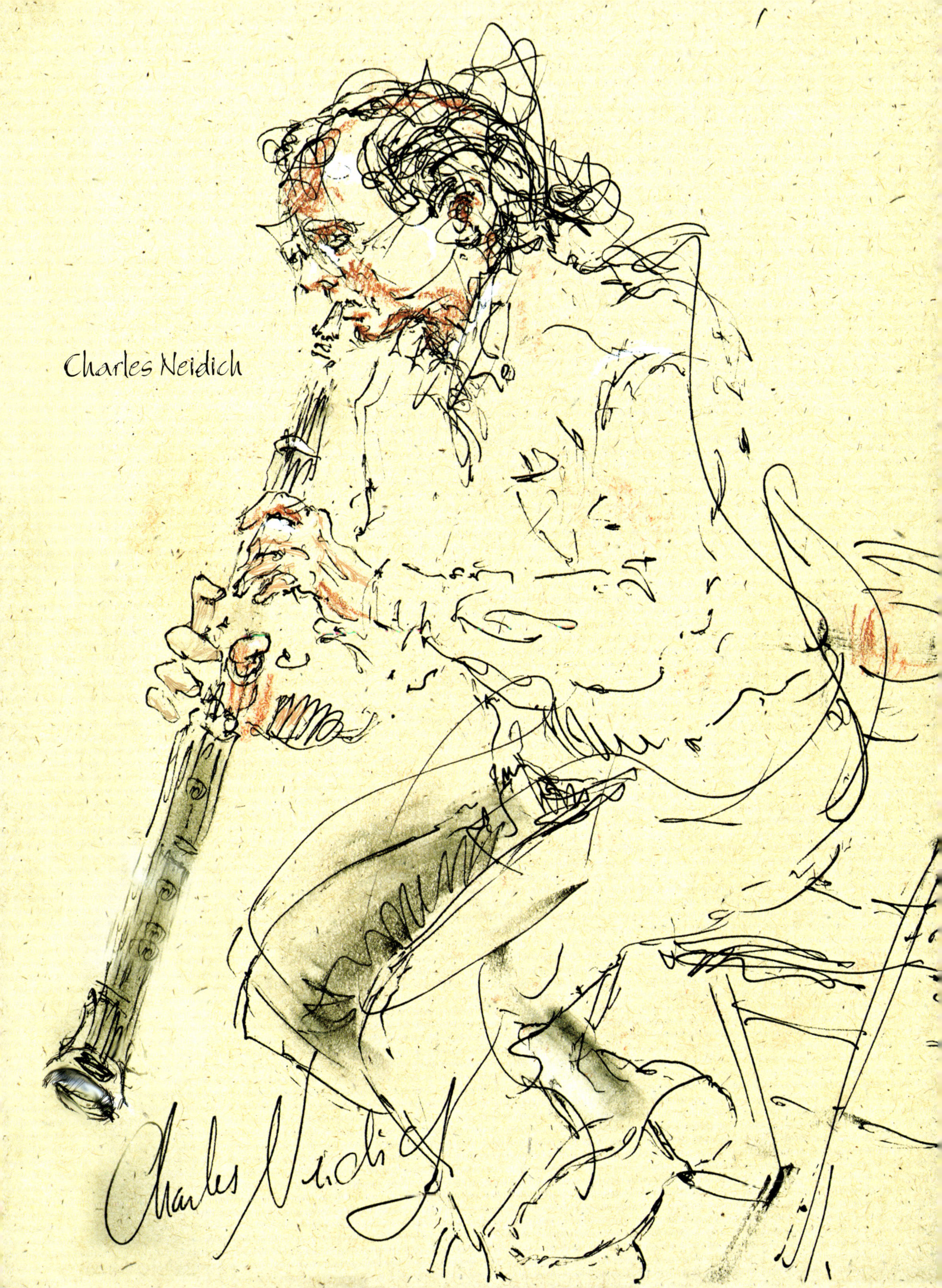

Charles Neidich

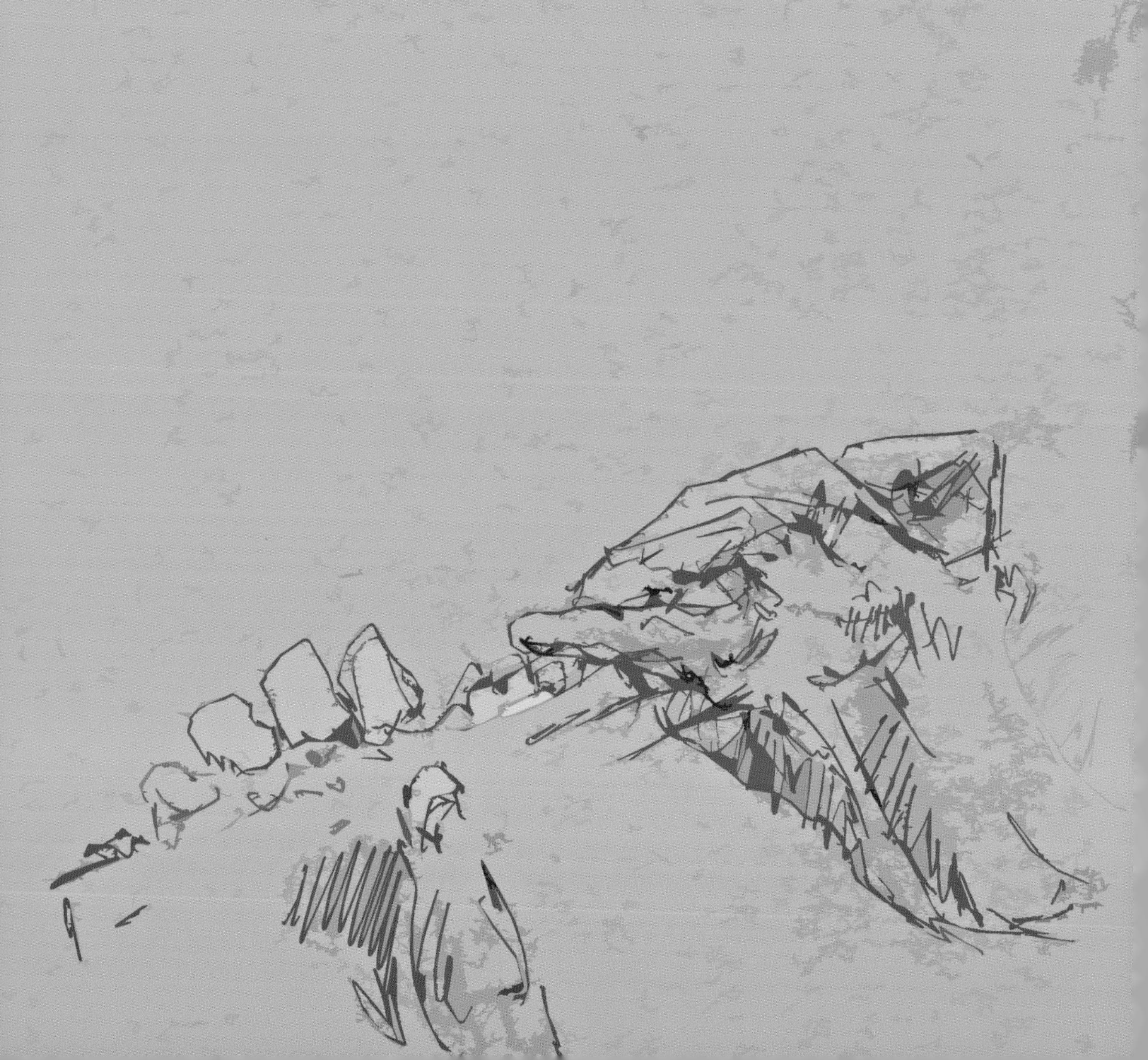

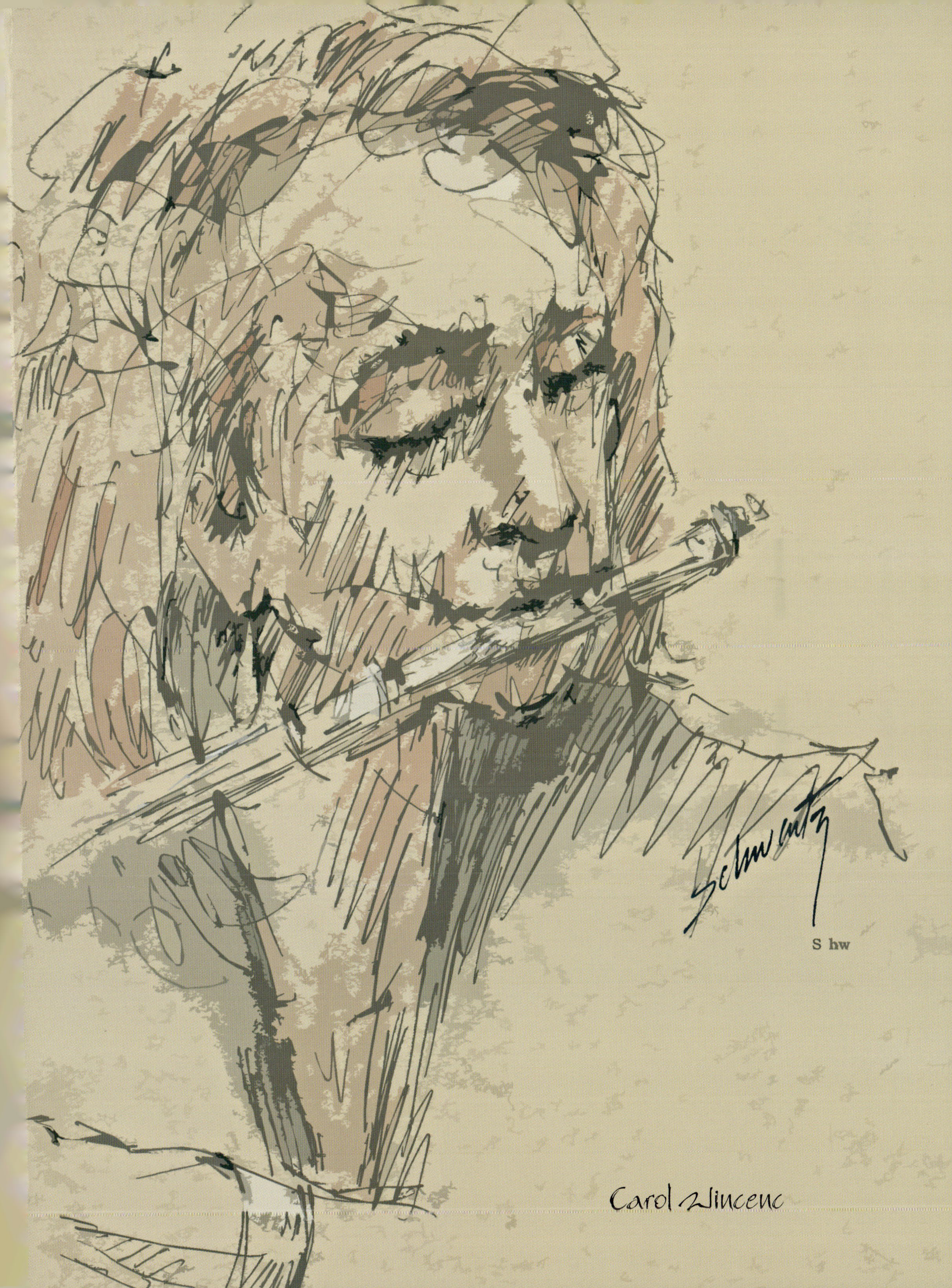
Schwartz
S hw
Carol Wincenc

solschwartz.com

ISBN: 978-1-4675-6683-4

Design/production, Studio Two
studiotwo.com